DESTROYERS

DESTROYERS

AN ILLUSTRATED HISTORY OF THEIR IMPACT

Eric W. Osborne

A B C ☰ C L I O

Santa Barbara, California   Denver, Colorado   Oxford, England

Library of Congress Cataloging-in-Publication Data
Osborne, Eric W.
Destroyers : an illustrated history of their impact / Eric W. Osborne.
   p. cm. — (Weapons and warfare series)
Includes bibliographical references and index.
ISBN 1-85109-479-2 (hardback : alk. paper) — ISBN 1-85109-484-9 (eBook)
1. Destroyers (Warships)—History. I. Title. II. Series.
V825.O83   2005
359.8'354—dc22
2005007481

05 06 07 08 / 10 9 8 7 6 5 4 3 2 1

This book is also available on the World Wide Web as an eBook.
Visit abc-clio.com for details.

ABC-CLIO, Inc.
130 Cremona Drive, P.O. Box 1911
Santa Barbara, California 93116-1911

This book is printed on acid-free paper.
Manufactured in the United States of America

CONTENTS

PREFACE AND ACKNOWLEDGMENTS

THE DESTROYER, a comparatively small vessel of great speed and moderate armament, is one of the most recent additions to world navies, but it has evolved to become the most numerous and important type of surface combatant in the forces of the world's major maritime powers in the present day. Even so, far fewer studies are released on the development of this type of ship than the larger warships such as battleships and aircraft carriers. This fact is partly the result of the sense of glamour that surrounds the larger, more powerful vessels. Many of these studies examine the history of warships in general where destroyers are dealt with in only a single chapter that, through the nature of these works, is a relatively small part of a larger whole. These works, although many are of good quality, have three chief drawbacks that detract from their usefulness in highlighting the history and importance of the destroyer. First, the coverage oftentimes centers on technological development and does not take political developments or foreign policy in individual countries that effect the development of the destroyers into account. As a result, readers are left with a history of destroyers that is detached from the events that govern their construction. Second, these works do not provide detailed information on the performance of destroyers in battle and how their design changed on the basis of that experience. Oftentimes, the reader is provided only with a summary of the combat roles of destroyers, without specific examples that lead to a better understanding overall. Last, these books fail to incorporate information about how these ships were operated and the people who crewed them. Destroyers, like all warships, are communities where people work constantly to make their vessels as effective as possible in conditions that have been far from comfortable until recent years. Without the inclusion of the human element, the reader cannot fully appreciate the rigors of life at sea and its impact on the performance of the destroyer. Other works that focus solely on destroyers seek to address these problems with more in-depth examination, but most deal with specific time periods of the destroyer's history, such as the performance of U.S. destroyers in World War II. These studies, although far more detailed, are also of limited value for those who seek a complete history of these vessels.

This work seeks to remedy the problem of coverage through the use of secondary sources to include technological, wartime, social, and diplomatic and political histories as part of a larger whole that examines the development of the destroyer from its inception to the modern day.

Chapter 1 serves as a background to the introduction of the destroyer and has two sections. The first is a history of the sloop in the eighteenth and nineteenth centuries during the Age of Fighting Sail, being the period when warships were propelled by sails. The sloop, also known as the corvette, of this era is oftentimes viewed as the forerunner of the modern destroyer. This section includes discussion on the technological aspects of sloops and life at sea. It also showcases the duties of sloops through examples from wars of the era. The roles included scouting, commerce protection through acting as an escort for merchantmen and hunting down commerce raiders, preying on enemy commerce, and courier service through delivering dispatches. The second section entails a discussion of technological development in the nineteenth century that effectively ended the Age of Fighting Sail and ultimately made possible the creation of the destroyer.

Chapters 2–4 discuss important innovations in design and changes in the roles of destroyers that mark watersheds in their development. Chapter 2 covers the period from the introduction of the first torpedo boat destroyer in 1882 to 1914, by which time the destroyer was the most numerous type of warship in world navies. The technological developments and consequent changes in shipboard life were enormous in this period. Destroyers became increasingly large and expensive and much more effective as warships. The increase in size allowed them to operate for much longer periods at sea and thereby provide more effective protection for battle fleets on extended operations in time of war. Sailors in this period had to endure harsh conditions aboard their small vessels while increasingly specializing in certain technical subjects to properly and efficiently man the ship. By 1914, destroyers were charged with protecting battle fleets from torpedo attacks and launching assaults of their own.

Chapter 3 examines the era from 1914, the beginning of World War I, to the conclusion of World War II in 1945. One of three central themes is an examination of the technological changes in destroyer design and the additional duties that were charged to them as a result of technological change in naval warfare as a whole. By the end of World War II, the importance of destroyers had expanded far past their previous roles or those of their antecedent, the sloop of the Age of Fighting Sail. Destroyers served as escorts for convoys against submarine attacks, light gun support for amphibious operations, antiaircraft (AA) batteries to protect larger vessels from aircraft attacks, and minor surface combatants. A second key subject is the impact of international law on destroyer development that limited their size and armament. Last, I continue the examination of shipboard life in a time when the destroyer became an increasingly more complicated weapons system. By the end of World War II, the men who crewed destroyers were charged with a multitude of tasks that were vital to the function of the world's battle fleets.

Chapter 4 treats the evolution of the destroyer from 1945, the end of World War II, to the present day. This period is a confirmation of the continued importance of these ships. The dawn of the missile age and computerized systems led to a renaissance in destroyer design and cemented its place as the backbone of world navies. One of the chief reasons behind the importance of destroyers in the postwar era was the fact that they were cheaper surface combatants to build than cruisers and aircraft carriers. Destroyers, although smaller, retained the weapons and systems necessary for the strategic requirements of the world's major powers. This section also details the further changes in training for sailors who were brought on by the missile and computer ages. Today's sailors, who enjoy shipboard conditions that are far improved from those of the past, must be more knowledgeable than their counterparts from the middle twentieth century. The conclusion stresses the great importance of these vessels not only as tools for war but also as instruments of peace through the projection of power overseas by the Great Powers.

The final part of this work is a reference section that contains the design specifications and fate of the most important destroyers built. Each entry includes a picture, description, and major characteristics. The technical specifications include the dimensions of the hull, armor, armaments, means of propulsion, crew complement, the number of each vessel built, and a description of the fate of each destroyer. This information provides more detailed information than that included in the text and serves to strengthen the reader's under-standing of the appearance and mechanics of the destroyer.

I owe a great debt of gratitude to a multitude of people whose support has made this work possible. The professional assistance and encouragement of Spencer C. Tucker, aside from the opportunity he has given to me to write for this series, has been invaluable. I would also like to thank Alicia Merritt, senior acquisitions editor at ABC-CLIO, and the publishing house's editorial staff for their consistently helpful guidance.

In addition to the aid of professionals, this work was possible due to the help of family and friends. The encouragement of Iana, my wife, has been invaluable. Combined with her efforts has been the unwavering and ever-present support of my parents, Dr. and Mrs. Larry Osborne, my brother, Jack E. Osborne, and my extended family.

Eric W. Osborne

INTRODUCTION TO
ENCYCLOPEDIAS OF WEAPONS
AND WARFARE SERIES

WEAPONS BOTH FASCINATE AND REPEL. They are used to kill and maim individuals and to destroy states and societies, and occasionally whole civilizations, and with these the greatest of man's cultural and artistic accomplishments. Throughout history tools of war have been the instruments of conquest, invasion, and enslavement, but they have also been used to check evil and to maintain peace.

Weapons have evolved over time to become both more lethal and more complex. For the greater part of man's existence, combat was fought at the length of an arm or at such short range as to represent no real difference; battle was fought within line of sight and seldom lasted more than the hours of daylight of a single day. Thus individual weapons that began with the rock and the club proceeded through the sling and boomerang, bow and arrow, sword and axe, to gunpowder weapons of the rifle and machine gun of the late nineteenth century. Study of the evolution of these weapons tells us much about human ingenuity, the technology of the time, and the societies that produced them. The greater part of technological development of weaponry has taken part in the last two centuries, especially the twentieth century. In this process, plowshares have been beaten into swords; the tank, for example, evolved from the agricultural caterpillar tractor. Occasionally, the process is reversed and military technology has impacted society in a positive way. Thus modern civilian medicine has greatly benefitted from advances to save soldiers' lives, and weapons technology has impacted such areas as civilian transportation or atomic power.

Weapons can have a profound impact on society. Gunpowder weapons, for example, were an important factor in ending the era of the armed knight and the Feudal Age. They installed a kind of rough democracy on the battlefield, making "all men alike tall." We can only wonder what effect weapons of mass destruction (WMD) might have on our own time and civilization.

This series will trace the evolution of a variety of key weapons systems, describe the major changes that occurred in each, and illustrate and identify the key types. Each volume begins with a description of the particular weapons system and traces its evolution, while discussing its historical, social, and political contexts. This is followed by a heavily illustrated section that is arranged more or less along chronological lines that provides more precise information on at least 80 key variants of that particular weapons system. Each volume contains a glossary of terms, a bibliography of leading books on that particular subject, and an index.

Individual volumes in the series, each written by a specialist in that particular area of expertise, are as follows:

Ancient Weapons
Medieval Weapons
Pistols
Rifles
Machine Guns
Artillery
Tanks
Battleships
Cruisers and Battle Cruisers
Aircraft Carriers
Submarines
Military Aircraft, Origins to 1918
Military Aircraft, 1919–1945
Military Aircraft in the Jet Age
Helicopters
Ballistic Missiles
Air Defense
Destroyers

We hope that this series will be of wide interest to specialists, researchers, and even general readers.

Spencer C. Tucker
Series Editor

DESTROYERS

CHAPTER 1

The Technological Revolution Leading to the Development of Destroyers, 1750–1860

THE DESTROYER IS A VESSEL whose roles have changed markedly since its development in the late nineteenth century. In general, a destroyer is designed as a small, lightly protected and armed warship capable of high speed. The type, unlike other ships such as battleships and cruisers, is a relatively new weapons system in the history of naval warfare. Few precedents exist in the Age of Fighting Sail, although some naval historians equate sloops, also known as corvettes, as forerunners of the destroyer. Sloops were designed principally to act as escorts for merchantmen, commerce raiders, and scouts. In an era when long-range communication, such as radio, did not exist, sloops were also used to carry dispatches between overseas bases and information from these to the naval leadership of their respective countries. Destroyers eventually counted the first three of these duties of sloops, but primarily the role of escort, among the myriad of roles that have been attached to them over the course of naval history from the late nineteenth century, when the modern destroyer was created, to the present day.

In the eighteenth century, *sloops* were small, fast warships that mounted a battery of light guns on a single gun deck. These vessels

1

ranked low on the ratings system of the day that gauged the fighting capacity of vessels. First-rate vessels—those that were the eighteenth century equivalent of a modern battleship—mounted 100 guns or upward; second rate between 90 and 98 guns; third rate, 64–74; fourth rate, 50–60; fifth rate, 32–44; and sixth rate, 20–28. Small frigates normally carried between 24 and 30 guns while larger ones mounted 50–60 cannons. Sloops mounted between 8 and 24 guns, meaning that the larger vessels of the type fell into the sixth rate. Smaller sloops fell outside the ranking system.

The weapons carried by sloops were normally cast-iron, smooth-bore, muzzle-loading cannons. The alternative to iron in this era was bronze, which had the advantage of being easier to cast. It also better withstood the shock of firing due to its greater elasticity. Bronze cannons, however, were immensely expensive to produce and consequently fell out of favor. They could be four times as expensive as a piece made of iron. Whether they were made from iron or bronze, naval cannons were capable of firing a variety of projectiles. Solid shot, being a solid, round ball of iron, was designed to inflict damage to the hull of an enemy vessel. Oftentimes, hits from this type of projectile did not produce holes large enough to sink a vessel. They were more of a danger to the crews of warships in the Age of Fighting Sail as they splintered wood upon impact, producing deadly projectiles that could kill crewmen. This effect was preferable to sinking a ship, as most navies of this era preferred instead to capture vessels to incorporate the prize into their own force. To that end, a further type of projectile, known as chain shot, was designed to strike at the rigging of an enemy ship with the object of dismasting it, rendering the vessel incapable of maneuver and easy prey for capture. Chain shot, as with all types of shot, weighed approximately the same as round shot of the same size of gun for which it was being used. A typical chain shot consisted of two balls of equal size attached by a length of chain. Once fired, the chain between the two balls could slice though a vessel's rigging. Vessels in the Age of Fighting Sail also carried shot for close-range actions designed to kill the crew of the opposing ship. Grapeshot consisted of a collection of small balls contained in a stand enclosed in canvas. Once fired, the balls would separate from the stand to form a deadly hail of projectiles. Another type of close-range, antipersonnel weapon was canister shot, which comprised scrap metal or musket balls packed into a canister. Like grapeshot, this type, once fired, would produce a deadly, tightly packed group of projectiles. All of these were fired through inserting a charge of gunpowder into the weapon along with the projectile.

Sloops carried cannons on the main deck. These guns were placed on carriages and sighted through ports cut into the sides of the hull. The dominant gun carriage employed in a sloop was known as a truck carriage for its four free-moving wheels that were necessary due to the recoil of the weapon once fired. To prevent the larger guns from recoiling into their crews, they were lashed by heavy ropes, known as breeching, to the hull. These ropes were also necessary at times other than combat. The pitching and rolling motion of a sloop in a heavy sea necessitated ropes to keep the guns in place. Otherwise, a cannon might roll down the length of the main deck, wreaking havoc and sometimes death. Sloops also carried lighter antipersonnel guns on the main deck where they were attached to the bulwarks, or rails, of the hull. These were commonly known as swivel guns due to the mount on which they were placed that allowed the operator of the weapon to turn it by hand.

The size of these weapons varied among the world's great naval powers largely because officials disagreed over which type of gun proved best in combat. By the outbreak of the French Revolution and the Napoleonic Wars (1793–1815), many sloops of the British Royal Navy employed 6-pounder guns as their primary armament. In this age, guns were rated by the weight of the ball that they fired rather than the diameter of the bore. A 6-pounder, consequently, fired a solid shot that weighed 6 pounds. The 6-pounder guns of the British Navy varied in size from 6 feet to 8 feet, 6 inches long. They weighed between 17 and 22 hundredweight (cwt), meaning that their weight varied from 1,904 pounds to 2,464 pounds. By comparison, the main armament of some frigates of the Royal Navy, being the predecessors of modern-day cruisers, was the 12-pounder gun that measured between 7 feet and 9 feet long and weighed between 2,352 pounds and 3,808 pounds.[1] In addition to these guns, some sloops of the late eighteenth century, and especially the early nineteenth century, carried a relatively new weapon called the carronade. This weapon was named after the Carron Company of Scotland that produced a prototype model in 1776. These were short pieces that had a large muzzle bore. They were particularly useful in smaller ships like sloops due to their lighter weight. In the British Navy, the typical carronade of sloops was the 24-pounder that weighed 1,456 pounds as opposed to the 1,904 pounds of the smallest 6-pounder long gun.[2] Carronades were designed to fire heavy shot at close range to smash through the hulls of opposing vessels. Their chief drawback in battle was shorter range against regular long guns.

Regardless of the type, guns were carried to sea on an extremely complex weapons system comprising two major parts: hull and rigging. By the beginning of the nineteenth century, the hulls of sloops exceeded 100 feet in length and displaced between 400 and 600 tons. These ships were constructed entirely of wood, the dominant material being oak due to its extreme strength and, consequently, its ability to resist cannon fire. Some sloops, however, were also built with fir and teak. The first step in the construction was to lay down the keel, the backbone of a ship. It was the lowest piece of timber in the hull and extended the length of the hull down the centerline. The keel did not consist of one piece of wood. Instead, it was made of several pieces that overlapped. These were attached together by joints known as scarphs. Once the keel was finished, shipbuilders began to construct the frame, which was composed of giant ribs that were attached to the keel. These, like the keel itself, were made out of several pieces of timber joined together. The decks were then constructed on longitudinal frames within the ribs. These frames as well as the decks themselves had to be made of the strongest material available to support the ship's ordnance. This process was followed by the fitting of hull planks to the outside of the hull as the skin of the vessel. To prevent leaking, these planks were sealed using a combination of rope and pitch inserted into the cracks. Beginning in the 1770s, the hulls of sloops were fitted with a copper sheathing below the waterline to prevent rotting. An equally important use for sheathing was to curtail the growth of marine organisms such as barnacles on the hull that created excess drag on the ship and consequently impeded speed.

The layout of the hull varied according to the type of sloop. All versions had two decks, one being the main deck where the armament was placed, the other (lower) deck intended for the storage of supplies and crew accommodations. Beyond this universal construction, some large sloops had quarterdecks and forecastles. A quarterdeck is a deck in the stern portion of a vessel that is situated higher than the main deck and, in the Age of Fighting Sail, was usually reserved for officers. It was designated also as an area for conducting official and ceremonial functions. A forecastle is a deck in the bow of a ship that is, like the quarterdeck, raised higher than the main deck. This area can be used to accommodate crew members. A more common hull configuration, however, was the flush deck, being a hull that simply has the main deck as its highest deck.

Coupled with the hull was the rigging. Mounted on giant masts, the sails of the vessel provided the mode of propulsion by harnessing the wind. Sloops carried either three or two masts depending on the size of the ship. Ship-rigged sloops were those with three masts, being the foremast, or mast in the forward part of the hull; the mainmast located amidships; and the mizzenmast sited in the stern. Brig-rigged sloops, with two masts, carried them forward amidships and aft amidships. These masts were, like the other parts, made out of several pieces joined together and rested on giant blocks of wood in the bottom of the hull. The largest was the mainmast in ship-rigged sloops. Masts were held in place at first by rope, but in the early nineteenth century this practice gave way to the use of iron bands. Attached to these giant masts were cross yards from which sails, made of canvas, were hung to catch the wind. The rigging of sloops could yield speeds in excess of 14 knots.

Daily life for the sailors who manned these vessels was demanding and harsh. These men constantly drilled to ensure maximum efficiency in combat. This practice was especially necessary given the lack of formal training prevalent among seamen. Although many of the ordinary sailors in the Age of Fighting Sail were recruited from the merchant service, there were also a great number of individuals with no experience at sea. These men included foreigners in search of a living in the employ of another country's navy, prisoners, conscripts in the case of navies such as that of France, and civilians seized for the service by means of impressment. The work of impressments entailed the use of so-called press gangs composed either of sailors already in naval service or men who were specifically employed for the job. The unfortunate individuals captured by such groups, as well as all other new seamen, had little or no knowledge of how to operate a warship. Practical experience through drill at sea was also important for officers, as there were few naval schools in the late eighteenth and early nineteenth centuries. Those that did exist, like Britain's Royal Naval College at Portsmouth, founded in 1729, did not enjoy high enrollment until the nineteenth century due to the aversion of officers to formal studies.

The conditions under which the officers and crews worked and lived offered very little comfort at the end of a trying day of work. The best-disposed of the crew was, of course, the captain, who enjoyed a cabin located in the stern of a sloop that spanned the beam of the hull. The best-disposed sloop commanders were those who had charge of a sloop that possessed a quarterdeck. In these vessels, the captain's cabin was located underneath the quarterdeck and had windows that enclosed the rear, sternmost portion of the room. In flush-decked vessels, the commander's cabin oftentimes did not have stern windows, as the cabin was located on the lower deck. Officers also had their own cabins, which were small and placed on either side of the vessel on the lower deck. Oftentimes, the rooms allotted to the officers were no more than canvas curtains cordoning off an area for the individual. Some were more elaborately built, being canvas stretched over wooden beams to create makeshift walls. Aside from these accommodations, sloops were very cramped vessels; most of the interior space was filled with the ship's equipment and stores. In sloops, the lesser officers and men consequently slept in hammocks strung from beams on the lower deck. The crews also ate their meals on this level. This lower deck was generally lacking in natural light.

Adding to this discomfort was the state of the vessel itself. Crewmen lived in a constantly damp and dirty environment where rats and other vermin were commonplace. Many of these unwelcome passengers made their presence known when the crew ate their meals. Oftentimes, their bread, stored in casks below decks, was moldy and inundated with weevils. These insects were so prevalent that crews took it as commonplace to break apart a biscuit at its center, where most of the weevils were, and simply scrape them out with a knife. Equally poor was the meat, which was procured from local slaughterhouses before a ship set sail and then stored in casks. Meat was frequently infested with worms over the course of a voyage and, although it could be eaten, was certainly no comfort to the crew. Salting the meat before packaging it, which became a common practice to make it last longer, could extend the life of food, but crewmen oftentimes could not taste the meat due to the heavy salt. Indeed, the poor diet of the crew was a major reason for a variety of potentially fatal illnesses. One of these was scurvy, which resulted from a lack of vitamin C in the diet and persisted through most of the Age of Fighting Sail. This disease quickly produced bleeding gums and would oftentimes open previously healed wounds.

Hygiene was sometimes a problem for those who manned sloops in the Age of Fighting Sail. The toilets of these ships, known as heads, were originally made up of planks with a hole in the center that were located at the sides of the vessel in the bow. Later, heads were placed in the bow below decks with sluices that led out of the ship. Sometimes, officers and crew alike used these facilities, which were uncomfortable as the pitching motion of a sloop or heavy winds made them difficult to use. The result was that in periods of heavy seas the bilge of a sloop, being the lowermost portions of the hull, might contain human excrement, as the men could not relieve themselves in the heads. In many sloops, this arrangement might be alleviated for officers through the use of chamber pots contained in their living quarters on the lower deck. This, however, was little better than the head due to the same problem of the pitching and rolling motion of the vessel. Only the captain, who sometimes had a toilet within his cabin, was better off than the rest. Even he, however, had to endure the foul stench that sometimes arose from the ship while at sea. This was particularly a problem when sloops, as well as any other vessel, were in stormy seas when men could not relieve themselves in the head due to the pitching motion. Oftentimes, crewmen would relieve themselves in the hold in these conditions. The smell could also be bad when at anchor in a harbor after protracted periods at sea. Ships that were not well-cleaned did not benefit from the wind generated from the ship's movement through the seas, as ventilation in the hull of a sailing vessel was oftentimes poor. Consequently, the odor was not carried away.

Bathing in these conditions offered little comfort. Due to the lack of fresh water aboard, the officers and men all washed with saltwater. The sailors, however, did not bathe frequently, which added to the poor hygiene onboard. Oftentimes, when they did, they only had the opportunity to wash their hands and faces, and soap was not a required part of a ship's stores in the Age of Fighting Sail. Clothing regularly went unwashed. This state of affairs contributed to the spread of fleas and lice. As with the lack of a proper nutritional diet, this problem could prove deadly, as lice carried typhus.

Many of these conditions were partially alleviated either at the outbreak or during the French Revolution and the Napoleonic Wars. Food became more tolerable owing to better storage, and hygiene was somewhat improved. Medical problems like scurvy were also dealt with, as in the case of the British Royal Navy in 1795, when lemons and oranges became a mandated part of a sailor's diet. Even so, conditions in cruising warships remained harsh well past the Age of Fighting Sail.

In addition to all these hardships, sailors had to endure a rigid system of discipline where infractions were often dealt with through a variety of painful, sometimes fatal punishments. Many of these were given to officers and men through a court-martial, a hearing in port where a panel of officers deliberated the fate of an individual accused of either breaking a captain's disciplinary code, in the case of lesser officers and ordinary seamen, or behaving poorly in battle. One common punishment was flogging, where an individual was tied down and whipped on his back. In the British Royal Navy at the end of the eighteenth century, convicted people could be sentenced to between 100 and 1,000 lashes. These lashings could dreadfully injure a person to the point of death. This practice was also common while at sea, where offenses that warranted flogging included drunkenness, sleeping on duty, neglect of duty, disobedience, and theft. Another punishment at sea was keelhauling, where an individual would be tied to a rope, weighted down, and dragged underneath the keel of a ship from one side of the vessel to the other. The chances of surviving keelhauling were slight. In addition to flogging, which carried with it a chance of death and keelhauling that virtually ensured it, officers and men alike had to be wary of the death penalty. Among the reasons for capital punishment were cowardice in battle and mutiny. The method varied based on the rank of the convicted individual. Seamen were oftentimes hanged from the rigging of a ship; officers were shot.

Nevertheless, despite the rigid discipline and poor conditions, a well-trained crew ensured that a sloop would have both the speed and the effective firepower to successfully accomplish its vital roles. These were exhibited in the late eighteenth and early nineteenth centuries through the French Revolution and Napoleonic Wars and other conflicts that took place in the same period. Perhaps the most important role was commerce protection. Sloops traveled with convoys of merchantmen to keep them sailing in an orderly fashion as a group and to ward off potential commerce raiders. As larger frigates were oftentimes used to raid commerce, sloops could be accompanied by frigates on this duty. This task was especially vital to Great Britain, which relied on a large portion of its wartime supply from overseas.

Sloops were also used as parts of squadrons tasked with hunting down commerce raiders. One case took place in the War of 1812 that pitted the United States against Great Britain. The United States, as it did not possess a fleet large enough to meet that of Britain in a pitched engagement, used its vessels to prey on Britain's merchant shipping with the object of causing economic hardship that might damage its war effort materially or sap its population's will to fight. One of these commerce raiders was the frigate *Essex* under the command of Captain David Porter. *Essex* raided British shipping in the South Atlantic and off the Pacific coast of South America. From 12 December 1812 to 13 July 1813, Porter captured 15 vessels of varying types that were primarily part of the British Pacific whaling fleet.[3] On 28 March 1814, off the coast of Valparaiso, Chile, *Essex* engaged the British frigate *Phoebe* and the sloop

Cherub that had been dispatched to hunt down *Essex*. In the opening phase of the battle, *Cherub* closed to short range at the stern of *Essex* and fired broadsides into the U.S. vessel. The sloop, however, later was forced to bear off as the fire from *Essex* proved damaging. Nevertheless, the long guns of *Cherub* and *Phoebe* reduced *Essex* to shambles, as the U.S. vessel was armed largely with shorter-range carronades and could not close to proper range. As a result, Porter was forced to surrender his vessel.

Sloops also were used as commerce raiders. An example occurred during the Napoleonic Wars with the operations between 1798 and 1800 of the sloop *Netley*. Armed with 24-pounder carronades, *Netley* cruised in the English Channel off the French coast and also off the coasts of Spain and Portugal. *Netley* employed its high speed to run down merchantmen—either enemy ships or neutral vessels violating Britain's blockade of France—and forced them to surrender. Once the vessel had hauled down its colors, the sloop sent a boarding party that commandeered the merchantmen and all of its cargo as prizes of war. The vessel and cargo subsequently was sold to the profit of the officers and captain of *Netley*.

Sloops were also used during the French Revolution and the Napoleonic Wars in a corollary to commerce raiding: the imposition of blockades. In the Age of Fighting Sail, this consisted of deploying a cordon of warships around the coastline of an enemy power to prevent the entrance or exit of merchantmen carrying supplies. Great Britain was the principal user of this tactic and first employed a systematic blockade in the 1756–1763 Seven Years' War. During the French Revolution and Napoleonic Wars, the British attempted to deny France and its allies the use of the sea through a blockade of the entire coastline of those parts of Europe under the control of French revolutionary forces and later Napoleon. There were two objectives to this operation. The first was to starve France's war effort and consequently generate hardship for the people under French rule. The second was to prevent the warships of France and its allies from leaving their ports to prey on British shipping.

At the opening of the conflict in 1793, the British employed an open blockade strategy. While Britain's ships-of-the-line remained in a state of readiness in port, a squadron of frigates sailed within visual range of French ports. They were accompanied by sloops and smaller vessels such as cutters and schooners. Sloops, but mostly frigates, overhauled any merchantman they encountered to ascertain their destination and the nature of their cargo. If the cargo was proven to be contraband—meaning goods that could be used for military purposes by the French—the ship and cargo could be seized. In the case of enemy warships leaving port, sloops, schooners, and cutters dispatched the information to the battle fleet, which would sortie and attempt to destroy the enemy while at sea. This latter duty was later altered by the adoption of a close blockade strategy that did not greatly involve sloops. This plan entailed having ships-of-the-line sail at a distance farther out from French ports.

Sloops figured most heavily in coastal blockades, as the shallow draft of these ships—being the depth of water to which a vessel's hull sinks as it floats—allowed them to maintain station in shallow depths of water that could not be traversed by larger warships. Britain's blockading effort produced economic hardships for France. Although it did not force France to surrender, the blockade had outstanding results and led Napoleon in late 1807 to establish his Continental System as a reprisal to the British action. This system was an embargo of British goods entering Europe. The Continental System created great economic hardship for European people under the control of Napoleon and ultimately led to the rebellion of Russia in 1810 against the system. Napoleon's attempt to force Russia to heel led to his 1812 invasion of Russia, which proved a crushing defeat for the French emperor. Although the role of blockade did not translate to destroyers of the modern era, it was a very important role for its predecessor, the sloop, during the Age of Fighting Sail.

Regardless of the duty, the lives of sailors in battle in the Age of Fighting Sail bordered on the horrific. Solid shot not only damaged a ship but also killed and badly wounded members of the crew. The wooden sides and fittings of a ship when hit by solid shot splintered and created a hail of additional projectiles. A direct hit on a human being by such shot was almost always fatal. Sailors oftentimes had arms and legs ripped off of their bodies when hit by solid shot. Others were decapitated by the projectile. Sometimes, a solid shot would literally cleave an individual in half. The effects of grapeshot were equally as terrible. The relatively small balls of this type of projectile could sweep a ship's main deck of personnel. Some of these unfortunate sailors were almost obliterated by the damage caused by the multiple balls. Chain shot, if it was fired too low, also proved devastating to human beings, as it could slice several men in half rather than the masts that they were intended to destroy. If it cut through a mast, the crew had to contend with huge pieces of wood plummeting to the main deck. Adding to these threats was the possibility of fire, as solid shot could be heated beforehand. The potential effect on a wooden warship was devastating. Not only could the crew be incinerated, the ship's magazine—being the storage area for powder and shot—could blow up and obliterate everyone aboard. All told, the decks of a sloop in the Age of Fighting Sail might literally have blood running down their length as a result of combat. The experience of combat in this era is well described by one seaman who related a battle where "the whole scene grew indescribably confused and horrible; it was like some awfully tremendous thunderstorm, whose deafening roar is attended by incessant streaks of lightening, carrying death in every flash and strewing the ground with the victims of its wrath: only, in our case, the scene was rendered more horrible than that, by the presence of torrents of blood which dyed our decks."[4]

Many wounded seamen who survived the nightmarish experience of combat were confronted with being permanently crippled or dying from their wounds. Surgeons of the Age of Fighting Sail extracted splinters, set broken bones, and on many occasions amputated limbs. Oftentimes, the impact of an object severely damaged limbs to the point where the only way to provide a chance of survival for the wounded patient was to remove them. This procedure was also a distinct possibility for a badly wounded sailor given the state of medical science, which did not permit for overly complex reconstructive surgery. Amputation did not always ensure survival. Many subsequently died of shock or loss of blood in the operation. Aside from these horrors, seamen had to contend with the fact that medical science had not progressed far enough in the Age of Fighting Sail concerning infection. Many died due to the festering of a wound or fever from infection.

Sailors also suffered when their ship foundered from damage sustained in battle. This occurrence was rare, as the buoyancy of wood permitted a large amount of flooding before a warship was in danger of foundering. When it did occur, many sailors never made it off of their vessels, as they were trapped below decks, particularly if the vessel capsized. Others died in the water through exposure to the elements, which was a particular danger in areas of the Atlantic Ocean.

The period spanning the French Revolution and Napoleonic Wars was the golden age of warfare in the Age of Fighting Sail and perhaps the greatest contests that showcased the roles of the sloop. These conflicts, however, also represent the last great war at sea for sailing sloops and, indeed, all vessels of the Age of Fighting Sail. The years directly following the French Revolution and Napoleonic Wars were the beginning of an era of enormous technological innovation that transformed naval warfare, ended the Age of Fighting Sail, and made the modern-day destroyer possible.

Steam propulsion was the first innovation of the new age. The potential advantage of a vessel equipped with steam engines was enormous. A warship that possessed them was not limited in its maneuvering in combat by the wind, whose direction changed on a regular basis. The concept of steam propulsion was not new in the early nineteenth century. James Watt, a British inventor, produced the first moderately efficient steam engine in 1769. Even so, Watt's creation did not herald a revolution in naval propulsion overnight due to the fact that harnessing the power of steam was impeded by technological problems. Early steam engines were heavy and consequently could not be fitted easily inside a wooden-hulled warship. Such a weighty propulsion plant left little space for guns, stores, and crew. If the weight of the engine, weapons, supplies, and crew exceeded the buoyancy provided by the hull, the vessel would sink. Exacerbating this problem were the more conservative-minded naval officials of the period, who maintained that sails were far more reliable than the new invention of steam propulsion. Consequently, the first use of a steam engine in a vessel was not until 1783 when a French nobleman, the Marquis Jouffroy d'Abbans, financed an unarmed steamer named the *Pyroscaphe* in a trip up the River Sâone.

Others followed d'Abbans by launching steam-powered merchant vessels and, occasionally, warships. One of the earliest examples of a steam-engine warship came in 1793 in Great Britain when the Earl of Stanhope envisioned a vessel using steam-driven paddles. This experimental craft was the *Kent,* which proved to be a failure. By 1797 the ship's engine, after having suffered repeated breakdowns and yielding poor performance, was removed. Attempts to incorporate steam propulsion in warships also resulted in failure. In 1813, U.S. inventor Robert Fulton submitted plans to the U.S. government for a steam-powered warship. With the authorization of Congress in 1814, Fulton oversaw construction of *Demologos.* Commissioned into the U.S. Navy in June 1815, the hull of this vessel, composed of two separate hulls joined together in the configuration of a catamaran, measured 153 feet, 2 inches by 56 feet and displaced 2,475 tons. The armament consisted of 24 32-pounder guns. It was fitted with a steam engine in one of its hulls, while the other housed a boiler. Despite the groundbreaking design, *Demologos* was not a success. The propulsion plant, which delivered its power to one large paddle wheel housed between the two hulls, could produce a maximum speed of only 5 knots. This low speed obviated the vessel's use as a viable warship. The low speed meant the ship was never completed for service. It probably never went to sea after its trial, being its test run.

The early experiments with steam power made its use in warships a dubious proposition. Aside from mechanical unreliability and inability to produce high speed was the glaring deficiency of fuel consumption. A tremendous amount of fuel—coal at the time—was necessary to steam short distances in the early steam-powered ships. One such early vessel, *Rhadamanthus,* which was laid down in 1831 as one of the British Royal Navy's early steamers, is an example of the problem. This vessel was small, displacing only 813 tons, and shipped both a steam engine and sails for propulsion. On 21 April 1833, *Rhadamanthus* left Plymouth, England, and became the first British steamship to cross the Atlantic Ocean. By the time it reached the island of Madeira to recoal, it had consumed 320 tons.[5] This high consumption was only a fraction of what might have been consumed had the vessel not made part of the journey through the use of sails. The problem of fuel inefficiency is more evident through a calculation that revealed that *Rhadamanthus* required 188 tons of coal to steam for 10 days.[6]

Yet another problem handicapped steamers like *Rhadamanthus.* Early boilers were not well-machined and were subject to blowing up if too much steam pressure was built up. This possibility posed a threat, as boilers were seated at the bottom of the hull. The explosion of a boiler could blow a hole in the bottom of the hull or the sides below the waterline and cripple or sink the ship. Aside from material damage, the explosion could also be costly in human life by killing engineers and stokers who worked the engines and boilers.

Further compounding the inefficiency of early steam vessels was transferring the power of the engines to the water to propel the ship. The earliest machinery to accomplish this task was the paddle wheel, giant wheels containing blades that were much like those of a water mill and were connected to the engine plant and dipped into the sea. Normally one was mounted on each side amidships. The paddle wheel had numerous weaknesses when applied to warships. Foremost was the general inefficiency of the wheel, as the action of the large blades hitting the water expended power that could otherwise be used to propel the ship. There were attempts to correct this problem, such as the invention of the cycloidal wheel in 1833 that replaced the large blades of the wheel with narrower, staggered ones. Such innovations proved unable to fully surmount the problem.

In addition, in a stormy, rough sea a ship had the tendency to pitch and roll, and one of the wheels might consequently be far out of the water while the other was far more deeply submerged than normal. Such a situation would put an enormous amount of strain on the machinery as one wheel encountered far more drag from the water than the other. Finally, the paddle wheel had drawbacks in battle. As warships of the age still mounted weaponry on their sides, the paddle wheel in most cases decreased the number of guns that could be mounted on the ship. The wheels also proved vulnerable targets for enemy fire. Although most naval powers attempted to protect them by encasing the upper halves in armored boxes, the wheels could still be shot away and the vessel disabled.

Despite the drawbacks of steam propulsion and the paddle wheel, the world's major naval powers could not afford to ignore the steam engine. The British warship *Rhadamanthus* and others like it were invaluable, as the potential of steam power was great. In 1832, the year before its voyage across the Atlantic Ocean, *Rhadamanthus* had proved the value of steam power in a blockade of the Netherlands coast in support of French operations to expel Dutch troops from Belgium. The vessel was able to stay on station regardless of changing wind patterns. Aside from this practical consideration, it was better in the long run to embrace the new system rather than be left behind by other powers.

Before 1840, most steamers were small dispatch boats. British vessels such as *Rhadamanthus* were the order of the day. Indeed, France had set the precedent for this vessel in 1829 with the launch of *Sphinx,* its first steam-powered warship, at the port of Brest. The hull of *Sphinx* measured 151 feet, 6 inches by 26 feet, 4 inches and displaced 777 tons. Its engine, produced in Great Britain (the French did not start building their own steam plants until 1848), was capable of a maximum speed of 7 knots. The vessel also was equipped with sails. French shipyards over the next 10 years launched 23 warships that mirrored the design of *Sphinx.* Other naval powers such as Russia, the third largest naval power of the early nineteenth century, were slow to adopt steam power despite the recognized potential.

These early steam-powered vessels on the whole possessed so little armament that they could hardly be considered viable warships. The launch of the British warship *Gorgon* in 1837 marked a noted departure from the dearth of weaponry. Originally rated as a first-class paddle sloop but considered by many to be a frigate, it was a wooden-hulled warship that measured 178 feet by 37.5 feet and displaced 1,111 tons. The ship mounted two 10-inch smoothbore cannons, the size being the diameter of the gun barrel, and four 32-pounder cannons. Its steam engines and paddle wheels produced a speed of 10 knots. The portion of the paddle wheels above water was enclosed in lightly armored boxes to protect them from enemy fire. Typical of all steam-powered warships of the early age of steam, *Gorgon* was also equipped with sails because of the tremendous amount of coal needed to fuel the engines. British naval officials evaluated *Gorgon* as a good design, which led the British to construct larger vessels resembling it.

Construction on paddle wheel warships proceeded apace after 1837 by some of the world's maritime powers. Sloops comprised a large portion of the production programs of these powers. By 1860, France possessed 56 paddle wheel sloops, making it the largest force in the world. Great Britain operated 36 and the Austrian Empire (later the Austro-Hungarian Empire) maintained 13. The United States possessed two paddle wheel sloops.[7]

These ships, however, were approaching obsolescence by 1860 due to another innovation in propulsion that had a tremendous impact on warship design. The invention of the screw propeller negated the disadvantages that the paddle wheel posed to steam-powered warships. Technical plans for such a system had existed since the late eighteenth century. A step forward toward a viable screw propeller occurred in 1800 when English inventor Edward Shorter patented a two-blade propeller that was attached to a shaft. The device was fitted into a transport ship in 1802, with the shaft being cranked by some 10 seamen. The top speed attained was only 1.5 knots, but the test did show the viability of screw propulsion.

Shorter's work was taken farther by Englishman Francis Petit Smith and John Erickson, a Swedish-born inventor. In 1836, these two individuals, working independently of one another, produced designs for steam propulsion plants that used screw propellers. Smith's design led to the construction of the *Francis Smith,* which was equipped with a single screw propeller. The hull of this diminutive vessel measured 31 feet, 11 inches by 5 feet, 6 inches and displaced 6 tons. Due to its size, the vessel spent most of its successful career after launching in late 1836 on the canal system that ran through the British Isles. Erickson's design produced the *Francis B. Ogden,* which was only slightly larger than Smith's craft. Launched in 1837, the vessel measured only 45 feet by 8 feet, which classified it as a launch. It possessed two screw propellers that each measured 5 feet, 2 inches in diameter. Upon its first trial, the *Francis B. Ogden* attained a speed of 10 knots.

Larger ships soon followed those of Smith and Erickson. Smith's work attracted considerable attention in the British Admiralty, the administrative board of the Royal Navy, but it was not yet inclined to decide whether to adopt the screw propeller for warships. In 1838, the British Admiralty called for a further demonstration of the screw propeller in a vessel of larger size. This led to the construction in the same year of *Archimedes*.

Launched in October 1838, the ship measured 125 feet by 22 feet, 6 inches and displaced 237 tons. It shipped a steam engine and propeller along with a sailing rig in case the engine broke down. Between April and May 1840, *Archimedes* proved the superiority of the propeller over the paddle wheel in a series of races across the English Channel against paddle wheel ships. Despite the fact that one paddle wheel vessel was faster than *Archimedes* under certain weather conditions, the naval officer in charge of the races attributed this to the larger size and greater weight of the screw-propelled ship versus its paddle-wheeled competitor. His conclusion was that the propeller was in fact equal if not superior to the paddle wheel in speed and performance. On 3 April 1845, reinforcement for this conclusion was provided by a test between the screw-propelled steamship *Rattler* and the paddle-wheel equipped *Alecto*. The two vessels were lashed together stern to stern in a tug-of-war. *Alecto* first dragged *Rattler* along at a speed of 2 knots, but only due to the fact that *Rattler* had not started its engine. Once it did so, *Rattler* was soon towing *Alecto* at a speed of 2.8 knots despite *Alecto*'s propulsion plant being pushed to its operational limit. This experiment became much more famous than the trials of *Archimedes*, but in truth the British Royal Navy and other powers had already made their decision concerning the propeller. Paddle wheel warships remained in service well after the tests involving *Archimedes*. Even so, the British along with the world's other naval powers turned away from paddle wheels in favor of screw-propelled warships.

Besides its proven superiority over the paddle wheel in terms of speed, the propeller had other advantages that the world's navies seized upon. First, the propeller obviated the problem of reduced firepower that was inherent to paddle wheel ships. As the propeller was mounted under the stern, ships that used it had an unobstructed broadside and could thus mount more weaponry than paddle wheelers. Second, the propeller was far less vulnerable to enemy fire. In practical terms, the propeller also had the distinct advantage of being able to be fitted to preexisting sailing warships.

The major maritime powers thus embarked on a program of acquiring steam-powered, screw-propelled warships. A portion of these craft were converted ships from the Age of Fighting Sail, being old ships-of-the-line and frigates. Others were newly built, such as the French *Le Napoleon* that was launched in 1850 as the world's first purpose-built, steam-powered, screw-propelled ship-of-the-line.

In terms of warships the size of a sloop, the majority represented new construction. An example is a unit of the six-ship *Jason*-class of wooden screw corvettes. *Jason*, completed in 1860, measured 225 feet by 40 feet, with a draft of 8 inches by 19 feet, and displaced 2,431 tons. It was armed primarily with 20 8-inch muzzle-loading smoothbore guns. The vessel's steam engine could produce a maximum speed of 12 knots. This velocity could be supplemented by the vessel's sailing rig. Like all vessels of this period, sails were still retained owing to the high fuel consumption of the engines. By the time of the completion of *Jason*, the screw sloop, or corvette, was an integral part of battle fleets in several navies. Great Britain possessed 48 of them, while France operated 34 such vessels. Russia counted 26, which dwarfed the number of the United States, with 6. Other countries possessed still fewer screw-propelled, steam-powered sloops and corvettes than the United States.[8]

While naval powers incorporated the newest advances in propulsion into battle fleets, another innovation was the advent of iron-hulled vessels. The concept of iron as a material for ship construction was not new. Iron canal boats had been in use since the late eighteenth century, as many involved in maritime affairs recognized its superior strength over wood and its ability to better weather the elements. The first oceangoing iron ship was the British-built *Aaron Manby* that entered service in 1822. Constructed in sections of iron plates riveted to an iron frame, this paddle wheel steamer was relatively small, measuring only 106 feet, 9 inches by 17 feet, 2 inches and displacing 116 tons. Its size allowed for commercial travel between London and Paris, as it could steam laden with goods across the English Channel and travel via the Thames River to London and the River Seine to Paris. The vessel's career is a testimony to the advantages of iron construction. Its hull suffered little damage despite numerous groundings in shallow waters that would have caused great damage to wooden ships. The hull also required very little maintenance.

Given these advantages, iron was subsequently applied to warship construction as naval officials took note of the strength of iron and its potential to withstand enemy fire far better than the wooden walls of the past. The first application of iron to warship construction was the British gunboat *Nemesis*. Laid down in 1839 and completed in January 1840, the iron hull of *Nemesis* measured 184 feet by 29 feet and displaced 660 tons. This structure was revolutionary for its composition and for the fact that it incorporated watertight compartments, making the vessel the first warship fitted with this innovation. The vessel's means of propulsion consisted of a steam engine connected to paddle wheels on each side of the ship and a sail rig of two masts. Its armament originally consisted of two 32-pounder cannons and four 6-pounders. A crew of 60–90 officers and men manned the ship. This vessel was not designed as an oceangoing craft but rather one capable of shore and river operations. *Nemesis* proved its worth in these capacities during the 1841–1843 First China War, a British imperial conflict. The vessel was hit numerous times by enemy fire, but everything simply ricocheted off its hull. In one engagement, *Nemesis* was hit 14 times without significant damage. Even so, there was a major problem with ships built solely of iron that hampered its use in larger warships. Iron proved brittle, especially in cold weather, which meant that it could be a liability in war, as it had a tendency to crack upon the impact of larger projectiles.

Between 1840 and 1860, despite this difficulty, experimentation continued with iron-hulled warships. In 1842, U.S. inventor Robert L. Stevens endeavored to produce the world's first seagoing ironclad. Known as the Stevens Battery, it was never completed, but other nations pursued Stevens's goal. The world's first significant iron warship was the British-built paddle wheel steam frigate *Guadeloupe,* built in 1842 and ordered by Mexico. Although many of the iron-hulled, steam-powered warships proceeding *Guadeloupe* were frigates and still larger craft, the world's naval powers did extend iron construction to smaller ships. Great Britain's first iron-hulled sloops—termed corvettes at the time—were the three vessels of the *Volage* class launched between 1870 and 1875. Other naval powers produced iron-hulled steam sloops at the same time as the launch of the *Volage*-class units.

The delay between the appearance of *Guadeloupe* and vessels like those of the *Volage* class was the result of a temporary, generally worldwide, cessation in the construction of iron-hulled warships in the 1850s as concerns over the brittle nature of iron could not be overcome. This cessation ended due to two technological innovations that posed threats to wooden-walled vessels. The first was posed by guns that fired shells rather than solid shot. Indeed, the danger posed by shells to wooden walls had spurred the first use of iron for the hulls of warships. Tests of this ordnance were conducted by the British and the French between the middle eighteenth century and early nineteenth century. Beginning in the

1820s, thanks to the work of French Colonel Henri Paixhans, who developed the first truly reliable shell gun, the shell began to supplant shot. Shells were much more destructive than shot to wooden vessels. Round, solid balls of shot had the tendency to produce a clean hole that could be patched. A shell, on the other hand, was designed to lodge in the hull of a ship and then explode, creating an irregular size hole that could be patched only with great difficulty.

The growing interest of naval powers in shell guns in the following years necessitated the use of iron in the construction of warships. Iron was also necessary given the rise of another threat to wooden-hulled ships: rifled guns. Cutting grooves into the gun tube of a cannon produced spin on the projectile fired. In 1742 Englishman Benjamin Robins pioneered work in rifled guns. By the 1850s, rifled, muzzle-loading guns had gained favor due to their longer range and greater accuracy, although production remained low due to the higher pressure, over that of smoothbore cannon, created by rifled guns when fired. The extra stress created by the higher pressure was the result of the gun tubes of rifled guns being slightly smaller than the smoothbore variety to help produce the spin on the projectile.

The Crimean War (1853–1856) reinforced the need for iron in ship construction in order to counter the power of the shell gun and rifled guns. It also was the first large-scale conflict that tested in battle the new naval technology that had appeared since the end of the Napoleonic Wars. This war pitted Great Britain, France, the Ottoman Empire, and Sardinia against Russia. The fundamental causes of hostilities were the Russian efforts to expand into the Ottoman Empire's European possessions, something opposed by other European powers as it upset the balance of power in the region. The naval Battle of Sinope that occurred on 30 November 1853 proved the value of shell guns against wooden-hulled ships, as all of the warships involved were constructed of wood. A Russian force that employed both solid shot and shell virtually annihilated an Ottoman squadron that was equipped with only solid shot. This battle renewed world interest in iron-hulled vessels. The power of the shell gun also generated interest in iron armor. France was the first to develop viable armored vessels when it built floating batteries for use in the Crimean War. These batteries were wooden-hulled vessels with iron bolted to their sides. On 17 October 1855, three of these ships were used in the bombardment of Russian forts in the Black Sea. The iron resisted most of the hits registered on the floating batteries.

The Crimean War made the construction of corvettes like *Volage* possible by signaling a definitive end to the era of wooden-walled vessels and cementing iron construction—another technological innovation that led to the modern destroyer—as the new production method. It also generated greater interest in the use of iron for armor. The first manifestation appeared in August 1860 with the completion of the screw frigate *Gloire,* which had iron bolted to a wooden hull. Great Britain followed in December 1860 with the iron-hulled screw frigate *Warrior.* This concept would lead in the future to protection that would at times be used on sloops and later on destroyers.

Sloops were able to showcase new naval technology during the U.S. Civil War (1861–1865), which occurred on the heels of the age of the wooden-walled vessel. Warships the size of sloops participated in the conflict in various duties for the Union. The Union strategy to defeat the Confederacy, proposed by General Winfield Scott and accepted by President Abraham Lincoln, became known as the Anaconda Plan. The scheme rested on two operations to compel surrender. On 19 April 1861, President Lincoln declared a blockade of the coastline of the Confederate States of America to deny it any supplies from overseas. Among the vessels employed in this task were sloops. One of the more powerful vessels of the Union blockading force was the screw sloop *Niagra,* while the five screw sloops of the Hartford class also greatly enhanced the effort. Not only were these vessels useful in maintaining the blockade in deep waters off the Confederate coast; their shallow drafts also made it possible for them to patrol waters close offshore. The blockade proved effective in stemming overseas commerce. In the first year of the conflict, 800 vessels arrived in Southern ports as opposed to 6,000 in the last year of peace.[9] Although the blockade did not force the Confederacy from the war, it did lead to shortages in equipment and supplies such as artillery and medicines.

The second aspect of the Anaconda Plan in which sloops took part were coastal and river operations, as General Scott envisioned the capture of key strongholds on the tributaries of the Mississippi River and on the great river itself to split the Confederacy in two and to garner launching-off points for ground assaults deep into Confederate territory. An example of this duty is the April 1862 Union operation to capture New Orleans, the Confederacy's largest city and its most vital port. The Union naval force tasked with defeating the Confederate forces defending New Orleans—two forts and gunboats on the river—consisted of 17 ships commanded by Commodore David G. Farragut. Eight of these ships, and the most powerful of Farragut's force, were classed as either steam sloops or steam corvettes. They were vital to the Union victory over Confederate defenses and the subsequent capture of New Orleans, a grave blow to the Confederate war effort.

Aside from duties arising from the Anaconda Plan, sloops also engaged in the role of commerce protection. The Union used screw sloops to hunt down Confederate commerce raiders. On 19 June 1864, the Union steam sloop *Kearsarge* engaged the Confederate raider *Alabama* outside the port of Cherbourg, France, and sunk the Confederate vessel.

The U.S. Civil War proved to be the last instance where sloops were used in a major conflict in the roles assigned to them during the Age of Fighting Sail. Further technological innovation rendered the sloop an obsolete craft and paved the way for its successor, the destroyer. Although the technological innovations of the first half of the nineteenth century made a modern warship like the destroyer possible, the additional innovation of the self-propelled torpedo in the second half of the nineteenth century led naval officials to the new warship's development. The creation of the self-propelled torpedo heralded the age of the destroyer, a vessel that assumed some of the roles of the sloop, as well as new roles dictated by changes in naval warfare.

ENDNOTES

1. Brian Lavery, *Nelson's Navy: The Ships, Men, and Organisation, 1793–1815* (London: Conway Maritime Press, 1989), 80,82.

2. Ibid., p. 84.

3. Allan Millet and Peter Maslowski, *For the Common Defense: A Military History of the United States of America* (New York: Free Press, 1994), p. 102.

4. Dean King and John Hattendorf, eds., *Every Man Will Do His Duty: An Anthology of Firsthand Accounts from the Age of Nelson, 1792–1815* (New York: Henry Holt, 1997), p. 307.

5. David K. Brown, *Before the Ironclad: Development of Ship Design, Propulsion, and Armament in the Royal Navy, 1815–1860* (London: Conway Maritime Press, 1990), p. 8.

6. Spencer C. Tucker, *Handbook of 19th Century Naval Warfare* (Gloucestershire, UK: Sutton Publishing, 2000), p. 53.

7. James L. George, *History of Warships: From Ancient Times to the Twenty-First Century* (Annapolis, MD: Naval Institute Press, 1998), p. 65.

8. Ibid.

9. Spencer C. Tucker, *A Short History of the Civil War at Sea* (Wilmington, DE: Scholarly Resources, 2002), p. 19.

CHAPTER 2

From Experimental Vessel to Warship, 1860–1918

THE PRODUCTION OF the self-propelled torpedo, which ultimately led to the creation of the destroyer, was the result of decades of development. Since the late eighteenth century during the Age of Fighting Sail, experiments had been under way to produce a submerged weapon that could explode in proximity to or against a vessel's hull. Inventors hoped that the detonation of such a device would produce a hole below the waterline and lead to flooding that would sink the ship. Modern underwater warfare, and the path of development toward the torpedo, originated in 1778 during the American Revolutionary War. Locked in an imperial war with the American colonies, Great Britain's navy vastly outnumbered the paltry forces of the colonists. To offset this disadvantage at a relatively cheap price, U.S. inventor David Bushnell created floating mines designed to detonate upon impact with a solid object such as a warship's hull. They consisted essentially of kegs of powder that also contained a flintlock mechanism that would release upon the shock of the keg hitting the hull, detonating the mine. These early mines were limited in their use due to the technology of the age. They were defensive weapons, as they had no motive power of their own. One type relied on currents in inland waterways to sink enemy vessels at anchor. The drawback of using the flow of water as motive power was evident, however, upon their first use in the Revolutionary War. On 5 January 1778, David Bushnell released his floating mines down the Delaware River to destroy British ships that rode at anchor downriver. The river, however, moved so slowly that the mines took more than a week to arrive at the British position, by which time many of the warships had moved. Another model was the stationary mine, which was anchored by a chain. This mine had the obvious drawback of requiring an enemy craft to pass over its position. In addition to their having little offensive capability, these weapons also could be employed only in shallow waters such as coastal areas and rivers.

Experiments with varying types of mines continued in the early nineteenth century in Europe and the United States. In 1801 during the French Napoleonic Wars, U.S. inventor Robert Fulton attempted to convince Napoleon, the emperor of France, to buy his floating mines by arguing that the best way to defeat Great Britain, one of the emperor's principal enemies, was to prevent the passage into and out of the country's ports. While Napoleon rejected the scheme, the undaunted Fulton was able to convince the British to invest in his weapons. Attempts in late 1804 and the subsequent year, however, failed for essentially the same reason as Bushnell's attempt with floating mines: the weapon was at the mercy of the currents. Fulton was able to demonstrate to the British government the destructive potential of an underwater weapon on 15 October 1805, when he successfully detonated a mine against a vessel captured by the British. The force of the explosion tore the hull of the vessel in half, making it the first ship of large size to be destroyed by a mine. Despite this success, the British withdrew their support of Fulton. The problem of motive power remained one of the chief drawbacks of the weapon, which continued to render it largely a defensive weapon.

Attempts to increase offensive potential produced mines that were attached to vessels that could propel them toward a target. These were the earliest torpedoes. Two types predominated by the middle nineteenth century. The first was the towed mine, attached to the stern of a vessel by a rope or chain. The second became known as the spar torpedo, which consisted of a mine attached to the end of a wooden beam that projected a little more than 30 feet over the bow of the ship that employed it. Spar torpedoes showcased the potential of an offensive mine in the U.S. Civil War (1861–1865). The value of this type, however, was dubious. If an attacking vessel was successful in detonating a spar torpedo against the hull of an enemy ship, the nearby blast could easily damage the hull of the attacking warship. The ramifications of this problem were evident through the experience of the Confederate submarine *H. L. Hunley*. On 17 February 1864, *H. L. Hunley*, armed with a spar torpedo, sank the Union steam sloop *Housatonic,* giving it the dubious distinction of being the first warship destroyed by a submarine in history. The explosion, however, probably damaged the *H. L. Hunley's* hull, and it sank while trying to return to shore with the loss of its crew.

Naval officials of the great maritime powers in subsequent years believed that further development of the torpedo was necessary to make it a viable weapon of naval warfare. This development occurred in 1868 with the introduction of the Whitehead self-propelled torpedo. In 1865, Captain Giovanni Luppis of the Austrian Navy had plans for a remote-controlled craft fitted with a spar torpedo. An attacker could afford to lose the small boat provided that it was unmanned. Luppis's lack of success led him to solicit the help of British engineer Robert Whitehead, who in 1867 produced an improvement on the Austrian officer's idea. His invention dispensed with the remote-controlled craft through the inclusion of propulsion machinery and the explosive charge in one casing. His torpedo consisted of a metal tube in which a 300-pound explosive charge was housed in the front. Behind it was enclosed a compartment full of compressed air, stored at a pressure of 370 pounds per square inch, that drove a motor that could produce a maximum speed of 7 knots. Although the range of this weapon was only 200 yards at this maximum speed and only 300 yards at a reduced velocity, this development was an enormous improvement that addressed the old problem of motive power for an underwater weapon. In 1868, Whitehead showcased improved designs of torpedoes of both 14 inches and 16 inches in diameter that could travel up to 700 yards at the maximum speed of 7 knots. This convinced the British of the military potential of Whitehead's torpedo, and they bought the rights to Whitehead's invention.

British naval officials then faced the question of what type of vessel should be used to deploy the new weapon. A committee set up in 1872 to examine the question produced three ideas. The first envisioned the construction of very small launches that could be stored on the decks of capital ships—at this time meaning battleships—and deployed in battle. A second proposal was fitting torpedo tubes into the hulls of conventional warships such as battleships and cruisers. This latter proposal found favor, and by 1880 many warships of the British Royal Navy carried torpedoes as part of their armament. More important for the history of the destroyer, however, was the last suggestion, which called for the construction of specialized smaller boats designed to mount torpedoes as their principal armament.

In the early 1870s the British pursued the development of ships that conformed to the committee's third proposal while other naval powers, such as France, procured variants of Whitehead's torpedo and did the same. The efforts of the British would eventually lead to the first destroyer. As with most naval powers at this time, the envisioned vessel was intended for coastal defense against battle fleets supporting an invasion of the homeland. The small size of the vessel would not allow for the storage of large quantities of coal for fuel or provisions needed for operations in the open sea. In addition, the tiny craft would not be able to keep station in rough waters. The first British warship designed specifically for torpedo attack was *Vesuvius*, completed in 1874. The hull of *Vesuvius* measured only 90 feet by 22 feet by 8.5 feet, displaced 245 tons, and was fitted with only one torpedo tube, located in the bow below the waterline, that fired a 16 inch–diameter torpedo. To mask the ship's approach against an opposing vessel and thereby allow it to close within torpedo range, *Vesuvius* had a very low freeboard, meaning that the hull did not rise very high out of the water. It also was built without a funnel so as not to produce a silhouette on the horizon. Smoke from its engines was expelled out of vents on the sides of the hull.

This novel design, however, was not very successful. The draft—the measurement of a how low a ship rode in the water—was rather deep and consequently produced a large amount of drag. As a result, the ship's steam engine could produce a maximum speed of only 9.7 knots. Most newer battleships of this period, which were deemed the principal prey of a ship like *Vesuvius*, were capable of faster speeds. An example is the British *Neptune*, launched in 1874 and completed in 1881, which could attain a maximum speed of 14.22 knots. *Vesuvius*, consequently, could not viably attack the warships it was designed to destroy. A lightly armed, unprotected ship like *Vesuvius* had to rely on speeds in excess of its opponent not only to run the enemy down and enable a torpedo attack but also to flee in the face of large guns that could destroy it.

The British answer to the problem of speed came in 1877 with the launching of *Lightning*, the Royal Navy's first torpedo boat. Although France built the world's first torpedo boat a year earlier, *Lightning* is indicative of the design of these craft. The vessel, which measured 87 feet by 10 feet, 8 inches by 5 feet, 2 inches, was smaller than *Vesuvius* in the interest of greater speed. The hull of *Lightning* is representative of a very important technological innovation that is still in use today: steel hulls. As a building material, steel had been used for centuries in weapons and some tools. The advantages were that it was stronger and lighter than iron. The prohibitively expensive process of smelting steel, however, obviated its use in large construction jobs such as ships. This state of affairs began to change in the middle nineteenth century. A step forward in reducing the cost came in 1856 when Henry Bessemer devised a new furnace to produce steel from iron. By the early 1860s, the price of steel consequently dropped to the point that it was being used in limited quantities on warships. Variations in the quality of the steel produced from Bessemer's process, however, hindered its widespread employment. In 1865, this problem was surmounted by a new smelting process developed by Frenchman Pierre Martin, who created a furnace based on an 1857 design by German inventor Sir William Siemens for a gas furnace. The quality of the steel from Martin's furnace was better than that of the past and further lowered the cost of the material. In 1878, steel became still cheaper through another advance by inventors Sidney Thomas and Percy Gilchrist.

These improved methods collectively led to a greater use of steel in warship construction. The French initially led the way in the use of cheaper steel through the completion in 1878 of *Redoutable,* the world's first steel-hulled battleship. Other nations such as Great Britain, with vessels like *Lightning,* followed the French example. The steel-hulled warships that resulted led to a virtual end to hull construction using iron. By the early 1880s, most naval powers would shift the majority of construction to steel. Aside from the advantage of steel, *Lightning's* shallow draft as well as its very small displacement of only 32.5 tons proved significant, as its engine could produce a maximum speed of 19 knots. The steam propulsion plant of this craft, as with most warships in this period, was the compound engine. This plant was a great improvement over the early steamship period. Instead of a single, large, reciprocating piston, the engine used one high-pressure and two low-pressure cylinders. These greatly increased the power generated by the burning of coal in the boilers while requiring less coal to produce it.

The first viable version of the compound engine was patented in 1853 and mounted in some ships as experiments, but these had been largely unsuccessful. The key reason was that the engines were still made of iron that could not easily withstand the added pressures produced by the new process. The use of steel, however, removed this problem and signaled a step toward more powerful, fuel-efficient engines that would eventually make the retention of sails an unnecessary feature on warships. Steam was provided by the ship's coal-fired locomotive boilers. The original armament of *Light-*

ning consisted of two cages, each containing a torpedo, that could be lowered down the sides. This very tiny craft was intended to fire torpedoes after steering the ship directly at the target to offer the smallest silhouette and thus make it harder for enemy gunners to hit it. Essentially a steam launch, the vessel was manned by a crew of only 15 officers and men.

Although *Lightning* and others like it were still designed primarily for coastal defense, the destructive potential of the torpedo boat began to increase in subsequent years and caused a great deal of concern in British naval circles. Great Britain, the largest naval power in the world at the time, based the power of its fleet on the battleship. This large and expensive warship was designed to engage in gunnery duels with ships of generally equal strength. It was vulnerable, however, to torpedo attacks below the waterline. British officials recognized that the torpedo boat, being a cheap and small craft, could destroy the mightiest ships afloat with its torpedoes. By the early 1880s, this possibility was substantially greater owing to advances in weapons technology. One version of the torpedo at the close of the 1870s could travel at 18 knots with a maximum range of 600 yards. This advance was only the beginning of subsequent increases in speed, range, and destructive power.

Equally alarming to the British was the fact that other naval powers were building far more seaworthy hulls for torpedo boats, enabling them to function outside coastal waters. Russia and France, Britain's chief naval rivals, were building such vessels in large numbers. British officials considered war versus these two powers as the highest probability by the late 1880s. French torpedo boats were increasingly capable of operating in the English Channel and formed part of France's naval strategy at the time, which was shaped by the Jeune École (Young School) school of thought. This idea was the product of the introduction of the torpedo and originated in 1869 with the work of a French captain, Baron Louis-Antoine-Richild Grivel. He believed that naval warfare consisted of three distinct types: on the open seas between battle fleets comprised of capital ships, coastal warfare, and guerre de course. The latter—a war on commerce—was advocated by Grivel in the event of war with Great Britain. In his view, France could not contest the British on the high seas through a pitched battle between capital ships because of British numerical superiority. France's economy was not strong enough to produce battleships in a quantity to equal that of Great Britain. Attempts to achieve parity had failed during the 1850s and 1860s.

Grivel realized, however, that France possessed one strength that Britain did not, and it dictated the proper naval strategy for France. Although France was completely self-sufficient in the production of foodstuffs for its population, Britain was increasingly dependent on food from overseas. Grivel therefore recommended a guerre de course with a fleet comprised of small craft and cruisers rather than battleships to starve Britain into submission in the event of war. This concept also held true for British imports of raw materials for industry, as a large portion was garnered from overseas. Grivel's belief was adopted by Admiral Theophile Aube, who in 1886 became France's minister of marine. France subsequently embarked on the construction of torpedo boats, cruisers, and submarines to this end.

By the 1880s, Grivel's theory appeared to hold particular weight given the further decline of Britain's agricultural sector, as by this point the country relied on the majority of its food supply from overseas. Indeed, by 1891 Britain imported 80 percent of its annual foodstuffs.[1] The ideas of the Jeune École were particularly threatening given this fact. The strategy of the Jeune École also carried some weight given that by 1880 Britain was responsible for 26 percent of the world's industry, being the leader in production of pig iron and steel.[2] This industrial strength allowed Britain to maintain its large navy. A large number of torpedo boats employed in time of war might disrupt that valuable trade. By 1885, rivals of Britain possessed torpedo craft in numbers that might make such a disruption possible. The torpedo boat fleets of the allied navies of France and Russia numbered 115 and 50 at this time.[3] Many of these had limited seagoing ability.

Great Britain consequently pursued an idea to combat the torpedo boats of its rivals. Beginning in the early 1880s, as the threat posed by the torpedo boat assumed alarming proportions, British naval officials advocated the concept of the torpedo boat catcher. This vessel was designed to protect the capital ships of the battle fleet against torpedo boat attacks and evolved into the destroyer as a distinct type of warship. An example of an early catcher is the *Swift*, launched in 1885. This vessel was classed as a torpedo boat but was larger and more heavily armed than preceding warships. The hull measured 153 feet, 8 inches by 17 feet, 6 inches by 9 feet, 6 inches and displaced 152 tons. Although it carried three 14-inch torpedo tubes, one being fixed in the bow while the other two were carried on deck, *Swift* was also armed with four 3-pounder guns to attack enemy torpedo boats.

Spurred on in 1885 by an imperial crisis with Russia over Afghanistan, work moved forward toward a larger version of *Swift*. These vessels were *Rattlesnake* and its three sister ships. Completed in 1888, the hulls measured 200 feet by 23 feet by 10 feet, 4 inches and displaced 550 tons. Each ship was armed with one breech-loading 5-inch gun and six 3-pounder weapons to attack enemy torpedo boats.

The inclusion of the breech-loading weapon represents a further technological innovation in naval warfare that became a permanent feature on warships. Breechloaders had been in existence for centuries and were first tried at sea aboard the French battleship *Gloire* in 1858, but the French and other navies had reverted to the use of muzzle loaders owing to the poor seal between gun and breech, which allowed gases to escape while firing and could lead to the bursting of the gun. Advances in breechloaders in the 1870s led to the readoption of the weapon. This type of gun was far more destructive than the old muzzle loaders, as it could be loaded far more quickly.

In addition to its guns, *Rattlesnake* and its sister ships were also armed with four 14-inch torpedo tubes. Unlike later torpedo boat catchers, these ships also incorporated a .75-inch protective deck of armor to shield machinery and engines from plunging gunfire. They were manned by a crew of 66 officers and men. The maximum speed of 19.25 knots was provided by a new engine, yet another of the many technological innovations of the day. First introduced in the mid-1870s and perfected in 1881, this development was known as the triple-expansion engine. Its giant pistons compressed steam from the boilers in three stages. This process increased the power of the engine. Triple-expansion engines could generate steam pressures of 60 pounds per square inch as opposed to compound engines that produced between 25 and 30 pounds per square inch. The new propulsion plant also consumed less fuel due to greater efficiency. The result was that a ship equipped with the triple-expansion engine could steam greater distances without the need to recoal and could keep station against the increasingly seaworthy boats of opposing navies.

Although armed with torpedoes, *Rattlesnake* and craft of the same design became known in the British service as torpedo gunboats (designation: TGB). Between 1892 and 1894, Britain built another three classes of TGB that numbered 32 boats. Each class was progressively larger; maximum speeds ranged from 18 to 19 knots. An example is a vessel of the *Dryad* class that measured 250 feet pp (the length of a ship from the perpendicular bulkhead in the bow to that of the stern) by 30 feet, 6 inches by 11 feet, 6 inches and displaced 1,070 tons. It was armed with five 18-inch torpedo tubes, two 4.7-inch guns, four 6-pounders, and one machine gun. The vessel's triple-expansion engine produced a maximum speed of 18.2 knots. The crew complement was 120 officers and men.

These first torpedo boat catchers, despite being an innovative design, proved ineffective due to a host of problems. The biggest was that the vessels were too slow to hunt down the torpedo boats they were designed to destroy. For instance, French torpedo boats launched in 1887 were capable of a maximum speed of 20 knots. The early torpedo boat catchers were also still limited in range despite the increase in size and were not very seaworthy owing to their lightly built hulls and low freeboards. Finally, the torpedo boat catchers were unreliable. Their locomotive boilers strained to produce the steam necessary to attain high speeds and the vibration of the reciprocating triple-expansion engines could shake fragile hulls apart. With the exception of speed, problems would continue to plague destroyers up to World War I.

Despite such shortcomings, however, the need to pursue better designs received further reinforcement from experiences of torpedo attacks around the world. In the 1891 Chilean civil war, the battleship *Blanco Encalada* was sunk by the torpedo boat *Almirante Lynch*. This case merely reinforced the threat of the torpedo to big surface warships and was the first time that a self-propelled torpedo sank an armored vessel. Further reinforcement was provided at the same time by the alarming numbers of torpedo boats in world navies. By 1890, Great Britain had 186 torpedo boats, but France and Russia operated 220 and 152, respectively. Other powers also had high numbers of the craft. Germany possessed 143, while Italy maintained 129 torpedo boats.[4] These craft were increasingly seaworthy and carried torpedoes of increasing range.

This environment led the British in 1892 to establish a new design committee to examine designs of the torpedo boat catcher. Called in March 1892 by Admiral John Fisher, Third Sea Lord and controller of the navy, who placed great faith in technological innovation, it was tasked with the job of producing a ship capable of a maximum speed of 27 knots. This vessel became known as a torpedo boat destroyer (designation: TBD); the name was subsequently shortened to destroyer by the turn of the century. Basically an enlarged torpedo boat, its primary purpose remained defense of the battle fleet against torpedo attack, but as a portent of the future the idea existed that this vessel could also assume the torpedo boat's role of mounting torpedo attacks. These warships therefore maintained a mixed armament of guns and torpedoes.

The British Admiralty contracted with private shipyards to produce vessels of the type specified by the committee. In all, about 110 destroyers were produced by private firms between 1892 and 1902, testimony to the importance attached to them. Indeed, the large number of contracts absorbed such a large portion of naval spending in Britain that delays were experienced in the production of more powerful ships. The building program of 1893–1894 is an example, where construction was delayed on the two protected cruisers of the *Powerful* class, which would become the largest vessels of their type at the time of completion.

The two private yards that met with the most success were the firms of Yarrow and Thornycroft. The former produced what many scholars identify as the world's first destroyers. These were *Havock* and *Hornet,* which were both laid down in 1892 and completed in 1894. They measured 185 feet by 18 feet, 6 inches by 7 feet, 3 inches and displaced 275 tons. The principal armament consisted of one 12-pounder gun mounted aft and three 3-pounder guns distributed throughout the rest of the ship.

These guns were of a relatively new, quick-firing type. The concept stemmed from an 1881 British Admiralty advertisement for a gun that could fire an unprecedented 12 shots per minute. This weapon functioned in much the same way as small arms on land that fired cartridges. Both the propellant and the shell were encased in one body rather than the past method of loading shells and propellant separately into guns, meaning that the reload time for the weapon was much shorter. Quick-firing guns were necessary for destroyers to riddle opposing torpedo boats before they could attack with torpedoes. The guns were in completely exposed positions without shields for the gun crews, which would remain common practice in most navies until the years directly before World War I.

The ships also carried three 18-inch torpedo tubes, one being fitted in the bow; the other two were single launchers sited on the main deck. As an indication of the importance attached to gunnery, however, the deck tubes could be replaced by more guns. In essence, if torpedo tubes were replaced, the vessel would not have a torpedo armament owing to the unsatisfactory bow tube. Naval officials deemed it problematic following the launching of the vessels, as the destroyer proved faster than the torpedo at the time, meaning that the ship could run over its own weapon once fired. It was also exposed to enemy gunfire, as the method of torpedo attack consisted of a head-on approach. A hit on the bow torpedo tube presented the possibility of the torpedo detonating and destroying the ship. The

top speed was 26.7 knots, only a fraction below the Admiralty's requirement and thus acceptable, and was provided partially through
an early effort to streamline the hull. This innovation was the turtleback bow, distinguished by the main deck forward being a rounded
shape in order for seawater to cascade over it as the vessel, which
maintained a low freeboard, plowed through the water.

Besides being the first destroyers, one of the ships, *Hornet*, represents an example of destroyers as a testing ground for new technology. Destroyers, being cheap and quick to build, would oftentimes
be used in this capacity in subsequent years. Unlike *Havock*,
equipped with locomotive boilers, *Hornet* was fitted with new water-
tube boilers, a design that was pioneered by France. Instead of the
old boilers that burned coal to heat air in copper tubing that subsequently heated water and produced the steam that drove the engines, the water tube reversed the process. These boilers contained
the water within the tubing itself that passed through the fires of the
boiler. Steam pressure was consequently contained in the tubing
rather than outside and thus reduced the risk of a boiler explosion.
The results were twofold. First, the thickness of the boiler shell
could be reduced and thus saved weight. Also, steam pressure could
be increased more rapidly. This meant that a ship equipped with water-tube boilers could raise steam much faster and increase its speed
in a much shorter amount of time. These advantages constituted a
great increase in the effectiveness of destroyers, which relied on
speed to intercept torpedo boats. If used offensively in torpedo attacks, the destroyer would also benefit from being able to conduct
faster attacks, thus giving the opposing gun crews less time to react,
and being exposed for a lesser amount of time to the guns of a
slower opponent. The time necessary to build a ship with water-tube
boilers was longer, so *Havock* was technically the world's first destroyer, being launched five months before its sister ship. Despite
this drawback, the water-tube boiler proved a success. Although the
maximum speed of *Hornet* was only a fraction higher than its loco-
motive-boilered counterpart, the vessel was more reliable.

Both *Havock* and *Hornet* represented a far more viable solution to
the threat of the torpedo boat than past designs of the torpedo boat
catchers. This fact was proven during the 1894 fleet training maneuvers of the Royal Navy, during which *Havock* overtook two torpedo boats. On the basis of this success, these two ships proved to
be the first of a series of destroyers that have become known as the
26-knotters. Thornycroft's answer to Yarrow's vessels, *Daring* and
Decoy, were slightly faster but similarly armed. All subsequent de-

signs from private yards of this type were generally the same in dimension, speed, and armament to satisfy the requirements of the Admiralty. Even so, these destroyers were still not fast enough to catch some of the latest French-built torpedo boats. An example is *Forban,* launched in 1895; it could attain a maximum speed of 29 knots.

As a result, the British continued to develop the design of the destroyer with the chief requirement being speed. This effort led to new groups of destroyers. The first of these were known as the 27-knotters, totaling 36 vessels that were completed between 1895 and 1901. The 27-knotters were followed by the still faster 30-knotters that eventually numbered 65 triple expansion–engined warships. These were built primarily by those private firms that had enjoyed success through construction of units of the past types. The 30-knotters, completed between 1896 and 1902, possessed larger hulls to house the more powerful machinery needed to attain the extra knots sought by the Admiralty. An example of them is a design by Thornycroft that led to the launching in 1897 of some of the first of the type. The hull of *Desperate* displaced 310 tons, measured 210 feet by 19 feet, 6 inches by 7 feet and, like the previous type, was unarmored. It was armed with one 12-pounder gun, five 6-pounder weapons, and two 18-inch torpedo tubes. The triple-expansion engines of the craft produced a maximum speed of 30 knots. Crew complement consisted of 63 officers and men. Other firms built similar vessels of the same armament that accommodated an identical number of people. The chief differences between them lay in their hull dimensions.

Despite being great improvements over the old torpedo boat catchers and TGBs of the *Rattlesnake* type, both the 27-knotters and 30-knotters shared many of the design problems of their predecessors. Due to the great emphasis on speed, these vessels were lightly built and their engines strained to meet the requirements of the Admiralty. Oftentimes, these vessels ran their trials lightly loaded, as it was the only way to attain the necessary speed that would lead the Admiralty to purchase the vessels from their private manufacturers. If a destroyer failed to meet its designed speed, the ship might still be purchased, but with financial penalties based on how far short the speed fell from that specified.

As the engines were very lightly built to save weight, the strain at high speed oftentimes led to mechanical failure. This should not be surprising, as oftentimes the boilers needed nonstop stoking to the point where the furnaces glowed white-hot and the stokers needed colored glasses to protect their eyes from the heat and extreme light. The vibration of the triple-expansion engines, despite having been balanced to reduce the problem in 1892, received the steam from the boilers and produced enormous strain on the flimsy hulls. Their hull plating was only .125 inches thick, which meant that the shaking motion of the engine could tear or warp the plates and lead to flooding that might sink the ship. One of the most striking examples of the problem of great propulsion power in a light hull is that of the destroyer *Chamois*. The propeller of this ship flew off its shaft during trials, sliced into the thin plating of the stern, and produced flooding that sank the vessel.

Rather than strange misfortunes like that suffered by *Chamois*, the majority of the strain on a destroyer's hull was the product of day-to-day operations at sea. In rough seas, crewmen reported that the entire hull would visibly flex; either the deck or the keel, being the spine or bottom of the ship, could warp or split from the stress. Other accounts mention that plates would sometimes rupture or water would seep through the hull at the joints where each plate met the other. As these ships also still possessed low freeboards, crashing seas could easily damage the bridge and equipment mounted on the main deck. The conning position of these ships, which housed the wheel and telegraphs to communicate to the engine room, was normally surrounded by thin plate that was just as susceptible to the pounding seas as the hull.

The actual bridge from which the commander directed the operation of the ship was enclosed by canvas, which could easily be swept away by the sea as water traveled over the turtleback bow and crashed into it. In many instances, the forward section of the ship might completely submerge, leading some commanders to navigate from a secondary control position in the aft portion of the vessel. A specific example of this action comes from the experience of Commander Roger Keyes, who began his career as a destroyer captain and later became a noted commander of World War I. Keyes related that the bridge of one of his destroyer commands was oftentimes submerged feet deep in water as the ship plowed through heavy seas.[5]

In addition to these problems of seaworthiness, the small hull of a destroyer did not allow for the storage of appreciable amounts of fuel and provisions for the crew, resulting in a ship that had to port frequently for replenishment. The early destroyers, consequently, were still ships that could not operate for long periods of time at sea with the battle fleets that they were primarily meant to defend.

Added to all of these drawbacks was the fact that, despite being quicker, the 30-knotters were still only fractionally faster than France's fastest torpedo boats. The Admiralty was aware of this fact and commissioned work on 33-knot destroyers, but these were failures due to technological limitations posed by the triple-expansion engine. The 30-knotters proved to be near the limit of the capacity of the existing propulsion machinery. Three 33-knot destroyers were built, but none of them achieved the desired speed. Indeed, two of these spent more than a year running trials to attain the specified 33 knots while the strain on the engines of one of the destroyers during trials led to serious damage of the machinery.

A further technological innovation held the promise of breaking the threshold of speed set by triple-expansion engines and of relieving some of the structural problems experienced in the early destroyers that resulted from their use. As with the 27-knotters, the 30-knotters were also used as a proving ground for advances in propulsion and machinery. A subset of the latter type were equipped with turbine engines rather than the old reciprocating type. Invented by British engineer Charles Parsons, the turbine engine consisted of steam being passed from the boilers through a series of nozzles, where it gained velocity as it was pushed through them. This steam then passed through an engine that consisted of a series of blades attached to a rotor, which subsequently turned it and produced propulsion for the craft. The turbine made its debut on 26 June 1897, aboard *Turbina*, a 103-foot yacht, at the Naval Review at Spithead that was part of Queen Victoria's Diamond Jubilee. While naval vessels slowly steamed in a line-ahead formation—a straight line composed of vessels—as part of the naval review, *Turbina* broke from the group and steamed the length of the review line. Boats were dispatched to try and stop *Turbina*, captained by Parsons himself, but none could match the new craft's 34-knot speed. This display took place in front of Queen Victoria and assembled nobility from Europe, as well as high-ranking naval officials at the celebration.

The display of *Turbina* led the Admiralty to commission with private shipyards for the construction of destroyers equipped with the turbine engine. The result was the commission in 1900 of *Viper*, the first naval vessel in the world equipped with turbine engines. The hull of *Viper* measured 210 feet, 3.5 inches (pp) by 21 feet and displaced 344 tons. Like its predecessors, it was armed with one 12-pounder gun, five 6-pounder weapons, and two 18-inch torpedo tubes. The turbine engines produced an impressive maximum speed of 33.75 knots. In the same year, a second vessel, *Cobra*, was purchased by the Admiralty from another firm. In addition to the new turbine engine, this ship is significant as an example of the technological innovation of electricity. Introduced in the 1870s, electrical lighting in destroyers had previously been limited to machinery spaces. *Cobra* had electrical lighting throughout, which would become a common feature for destroyers along with the use of electricity to power systems. At the time, however, the significance of electricity paled in comparison to the introduction of the turbine.

The introduction of the turbine engine was a great advance and had several positive aspects to recommend its future use, but there were also drawbacks that impeded its being immediately embraced as the propulsion system of the future. These engines were far more reliable than the triple-expansion type, whose huge pistons generally shook apart themselves and the hull of the destroyer after extended use at high speeds. The turbine was also obviously faster. Even so, early turbines suffered from poor fuel efficiency. *Viper* consumed 6 tons of coal an hour simply to maintain 22 knots.[6] Such consumption meant that the boilers had to be fed at a very quick pace to maintain speed. A reflection of this fact presents itself in a proposal that *Cobra* needed a 59-man engine room staff, with 48 of them stokers. This requirement was indeed a daunting problem given that the entire crew complement of the reciprocating-engine destroyers was 63 officers and men. The Admiralty gave weight to this problem by contracting for a third turbine vessel, *Velox,* equipped with turbines for its highest speed and triple-expansion engines for normal cruising. Adding to the problem of fuel consumption was the fact that turbine engines could not be reversed so that the ship could back up. Instead, the only solution was to fit ships with separate turbines for generating propulsion ahead and in reverse.

These turbine vessels also suffered, as their predecessors did, from lightly built hulls to attain high speed, which ultimately detracted from their seaworthiness. In very few instances are the early problems of light hulls and seaworthiness better seen than through the operations of *Viper* and *Cobra*. On 3 August 1901, during fleet maneuvers, *Viper* was caught in poor weather conditions and struck a reef that lay near one of the islands in the English Channel. The collision ripped the bottom out of the hull, and the vessel was deemed a total loss. *Cobra* had an existence that was of greater brevity. Weeks after the demise of *Viper, Cobra* encountered heavy seas two hours after leaving port. The result was that the ship buckled amidships and broke in half with the loss of most of its crew. The loss of both ships was entirely unrelated to the introduction of the turbine, but their brief careers, particularly that of *Cobra,* called into question the British practice of speed as the ultimate consideration for destroyers at the expense of structural integrity.

The technical problems resulting from the design of early destroyers led to severe mechanical wear and considerable danger to ships and crews. Life aboard destroyers was a hard and dangerous affair given the nature of small ships being pressed to their limits. Seasickness was common aboard these craft as they pitched and rolled. In addition to simple nausea was the generally unhealthy conditions aboard that could make life miserable. These vessels possessed no inside insulation on the sides, meaning that the interior could be cold. Oftentimes, the cold produced condensation inside the hull. The discomfort of breathing while in these surroundings was magnified by the low freeboard. These vessels did not possess a great deal of ventilation because water pouring over the deck could pour down the ventilation shafts and flood the ship. All told, this was a perfect environment for contracting tuberculosis, and the contraction rate of it among destroyers was indeed high.

Little relief was experienced in climates that were warm or hot, as the ships became a furnace. The suffering of crew members was not alleviated by amenities aboard the ship, as they possessed none. The small size of the hulls led to little space for officers and men to eat and sleep. Those crewmen lying down in bunks, which were stowed to save space when not in use, who did try to rest could rarely do so owing to the pitching and rolling, the noise and vibration of the engines (with the exception of the turbine ships), and the heat they produced. Even the basic necessity of relieving one's self and washing were difficult. Although officers had a toilet, the men of the first destroyers made use of an open earth-closet erected in the fore section. This improved somewhat in types such as the 27-knotters and later classes that included toilets for the crew, but even then there was little relief. Most washing for crewmen consisted of using a bucket of water on the main deck. Little distraction was provided in the face of these conditions. Once again owing to the size of the hull, these ships lacked facilities such as libraries and barber shops that were found on bigger ships of the era.

Life while in port offered little comfort. A universal procedure for destroyers and large warships alike was the process of refueling with coal. Although this was a dirty business on any ship, the small size of destroyers made it doubly harsh. Coal was hauled in bags onto the decks of destroyers and dumped down chutes to the bunkers that held the ore. This process created clouds of coal dust that blanketed all the exterior and interior surfaces of the craft and choked the sailors. In these conditions, it is not surprising that the Admiralty offered hard-lying money, an appropriately named compensatory pay, to destroyer crews in addition to regular wages.

This money was considered necessary due not only to poor living conditions in general but also to the destroyer's light construction, which placed crewmen in far more danger. The reciprocating triple-expansion engines of the majority of these ships posed the most severe problem. As the ships reached full speed and the machinery strained, stokers and other engine-room personnel would hurriedly try to pour oil on the machinery to lubricate it and avoid a breakdown. One individual described this as a situation where one would "pour on the oil and trust in Providence."[7] Breakdowns could lead to catastrophic situations as the machinery commenced to tear itself and the ship apart as it continued to move. One destroyer of this period experienced a piston punching through its keel, and another had a piston break loose and launch itself through the main deck. Aside from the problem of maintaining machinery, destroyer crews also faced the horrible possibility of a collision with another vessel that could slice through the light hull. In some cases, collisions resulted in the ship being completely carved in half by larger warships.

Despite all the difficulties, the value of the destroyer was recognized by the British and all the other naval powers of the era. Nations consequently embarked on destroyer production in the wake of the launching of Britain's first craft. By 1892, France had experimented heavily with the torpedo and built large numbers of torpedo boats as a consequence of Jeune École thought. Among the types pursued by the French, in tandem with the continued construction of torpedo boats, was a design for a ship that was much like the British *Havock*. France's first true destroyers were the four ships of the *Durandal* class that were launched between 1899 and 1900. The hull of *Durandal* measured 188 feet, 8 inches by 20 feet, 8 inches by 10 feet, 5 inches and displaced 296 tons; its appearance resembled that of the British boats through its turtleback bow. Its armament consisted of one 2.5-inch gun and six 1.8-inch weapons as well as two 15-inch torpedo tubes. Like all of France's first destroyers, the ship was equipped with triple-expansion engines that produced a maximum speed of 26 knots.

The intended use of the *Durandal*-class destroyers was ambiguous owing to chaos in the strategic planning of French naval officials by the turn of the century. The influence of the Jeune École had declined somewhat, but debate raged between advocates of it and traditionalists who based naval power on numbers of capital ships. As a result, the intended purpose of the early destroyers wavered between the Jeune École's commerce warfare and the concept of protection of battleships as succeeding ministers of marine pursued their own policy on how best to combat Britain in time of war. Nevertheless, the general value of torpedo craft did not waver and resulted in the launching between 1899 and 1902 of another three classes of destroyers that numbered a total of 32 ships. Regardless of their purpose, these ships and the torpedo boats in existence continued to pose a threat to Britain.

Russia, one of the principal builders of torpedo boats, also turned to the procurement of destroyers. Between 1899 and 1902, the Russians contracted for seven classes of destroyers that numbered 44 vessels. Only two of these, however, were indigenous Russian designs. The majority of Russia's first destroyers were built in British, French, and German yards to the designs of private shipyards in the respective countries. The majority of these craft were fast but limited in range in the same way as destroyers of other countries. An example is *Pruitki,* known more commonly as *Sokol,* designed by the private British firm Yarrow. At the time of its completion in 1895, this vessel was one of the fastest with a maximum speed of 30.2 knots. This craft employed weaponry similar to British vessels, but it was also equipped with a ram in the bow to run down opposing vessels. Russian-built destroyers were slower, averaging around 26 knots. They were marked by the inclusion of mine-laying machinery, which was a feature that would become common to many domestically constructed Russian destroyers in subsequent years. This represents a belief shared by some other powers in the expansion of roles for destroyers in war. In Russian naval circles, they could not only be used in the traditional context of defense against torpedo boats and the newer idea of launching torpedo attacks; they could also be employed as minelayers.

Other powers built fewer vessels than the British, French, and Russians. The United States had possessed at the close of the U.S. Civil War (1861–1865) a fleet of 671 warships, second only to Great Britain. The end of the American conflict, however, resulted in the scrapping of many of these vessels and a low level of naval expenditure as Americans reverted to the belief in a navy being used for coastal defense. A large navy was therefore deemed unnecessary. In addition, available funds after the war were devoted to the army and the development of the western frontier of the North American continent. By the late 1870s, the U.S. Navy consisted of a collection of obsolete warships, a fleet smaller than that of Chile. Experimentation with torpedo boats did not occur until 1887 with a wooden-hulled craft that was followed by a conventional steel-hulled model in 1900.

Destroyers, due to a lack of funding and a concentration on battleship construction, followed later, in the late 1890s. The first U.S. destroyer, although officially classed as a torpedo boat, was *Farragut*. Completed in 1899, its hull measured 214 feet by 20 feet, 8 inches by 6 feet and displaced 279 tons. It was armed with four 6-pounder guns and two 18-inch torpedo tubes. The triple-expansion engines yielded a maximum speed of 30 knots. Only two other one-ship classes were commissioned before 1902, suggesting that they were experimental craft. A third was not commissioned until 1908 due to serious problems with its propulsion machinery. At best, these vessels can be regarded as providing useful experience for future destroyer production that would greatly improve the performance of destroyers around the world.

The bulk of the remaining destroyer production of the world in the late nineteenth and early twentieth centuries came from countries that were new naval powers in comparison to the British, French, Russians, and Americans. The first of these—and a growing threat to British naval supremacy in the late nineteenth century—was Germany. Although constituted as a unified nation only in 1871 and possessing a history as a land-based military power, Germany was one of the forerunners in experimentation with torpedo technology. Its first ships were designed for coastal defense to prevent amphibious invasions, an example being spar torpedo boats in the early 1870s followed in 1876 by the torpedo cruiser *Zieten*. By the 1880s, Germany was commissioning a host of torpedo boats for coastal defense that were built in German as well as British yards. Germany's first destroyer, completed in 1898, was *D10* and was designed and built by the British shipyard Thornycroft. As such, it closely resembled the British 30-knotter type.

Subsequent destroyer production took place in an atmosphere of radical revision of Germany's naval strategy. The succession of Kaiser Wilhelm II in 1890 had begun this course as he believed in the policy of Weltpolitik (world power), referring to the projection of German influence around the globe. The policy contributed to the buildup of a navy for Germany and was further influenced by the ideas of U.S. naval theorist Alfred Thayer Mahan, who wrote that to be considered a true world power a nation must possess a fleet that can command the seas. The appointment of Admiral Alfred von Tirpitz as secretary of the state for the navy, who was also a believer in an oceangoing navy, in 1897 led to new naval building programs to this end. In 1898, Germany passed the First Naval Law that dealt primarily with the construction of capital ships. Destroyers were included in the 1900 Second Naval Law that called for a fleet comprising 38 battleships, 20 armored cruisers, 38 light cruisers, and 96 destroyers by 1920. These plans heralded the beginning of a naval arms race with Great Britain that would be one factor leading to the outbreak of World War I.

The first of these destroyers, and Germany's first domestically built units, were the 12 destroyers of the German S.90 class. Constructed by the German firm Schichau between 1898 and 1901, these ships were unlike the British models in two respects. First, the armament resembled an enlarged torpedo boat. It was composed of three 17.7-inch torpedo tubes and three 1.9-inch guns. The light gun armament was due to the fact that Germany emphasized the role of torpedo attacks on capital ships for destroyers rather than defense versus opposing torpedo boats. Second, the Germans focused on the production of more strongly built hulls at the expense of some speed to provide greater seaworthiness. The result was a vessel whose triple-expansion engines produced a maximum speed of 26.5 knots.

These ships were, however, far better sea boats than their British counterparts due in part to the use of a raised forecastle instead of a turtleback bow. This greatly increased the freeboard, meaning that water did not cascade over the bow with the same ferocity as on turtleback boats. It also allowed for the storage of greater provisions and better crew accommodations. This hull configuration, which was also being developed in the United States, would soon make a great impression on other naval powers. Between 1901 and 1902, three more classes were built for a total of 20 additional ships. These were generally armed in the same manner and were slow in relation to their British rivals.

Japan also embarked on the construction of destroyers. Following the 1853 arrival of a U.S. naval force under the command of Commodore Matthew Perry, the Japanese looked to transforming their country from a largely medieval one into a modern industrialized nation to combat Western influence that threatened their security. Naval construction was at first difficult owing to internal instability, a result of quickly implemented reforms. A proposed naval construction plan in 1873 was consequently shelved, and the first orders for a new naval program were not placed until two years later. The majority of these first ships were built through contracts with foreign shipyards, as those of the Japanese were not yet very advanced and the economy was still in the process of industrialization.

In 1879 the Japanese contracted for four torpedo boats with the British shipyard Yarrow. Others followed with various firms as the Japanese embraced the ideas of the French Jeune École on the value of small craft armed with torpedoes. These vessels also found favor with Japanese government officials because they were cheap to build and offered the possibility of a weaker naval power successfully combating a more powerful enemy. An 1896 10-year naval expansion bill heralded the beginning of the domestic Japanese destroyer program. This legislation called for 23 destroyers and eventually led to the construction by 1902 of four classes that comprised 15 ships. All of them were British designs and thus resembled British craft. An example is the two-ship *Shirakumo* class. The *Shirakumo* measured 216 feet by 20 feet, 9 inches by 6 feet and displaced 342 tons. It was armed with two 12-pounder guns, four 6-pound pieces, and two 18-inch torpedo tubes. Possessing a turtleback bow, its triple-expansion engines produced a maximum speed of 31 knots.

Italy also pursued the construction of vessels armed with torpedoes. Like Germany and Japan, the country was still in the process of becoming a modern industrialized power in the second half of the nineteenth century. Following the process of Italian unification that began in the early 1860s, naval construction was low. The Italian Navy had suffered a serious defeat to the Austrians in the 1866 Battle of Lissa during the Austro-Prussian War. This loss brought disfavor on the navy and a decline in naval expenditures. By the early 1880s, the budget of the Italian Navy was still below that before the Battle of Lissa. Nevertheless, the Italians did invest in torpedo technology.

In 1878 the Italians procured their first torpedo boat from Thornycroft of Britain and constructed their first craft seven years later. Due to Italy's geographic position, small craft like torpedo boats were desirable, as they did not experience as many problems with seaworthiness. The Mediterranean Sea encounters far less stormy weather than areas such as the North Sea and the Pacific Ocean. In addition, the size of the Mediterranean obviated some of the problems of endurance, as there were smaller areas of operation. Despite the interest in torpedo boats, however, the Italians were latecomers in the production of destroyers. Capital ships were under construction in Italian shipyards in the late nineteenth century, but

Italian constructors had little experience with small craft. As a result, the first Italian destroyer, *Fulmine,* was an experimental vessel. Commissioned in 1900 on a purely Italian design and in an Italian shipyard, it was not deemed successful. The hull of *Fulmine* measured 203 feet, 11.5 inches by 21 feet by 7 feet, 6.5 inches and displaced 293 tons. It was armed with five 2.2-inch guns and three 14-inch torpedo tubes. Its designed speed was 26.5 knots, but its triple-expansion engine could produce a maximum speed of only 24 knots.

Following this unsuccessful design, the Italians turned to foreign constructors. The six-ship *Lampo* class, commissioned between 1900 and 1902, was designed and built by the German firm Schichau. Although these warships were built by one of the best destroyer firms in the world, they proved generally unseaworthy. Even so, Italian constructors were able to use them to garner experience in destroyer design. The result was a joint venture with the British firm Thornycroft that produced the *Nembo*-class destroyers. This six-ship group, the first two being launched in 1901, measured 210 feet by 19 feet, 6 inches by 7 feet, 6 inches and displaced 325 tons. These first two vessels mounted one 3-inch gun, five 2.2-inch guns, and two 14-inch torpedo tubes. Their engines produced an impressive maximum speed of 30.2 knots. With these vessels, Italy was edging toward the construction of new, successful destroyer designs that were entirely the product of domestic shipyards.

The Austro-Hungarian Empire, the other naval power in the Mediterranean, was also in the process of building a modern navy that included destroyers. Although primarily a land-based power, it had a navy that had proven itself in the 1866 Battle of Lissa, and construction proceeded for new vessels in the wake of that engagement. The empire's first torpedo boat was launched in 1875, and Austria-Hungary did turn to the procurement of destroyers in the late nineteenth century, but these resembled the British torpedo boat catchers of the mid-1880s more than actual destroyers. Seven vessels were launched between 1887 and 1896 and were built by German, British, and Austro-Hungarian yards. All were experimental craft, as the empire's destroyer knowledge was still limited. They were as a whole heavier and slower than those of other nations. *Meteor,* launched in 1887, is a good example of the design characteristics of these ships. Built by Schichau, this vessel's hull measured 187 feet by 22 feet by 8 feet, 6 inches and displaced 435 tons. Its armament consisted of nine 1.8-inch guns and two 17.7-inch torpedo tubes, while the triple-expansion engine could produce a maximum speed of only 17.5 knots. This low speed is primarily the reason why these vessels cannot be considered true destroyers. The state of Austro-Hungarian production would improve with time, but these vessels exhibited the fact that the empire had much ground to cover to produce a ship comparable to those of other navies.

By the turn of the twentieth century, the combat role attached to the destroyer began to change in the face of technological advances. The original mission of the destroyer, with the notable exceptions of the French and Germans, who viewed them from an early stage as offensive warships, was to hunt down and destroy enemy torpedo boats that attempted to launch torpedo attacks against the battleships of a fleet. New destroyers, however, were far better craft overall than the torpedo boats that they were designed to destroy. The result was a move away from the production of torpedo boats in favor of construction only of destroyers. Their torpedoes allowed them to assume the offensive duty of the torpedo boat while retaining their original function as defensive units against opposing torpedo craft. Destroyers became progressively better vessels in light of this shift and would consequently become one of the most important units of every nation's battle fleet.

Further advancement in the design of destroyers had been initiated in part by the Germans with the introduction of the raised forecastle. Throughout the period between 1902 and 1914, other naval powers pursued similar improvements. One of these was the United States, which built ships of the same hull configuration as the Germans. Naval constructors in the United States had been working on improving seaworthiness at the same time as those in Germany and produced the same innovation. The five ships of the *Bainbridge* class were all commissioned in 1902 and were the first multiple-unit class of destroyer in the U.S. Navy. The hulls measured 250 feet by 23 feet, 7 inches by 6 feet, 6 inches and displaced 420 tons. Their armament consisted of two 3-inch guns, five 6-pounder weapons, and two 18-inch torpedo tubes. Equipped with the raised forecastle, the triple-expansion engine of this ship produced a maximum speed of 29 knots. Like the Germans, U.S. constructors saw a slight decrease in speed as acceptable in exchange for greater seaworthiness and habitability that would enable these ships to travel to far-flung U.S. bases like those in the Pacific Ocean.

Significantly, these vessels still lacked the seaworthiness necessary to remain at sea for extended operations. They were, however, able to project U.S. power by traveling to distant possessions. The vessels of this class spent the majority of their careers based in the

U.S. possession of the Philippines. The *Bainbridge* class was the beginning of a great increase in U.S. destroyer production that focused primarily on craft designed for the role of defense against torpedo attacks, as the battleship was the mainstay of the U.S. Navy. The 11 additional units, of five classes, that were commissioned by 1903 were generally similar to the *Bainbridge* class in terms of armament, although three of the groups were a reversion to the turtleback bow arrangement.

Subsequent vessels became progressively larger in the continuing quest for greater seaworthiness. In 1908 and 1909, the five-ship *Smith* class was launched. Each unit measured 293 feet, 8 inches by 26 feet by 8 feet and displaced 700 tons. The armament consisted of five 3-inch guns and three 18-inch torpedo tubes. These vessels were the first U.S. destroyers equipped with turbine engines and could steam at a maximum speed of 28 knots. The proceeding 10 ships of the *Paulding* class, launched between 1909 and 1910, were virtual repeats of the *Smith* class. The key difference was the use of oil-fired boilers rather than those that used coal. These ships are therefore significant as the first U.S. destroyers to employ this fuel. All subsequent destroyer classes employed oil rather than coal. Following a repeat class of 11 ships launched between 1910 and 1912, the United States produced the first of what became known as the 1,000 tonners. These vessels were built especially for seaworthiness and endurance. The first group of the 1,000 tonners was the *Cassin* class comprising eight ships. The hull of *Cassin* measured 305 feet, 5 inches by 30 feet, 2 inches and displaced 1,010 tons. It mounted four 4-inch guns and eight 18-inch torpedo tubes, making it the most heavily armed type of U.S. destroyer to date. To stay at sea for the longest time possible, *Cassin* was equipped with reciprocating engines for cruising and turbines when it was necessary to attain the ship's maximum speed of 29 knots. The final class of six ships that were laid down before the outbreak of World War I in August 1914 were merely improvements on the design of the previous group. Two of these were launched before the beginning of the conflict. The *Cassin* class and those similar to it represent the culmination of a tremendous effort to make destroyers more seaworthy vessels capable of extended operations at sea with battle fleets. Other navies embarked on the same course.

Great Britain, in the midst of a naval arms race with Germany, altered its construction plans for destroyers in much the same way as the United States. By the early twentieth century, British naval officials realized that the emphasis on speed at the cost of seaworthiness, endurance, and habitability had produced vessels that could not fulfill their desired function. Indeed, the emphasis on high speed had always been unrealistic, as the first British destroyers could attain their maximum speed while on trials only in calm weather conditions. These conclusions were concretely reached following a 1901 visit of British destroyers to the German naval base of Wilhelmshaven. While there, the British saw firsthand the raised forecastle hull configuration of the S.90 class, and this led designers to pursue the same course to make British vessels more seaworthy.

In 1902, the British laid down the first of the *River*-class destroyers. These ships are considered by most scholars as the world's first oceangoing destroyers. Although the German S.90 class and the U.S. *Bainbridge* class preceded the British ships, the *River* class proved to be the most seaworthy and with the greatest endurance. The units of this 34-ship class were generally similar to one another, slight differences occurring from the fact that the British contracted with six different shipyards to build them. Completed between 1904 and 1905, the hull of the first set of these ships measured 233 feet, 4 inches by 23 feet, 6 inches by 9 feet, 8 inches and displaced 550 tons. Their original armament was the same as the previous 30-knotters, being one 12-pounder gun, five 6-pounder guns, and two 18-inch torpedo tubes. Equipped with the raised forecastle, these ships could attain a maximum speed of 26 knots. This power was provided, with the exception of one unit equipped with turbines, through a reversion to triple-expansion engines, as vessels like the previous *Viper* were still in the experimental stage.

The reduction in speed was deemed acceptable given the advantages that it presented. First, these ships were able with their raised forecastles to maintain their highest speed in a seaway. In reality, this velocity was the same as the 30-knotters given that they could steam indefinitely at their highest speeds. The loss of some power in favor of a larger, stronger hull also allowed improvements in the structure of the bridge, which was in the process of becoming a properly enclosed superstructure rather than being enclosed partially by canvas. In addition, the surrender of some power decreased mechanical breakdowns as the triple-expansion engines of the units were no longer pushed to enormous limits to produce speeds almost in excess of their ability. Finally, the raised forecastle and internal arrangement of the hulls of the *River*-class units allowed for shipping 132 tons of coal, a great improvement. All told, these ships had a cruising radius of 2,000 miles. All other naval powers, given these advantages, would after 1904 incorporate design features of the

River class into their own ships. Great Britain was once again billed as the world's leading destroyer designer.

Subsequent British destroyer development followed along the lines of the *River* class, although there were some notable exceptions in the years directly following that group's completion. These were the result of John Fisher, First Sea Lord of the Admiralty. Throughout his 1904–1910 term in office, Fisher experimented with destroyer design and ultimately their combat role. Always a believer in employing the latest technological innovations, Fisher oversaw the next three destroyer designs, which produced mixed results. The smallest were the 36-ship *Cricket*-class destroyers. Launched between 1906 and 1909, their hulls measured 180 feet by 17 feet, 6 inches by 6 feet and displaced 255 tons. They were armed with two 12-pounder guns and three 18-inch torpedo tubes. Their engines represented a return to turbines, a feature of all future British destroyer classes of this age, and these could produce a maximum speed of 26 knots. This feature is a reflection of Fisher's belief in employing new technology.

A further example of this is the use of oil-fired boilers rather than coal-fired ones. This feature made the *Cricket*-class destroyers the first in the world to use oil fuel. Despite this advance, these ships were of limited value. Fisher had intended them to be coastal destroyers that supplemented the second class of larger ships. As a result, these craft were not very seaworthy and were a sharp contrast to the destroyer production programs of other countries. The larger counterparts of the *Cricket* class also suffered somewhat from Fisher's direction. The first of these were the 12 units of the *Tribal* class. Launched between 1907 and 1909, the dimensions and displacements varied because the British continued the practice of contracting with private shipyards. One unit, *Afridi*, will suffice as an example of these ships. Its hull measured 250 (pp) by 24 feet, 6 inches by 10 feet and displaced 855 tons.

Owing to Fisher's belief in the efficacy of large-caliber guns, *Afridi* mounted two 4-inch guns, three 12-pounders, and two 18-inch torpedo tubes. Its oil-fired turbine engines could produce a maximum speed of 33 knots. The principal problem with these vessels was their armament. Although the smaller guns were a quick-firing model, the largest guns were regular breechloaders as the technology had not progressed to the point where guns of this size could be made effectively with the quick-firing advance. Since British destroyers were primarily designed to ward off torpedo attacks, the rate of fire was crucial to sinking enemy vessels before they closed into torpedo range. This defect, however, was a slight one in comparison to the one-ship *Swift* class.

Swift represents not only Fisher's desire for a large vessel to lead destroyers into battle but also his belief that larger destroyers could assume the duties of light cruisers. These roles include commerce protection and scouting. The hull of this ship measured 353 feet, 9 inches by 34 feet, 2 inches by 10 feet, 6 inches and displaced a very large 2,170 tons. It was armed with four 4-inch breechloaders and two 18-inch torpedo tubes. Its maximum speed was 35 knots. This vessel proved a technological failure. Fisher wanted a ship that could reach 36 knots, as he was a firm believer in speed as an advantage in battle, but *Swift* could not attain it. Indeed, while the ship was launched in 1907 and completed sometime later, the Admiralty did not accept the ship until 1920. In addition, the high fuel consumption and low seaworthiness of the craft made it impossible to assume the duties of a light cruiser. *Swift* was an extreme design and was not attempted again, but the concept of the destroyer leader would persist, and new vessels would be constructed with this task in mind.

Following the construction of two more *River*-class destroyers that represented a reversion to the use of turtleback bows, the Admiralty returned to designs that more closely matched that of the *River*-class destroyers. Sixteen ships of the *Beagle* class were launched between 1909 and 1910 and were a more heavily armed version of the *River*s. They are primarily significant for the fact that they were the last British destroyers to use coal rather than oil. This reversion was a result of fears in the British government over the availability of oil from the Middle East in time of war. Between 1910 and 1914, the British designed five more classes of destroyers, with 85 units being complete before the outbreak of war. The last of these, the *M* class, as all of the vessels in the class had names beginning with "M," is a prime example of the state of British destroyer technology by World War I. Only one unit, *Miranda*, was launched by August 1914. Its hull measured 269 feet, 6 inches by 25 feet, 7.5 inches by 9 feet, 6 inches and displaced 850 tons. Its gun armament consisted of three 4-inch guns, which were now a new quick-firing model. The larger, uniform gun armament was the result of the Admiralty's belief that the old 12-pounder gun was too small because the size of gunnery weapons had increased substantially by this time. These guns had small shields mounted around them to protect the crew from flying splinters that were generated by exploding shells. They could not resist a direct hit, however, from even light naval ordnance. Nevertheless, the practice of using gun shields would eventually become a standard practice for most navies. In addition to its guns, the ship also carried four 21-inch torpedo tubes in twin launchers on the main deck. The vessel's turbines could produce a maximum speed of 35 knots.

The *M*-class vessels would see substantial service in World War I against the naval forces of Germany, Britain's chief rival in the years directly preceding the conflict. Four more classes of German destroyers comprising a total of 12 ships were launched between 1903 and 1905, and these possessed the same armament as the *S.90s* and only a slight increase in speed. These destroyers formed part of the ambitious naval building program launched by the Naval Laws that had by the early twentieth century achieved substantial results.

By 1905, the Germans had created a navy so large that it surpassed that of France and rivaled the United States, which by that time was the second largest navy in the world. Sixteen more classes of destroyers followed from 1905 to 1914 for a total of 88 units launched by August 1914, each being improved versions of the preceding type. Other units from the last of these classes were launched shortly after the beginning of hostilities. These vessels generally mounted fewer, slightly smaller guns than their British counterparts as a reflection of the continued German belief in the primary role of destroyers as being for launching a torpedo attack. Several of the types employed triple-expansion engines rather than turbines that comprised most of the destroyer production in other navies in the last nine years of peace.

Many of these were either coal-powered or employed both coal and oil fuel. They also had the unusual feature of a second auxiliary rudder placed beneath the bow in case the other was rendered inoperable in combat. The last class of destroyer in the process of launching in peacetime, the *S.31* class, is indicative of all of these traits. The hull of *S.31* measured 261 feet, 2 inches by 27 feet, 4 inches by 9 feet, 2 inches and displaced 802 tons. It mounted three 3.45-inch guns, six 19.7-inch torpedo tubes, and 24 mines. This latter weapon represents the German belief that these vessels could assume the role of minelayer in addition to its primary mission. Its turbine engines, a standard feature in German vessels by 1914, could produce a maximum speed of 33.5 knots. The type was also the first in the German Navy to switch completely to the use of oil fuel.

Other navies did not produce such large numbers of destroyers as the United States, Great Britain, and Germany in the years before World War I. From 1902 to 1908, the French Navy, which had been eclipsed in numbers by Germany in 1905, launched 23 more destroyers. The relatively small number in comparison to other naval powers was partially the result of construction delays that plagued French shipyards in this period. These destroyers were not well-suited to action at sea as their hulls were very lightly built. This design aspect was the result of a French belief at the time that destroyers were primarily coastal defense vessels.

The one significant French destroyer class in this period was the *Branlebas* class. The 10 ships of this group, launched between 1907 and 1908, were equipped with deck armor. This was a very unusual feature in destroyers due to their relatively small hulls in comparison to capital ships that did not allow for such an increase in weight. Nevertheless, the French were among the most technologically innovative of the age and managed to incorporate it. Their armor consisted of .75-inch steel plating over the deck that covered the propulsion machinery of the craft. This feature was designed to protect against small-caliber plunging shellfire that could punch through the deck and disable the destroyer. The feat was particularly impressive, as the maximum speed of the units of this class was 27.5 knots.

These ships, however, were also too small to maintain station at sea. In an attempt to catch up with the larger destroyer designs of other powers, the French next launched the *Spahi* class comprising seven vessels. Launched between 1908 and 1912, the hull of *Spahi* measured 212 (pp) by 19 feet, 10 inches by 7 feet, 7 inches, displaced 550 tons, and was powered by a triple-expansion engine that could generate 28 knots. It mounted six 2.5-inch guns and three 17.7-inch torpedo tubes. The idea of the armored deck was discarded. Two similar classes comprising six destroyers were launched afterward that were virtual repeats of the *Spahi* class, although the units of the *Chasseur* class are significant for being the first turbine-powered and completely oil-fueled French destroyers. The final two peacetime classes of 18 ships were larger versions and carried heavier guns, but their value was limited. The ships carried only two 3.9-inch guns and had weak hulls that made their use in heavy seas a problem.

Russia built a much larger number of destroyers between 1902 and 1914 than France, which was Russia's ally following the conclusion of a formal alliance between the two powers in 1894. From 1903 to 1905, the Russians contracted for 66 more destroyers that were largely built by German and French firms. The large output was in part the result of Russia's need to maintain more than one fleet to protect its vast geographic area, but it was also necessary due to the onset of the Russo-Japanese War (1904–1905). This conflict stemmed from a clash of imperial interests between Russia and Japan on the Asian mainland, principally Korea. The war proved devastating for the Russians, who lost the bulk of their fleet, including 21 destroyers, in the first defeat of a modern European power by an Asian nation. By the conclusion of the war, Russia had slipped from third to sixth on the list of the world's most powerful navies. Subsequent destroyer production before World War I was only able to address wartime losses. As a result, the Russian destroyer fleet by 1914 was only slightly larger than that of France.

The first new Russian destroyer was not ordered until 1909 in part because of the diversion of resources to combat popular unrest over the strain caused by the war. It, like all future destroyers, was designed and built solely in a domestic shipyard. This vessel, *Novik,* was launched in 1911 and was a continuation of the Russian tendency to build larger destroyers like the U.S. 1,000 tonners. Its hull measured 336 feet, 3 inches by 31 feet, 3 inches by 9 feet, 10 inches and displaced 1,280 tons. It was armed with four 4-inch guns, eight 18-inch torpedo tubes, and 60 mines in keeping with the Russian belief in using destroyers as minelayers. Its turbine engines produced a maximum speed of 36 knots. Due to its propulsion plant, this destroyer is significant for Russia as the first to use both turbines and oil fuel. The other group produced before the war, the nine-ship *Bespokoiny* class, was a variation of *Novik.* A difference, however, was the inclusion of two 1.8-inch guns. These were for use against enemy aircraft. The development of the airplane, while still in its infancy, had already gotten the attention of Russian naval officials due to the potential of air attack. World War I would provide a proving ground for antiaircraft armament such as that carried on these Russian craft.

Japan continued to build destroyers as part of its naval expansion program, but most of the units launched between 1902 and 1914 continued to be either ships contracted in British shipyards or those built in Japan to a British design. This was in part the result of the great degree of cooperation between Japan and Britain that was the result of the 1902 Anglo-Japanese Alliance, a defensive agreement. By 1909, the Japanese had 39 new destroyers at their disposal that remained a rather small design like those of the past. The next class, however, represented a Japanese move toward larger destroyers incorporating the most modern technology available. The two ships of the *Umikaze* class, launched between 1910 and 1911, possessed hulls that measured 323 feet, 3 inches by 28 feet, 1 inch by 9 feet and displaced 1,030 tons. As a result of their size and the incorporation of the raised forecastle, these are the first oceangoing destroyers of the Japanese Navy. They were armed with two 4.7-inch guns, five 3.1-inch weapons, and four 18-inch torpedo tubes. These ships were the first in Japanese service to employ turbines rather than triple-expansion engines. The turbines could produce a maximum speed of 33 knots. Only one other class of two ships was produced during the war, and these were scaled-down versions of the *Umikaze* class that were of limited value. Due to their smaller hulls, the ships were primarily capable only of coastal defense. These two ships of the *Sakura* class, however, are significant as they were the first destroyers built in a Japanese shipyard to a domestic design. This became standard practice in the years after World War I.

Italy, in the wake of its previous failure to produce an effective, domestically designed and built destroyer, looked for guidance from the British shipyard Thornycroft. A joint Italian-British design produced the six *Nembo*-class destroyers. Built entirely in Italy and launched between 1901 and 1904, these ships measured 210 feet by 19 feet, 6 inches by 7 feet, 6 inches and displaced 325 tons each. Most were armed with five 2.2-inch guns and four 14-inch torpedo tubes. These were followed by six more classes leading up to the war that comprised 20 ships and were all built in Italy to indigenous designs. The last four units were variations of the six-ship *Indomito* class launched between 1912 and 1913. The hull of *Indomito* measured 239 feet, 6 inches by 24 feet by 7 feet, 11 inches and displaced 672 tons. It was armed with one 4.7-inch gun, four 3-inch guns, and two 17.7-inch torpedo tubes. *Indomito* was the first destroyer for Italy to mount oil-fuel turbines. These could produce a maximum speed of 30 knots.

The Austro-Hungarian Navy built only one destroyer in the first five years of the twentieth century because the empire's shipbuilders were still experimenting with destroyer designs. This ship, the British-built *Huszar,* is significant as Austria-Hungary's first true destroyer. Its hull measured 224 feet, 4 inches by 20 feet, 6 inches by 6 feet, 3 inches, displaced about 390 tons, and mounted triple-expansion engines that generated a maximum speed of 28.5 knots. It was armed initially with one 2.5-inch gun, seven 1.8-inch weapons, and two 17.7-inch torpedo tubes. The Austro-Hungarians subsequently turned to domestic production of this design and produced another 12 warships. These were followed by the six ships of the *Tatra* class, all being launched by late 1913. Not only were these the empire's first destroyer design since *Fulmine*; they were also the first large destroyers for the fleet. The hull of *Tatra* was 273 feet, 11 inches by 25 feet, 7 inches by 9 feet, 10 inches and displaced 850 tons. It was the first destroyer for the empire that used turbine engines, which could produce a maximum speed of 32.6 knots. Mounted on this hull were two 3.9-inch guns, six 2.5-inch guns, and four 17.7-inch torpedo tubes.

By the outbreak of World War I on 1 August 1914, the destroyer was the most numerous type of warship in the navies of the maritime powers. Great Britain led the world with 228 destroyers in service. Germany operated 154 vessels and thereby had the second-greatest destroyer power. Russia possessed 105 destroyers, but many of these were of older designs. The other powers possessed fewer ships, but they would prove no less significant in the conflict that was about to unfold: France maintained 84 destroyers, although many of these were not capable of service in open seas; the United States operated 54, most being modern ships; Japan followed closely with 50; Italy had 32; and Austria-Hungary maintained 26.[8] All told, the combatant powers of World War I possessed 703 destroyers. These would prove invaluable not only in the primary tasks envisioned for them in the prewar years but also in new roles. By the end of the conflict, destroyers would be *multi-role* vessels that performed more duties than any other type of warship.

Destroyers throughout their history to this point had changed little in one aspect: Everyday life continued to be harsher than for sailors aboard bigger ships. The raised forecastles of destroyers had allowed for less cramped living and eating quarters, but amenities such as libraries on bigger ships were still impossible. All but the newest destroyers in operation by World War I continued to have electrical lighting in only the engine room areas, making the lives of officers and crewmen alike a dreary one after sunset, when only oil lamps were available.[9] Even these had to be used sparingly due to the threat of fire if the pitching and rolling in heavy seas broke one. Food remained much as it was in the age of sail in terms of quality. A common description by sailors of the meat of this era was that it resembled a piece of wood.

One of the few amenities aboard that had changed markedly for the better were toilet facilities. In most of the destroyers produced in the twentieth century, both officers and crewmen used enclosed toilets located below deck. Some ships had facilities for the officers equipped with washbasins while the crew still had to bathe on deck. Despite rough conditions, these ships were seen by young officers and crewmen as the first step in a career. There were never any shortages of men who volunteered specifically for destroyer duty given this fact. In addition, the discipline aboard was on the whole not as harsh as on bigger ships. Even the newest destroyers only had about 70 men aboard, while the newest battleships carried a complement of more than 1,000 officers and ratings. As a result, there was a sense of camaraderie in destroyers lacking in larger ships. Each individual knew the other as part of a close-knit community where all shared the same hardships. These men also bonded as part of the romantic air in the public sphere that surrounded destroyer men, who were seen as brave, tough, and dedicated to their duty despite adverse conditions.

Another aspect of life for sailors—recruitment and education—did change substantially by the outbreak of war. This did not appear until the early twentieth century. Before this time, the educational methods of some naval powers were ancient. The best example was France, whose naval training consisted of largely experience rather than schooling. Although the manning of the navy was partly voluntary and some soldiers in the army were conscripted into service, the majority of France's sailors were procured through the Inscription Maritime. This was established in 1681 during the age of King Louis XIV; the legislation enrolled all French sailors between the ages of 18 and 50 years. Most of these men saw five to seven years of service beginning at 20 years old. These men garnered almost all of their knowledge from experience aboard ship.

Although the recruitment methods differed somewhat than France, Great Britain and the United States pursued the same general method. Not until the twentieth century was detailed schooling really stressed. The change occurred here as a consequence of the vast number of technological innovations by the turn of the nineteenth century that made much more specific training necessary for the sake of efficiency in combat. Examples are numerous. One is the case of Russia, which by the turn of the century sought individuals with prior technical training. By 1900, 60 percent of the conscripts in Russia's navy were already experienced in some form of factory work to transition easily to operating machinery on board warships. When contrasted to the 2 percent of individuals with factory training in the army, it is clear that the Russians considered individuals with prior technical education as a necessity at sea.[10]

Other navies pursued the same course, including the greatest naval power at the time. The British increasingly screened incoming recruits to identify their aptitude for special skills. To supplement the numbers of skilled individuals, all navies by the end of the first decade of the twentieth century had specialized schools for the training of regular sailors in specific tasks such as engineering, gunnery, torpedoes, and damage control. The education of officers went up in tandem with that of the ratings. British naval schools were founded at Osborne and Dartmouth while specialized schools that were already in existence grew in importance and attendance. An example is HMS *Vernon,* the Royal Navy's torpedo school that became an independent institution in 1876. By the opening of the war, the training of destroyer men, like those in other navies, consisted in most powers of specialized training on land followed by on-site training aboard ship.

Despite the great numbers of destroyers produced from the 1880s to 1914, these ships had little opportunity to distinguish themselves in combat at sea. The Sino-Japanese War (1894–1895), sparked by the Japanese desire to imperially expand into the Korean Peninsula, involved only torpedo boats. Similarly, the 1898 Spanish-American War saw almost no usage of destroyers despite the fact that the Spanish had a few craft at the Battle of Santiago Bay. Destroyers experienced their first combat during the 1900 Boxer Uprising in China. This was an anti-foreigner revolt directed against an array of imperial powers that by this time had greatly diminished Chinese sovereignty in favor of their own interests. Numerous imperial powers dispatched destroyers as part of naval forces to quell the rebellion and rescue diplomats trapped in the Chinese capital of Peking (Beijing) by the Boxers. Even in this case, however, destroyers were not used in their roles of torpedo defense or torpedo attack.

The one instance where destroyers participated in their intended roles was the Russo-Japanese War (1904–1905). This was sparked by the Russian desire in early 1904 for a warm-water port in the Far East. The Chinese province of Manchuria, China itself, and Korea were possible sites. Russian interference in the region infuriated the Japanese since the Russians had forced them out of the same areas after the Sino-Japanese War on the pretext of protecting the peoples that populated them. The performance of destroyers in the naval aspect of this war, however, was not considered very successful by the combatants and the naval officials of other powers that acted as observers. The 8 February 1904 Japanese assault on the Russian naval base Port Arthur involved destroyers, but no Russian warships were sunk by the torpedo attacks conducted by the Japanese. In the 10 August 1904 Battle of the Yellow Sea, the opposing Russian and Japanese fleets operated eight and 17 destroyers, respectively. Like the previous engagement, there were no ships sunk by torpedoes. The largest battle of the war, the 27 May 1905 Battle of Tsushima, saw limited success, but it was not during the contest itself. In the closing hours of the battle, Japanese destroyers torpedoed crippled Russian battleships that were by this point dead in the water. The only other duty that destroyers fulfilled in this battle was one that was a minor and unenvisioned role: the offloading of survivors from sinking ships. The best example is the Russian use of a destroyer to rescue the wounded Admiral Zinovi Petrovich Rozhdestvenski from his crippled flagship, the battleship *Suvarov.*

These disappointing showings had not discouraged any of the great powers from building destroyers. The development of destroyers in the early twentieth century was spurred in part by the naval arms race between Great Britain and Germany, which was only one source of rising tensions in Europe. Since the unification of Germany in 1871, Europe had polarized into two alliances: the Triple Alliance of Germany, Austria-Hungary, and Italy; and the Triple Entente of Great Britain, France, and Russia. On 1 August 1914, events in the Balkans precipitated a chain of events that brought these two coalitions, with the exception of neutral Italy, into the conflict that became World War I. This war provided the first major test of destroyers as a modern weapons system since the Russo-Japanese War. Unlike that conflict, the participation of destroyers would prove vital to the naval aspect of World War I, as they were involved in almost every major operation of the war at sea both in their traditional roles and new ones that arose from necessity in time of war.

It is therefore fitting that the first shot of the naval war was fired on 5 August 1914 by the British destroyer *Lance* as it sank the German minelayer *Konigin Luise.* Further use quickly followed when destroyers composed the bulk of forces involved in the first full-scale naval engagement of World War I. Although the British had in the prewar years stressed the traditional role of torpedo defense for their destroyers, they were employed for surface engagement on 28 August 1914, at the Battle of Helgoland Bight. The British chose to strike a German naval force at the island of Helgoland, which guarded the approaches to the anchorages of the German High Seas Fleet. Arrayed against the German force of a few light cruisers and nine destroyers was a British force of 31 destroyers and two light cruisers that was later augmented by the arrival of capital ships. The resulting engagement had a profound effect on the entire war at sea. In exchange for suffering serious damage to one light cruiser and two destroyers, the British sank three German light cruisers and two destroyers. One of the sunken German cruisers, *Mainz*, was crippled by a destroyer's torpedo attack. These losses led to Kaiser Wilhelm II being far less willing to risk his fleet in a major action. He subsequently imposed severe restrictions on the operational movements of the German High Seas Fleet where the commander in chief was required to ask for the consent of the kaiser before engaging in a clash with British naval forces. Wilhelm's action largely removed the possibility of a major fleet engagement that had been predicted by both sides in the period leading up to the war. As a result, smaller vessels, particularly destroyers, became some of the principal combatants in the war at sea.

The only exception to the kaiser's rule—and for that matter the one opportunity in World War I that destroyers had to serve in both the fleet capacities of torpedo defense and attack—was the 31 May–1 June 1916 Battle of Jutland. This engagement proved to be the only major clash of battle fleets between the opposing sides. Destroyers formed the majority of the warships deployed in both fleets: of 151 British warships, 80 were destroyers; the Germans operated 63 destroyers in a fleet that numbered 101 vessels.[11] Both the British and German vessels launched torpedo attacks against the capital ships of their enemy and tried to defend against the same by sinking the opposing destroyers. The results of these attacks were, like the Russo-Japanese War, not very successful. Only one large vessel, the German predreadnought *Pommern*, was sunk by torpedoes during the Battle of Jutland. The effort of attacking and defending craft, however, provided some of the most savage fighting of the engagement.

Examples are numerous, but one of the more celebrated ones is the British destroyer *Shark*. This vessel was smothered by enemy fire and eventually crippled. Damage to the ship's engines rendered it dead in the water. The experience of *Shark*'s crew is a testimony both to the bravery of those who manned destroyers and the horrors that could be experienced aboard them in battle. Catastrophic damage was caused to *Shark*, as it lay motionless, by heavy-caliber guns that ripped into its unarmored hull. One shell from such a weapon blew the forward gun completely over the side of the ship and killed the gun crew. *Shark*'s captain ultimately fell victim to the explosions that wracked his ship and lost a portion of his leg. Finally, enemy destroyers employed in the role of defending capital ships from torpedo vessels closed in on *Shark* and scored a torpedo hit on the ship, whose light hull immediately broke in two and sank with the loss of all but five of the crew. Many of those who died in the sinking were probably trapped within the hull of their sinking ship. Such an experience is certainly an awful one, where any light that illuminated the interior of the ship is extinguished and men struggle to find a hatch on the main deck as an avenue for escape. Even if successful, a sailor would still be subjected to many dangers while adrift in the sea. These include oil slicks from their ship that may be set ablaze, marine predators such as sharks, and simple exposure to the elements.

Although vessels such as *Shark* were generally not successful in their mission of launching torpedo attacks, the mere threat posed by destroyers proved to be a pivotal feature of the engagement. By nightfall, after having suffered heavy damage at the hands of the British, the German commander in chief, Admiral Reinhard Scheer, ordered his destroyers to launch a torpedo attack against the British battle fleet while he executed a retreat. The order probably saved a great portion of the German fleet from destruction and forced the British commander in chief, Admiral John Jellicoe, to turn away from the impending attack. The result was a loss of contact between the two fleets and an end to the majority of the fighting, with the exception of some skirmishes. Destroyers, despite their lack of success in launching torpedo attacks, had proven successful in defense and their destructive potential realized by the opposing fleets. They were also proven as an integral part of battle fleet operations. The losses of both sides exhibit the heavy use of destroyers. The British lost 14 warships, eight destroyers, while five German destroyers were sunk out of their total of 11 destroyed vessels.

The destroyer, however, proved far more important in duties other than the fleet operations for which they had been designed. The most important was that of commerce protection, being an old duty of sloops in the Age of Fighting Sail. In this role, destroyers acted as a counter to the threat posed by the submarine. Like the destroyer, World War I proved to be the first great proving ground for this type of submersible. Germany put these vessels to good use, as they were well aware of the fact that Great Britain relied on overseas sources for its food supply and the majority of its munitions. The Germans believed that the use of submarines against British commerce could starve the country into submission and thereby lead to a German victory.

Destroyers proved to be the best weapon against submarines. They were difficult to hit using torpedoes, the submarine's primary weapon, owing to their shallow drafts, meaning that their hulls did not extend very low into the water and torpedoes could consequently pass under them without detonating. The ships also had the advantage of being extremely maneuverable and speedy. These attributes were necessary to run down an enemy submarine. As torpedo attacks in this era were primarily made on the surface or at shallow depth, destroyers would attempt to ram the submarine, break open its hull, and sink it. The possibility of ramming submarines was foreseen by some navies in the years before the war. Several U.S. destroyers were fitted with reinforced bows to ram submarines. In effect, destroyers proved to be a floating missile on the surface of the sea against attack from an enemy below it.

Even so, despite these attributes for submarine hunting, the destroyer was not an ideal weapons system for this task. In the first years of the war, there was no method of detecting an enemy submarine other than lookouts who might sight a surfaced vessel or its periscope. In addition, the use of ramming as the principal weapon against submarines was problematic, as it could cause as much damage to the attacker as the victim. In 1916, the destroyer came into its own as a more effective antisubmarine vessel with the advent of the depth charge. Pioneered by Great Britain, this weapon was a steel drum 18 inches in diameter and 30 inches long that weighed 400 pounds. Of this weight, 300 pounds consisted of high explosive contained in the drum. The depth charge was detonated by a device known as a hydrostatic pistol. This was pressure-sensitive and could be adjusted to fire at a certain depth, the range of the first depth charges being between 25 and 300 feet, and thus detonate the charge. These depth charges could either be rolled off racks on the stern or fired from mortars that could project them some 40 yards from the ship. This latter device became known as a depth charge thrower (DCT). Although a depth charge had to explode within 40 feet of the hull of a submarine to cause significant damage, the destroyer now had a viable weapon for use against what became its greatest enemy.

Upon the introduction of the convoy system in 1917, destroyers became escort vessels that patrolled the waters around convoys, which are groups of merchant ships in search of submarines. That same year, crude underwater listening devices known as hydrophones entered service. This innovation could not provide a precise bearing or range to a target but could detect the presence of a submerged vessel. Oftentimes, its value was reduced by the sounds of the destroyer that carried it. Nevertheless, hydrophones enabled destroyers to become more effective in their newfound role. Equipped with depth charges and hydrophones, destroyers allowed convoys to continue to arrive in British ports and thus keep the country in the war. A very large number of these were U.S. destroyers following the April 1917 U.S. entry into the war as an allied member of the Triple Entente. By war's end, the destroyer had accounted for a large portion of the 178 German submarines sunk in the conflict.

In addition to escorting merchant convoys, destroyers also acted as protection for troop carriers. During the opening days of the war, destroyers oversaw the transportation of the British Expeditionary Force (BEF) to France. Throughout the conflict, British destroyers continued to protect supply routes in the English Channel from both submarine attacks and assaults by German destroyers. The destroyers offered sterling service in this role. By the end of the conflict, only one transport was sunk by the Germans, and that vessel was empty at the time.

The protection of troop movements in the narrow waters of the channel meant that a corollary duty was coastal defense. On 3 November 1914, two British destroyers encountered a force of German capital ships en route to bombard the British port city of Yarmouth. The presence of these vessels unnerved the Germans and led them to bombard Yarmouth for a shorter time than was planned and at a greater range, thus reducing the damage to the city and the loss of civilian life.

Destroyers were also used in the North Sea and in the Mediterranean as gunfire support ships. In the case of the former, British destroyers bombarded German Army units in the first days of the war as they advanced through Belgium. British and French destroyers in subsequent months were used in the same capacity. The 1915 Dardenelles campaign provided further use of destroyers for gunfire support. This operation was mounted by Britain and France to force open a supply route to Russia through the Dardenelles Strait that leads into the Black Sea. Standing in the way of the effort was Turkey, which had become a member of the Triple Alliance, also known as the Central Powers, in December 1914. The campaign centered on an allied amphibious assault on the straits with the object of occupying the area while the Turks attempted to stave off the effort. Allied destroyers were used to bombard Turkish positions due to the threat posed to larger ships by Turkish torpedo attacks, which destroyers had a better chance of surviving given their shallow drafts.

The combat roles alone for destroyers give them a claim to being the most important vessels of the naval war, but this case is augmented by the variety of noncombat duties that fell to them. Destroyers were at times used as troop transports themselves, as in the case of the 1915 Dardenelles campaign in which seven destroyers were packed with troops of the allied amphibious force and towed boats full of more men. Destroyers were also given the ignominious task of torpedoing crippled vessels of their own fleet to prevent capture by enemy units. An example is the German battle cruiser *Lutzow*, which was so badly damaged during the 1916 Battle of Jutland that a destroyer had to torpedo the crippled vessel. In this situation, an additional role attached to destroyers was the rescue of those crewmen still aboard a sinking vessel. Destroyers were also used to search for survivors after the sinking of a warship. Upon the destruction of the British battle cruiser *Invincible*, a British destroyer was dispatched to retrieve any crewmen who may have escaped.

The myriad uses for destroyers in World War I necessitated the construction of a large number of additional destroyers during the war. Great Britain built the most destroyers for its large battle fleet and as convoy escorts. The British built 329 additional units during the conflict, but among the new destroyers to enter service were those procured from other powers that were under construction in British shipyards. Four destroyers similar to the *M* class that were being built for Greece were bought by the Admiralty. An additional four units that were under construction for Turkey were seized upon that country's joining the war as a Central Power. Last, the Admiralty purchased a destroyer under construction for Portugal.

British construction would comprise two types of destroyers: regular destroyers and large flotilla leaders. Those of the former category were the most numerous. The first British destroyers to enter service were the remaining units of the *M* class, numbering 12 ships, that had been under construction at the outbreak of the war. These were followed by 90 more *M*-class vessels, these being ordered and launched between 1915 and 1916 in the interest of launching more destroyers as quickly as possible by dispensing with the process of making a new design. The chief difference between these and the first batch was the incorporation of a 40mm pom-pom gun that was designed to fire explosive shells high into the air. This weapon was meant for use against airplanes. The airplane, although it was still a new weapon of war, was recognized by many naval officials for its destructive potential against warships. The incorporation of antiaircraft guns would soon become standard practice.

Repeating designs with slight improvements would be the trend for British construction of regular destroyers. The *R* class of 51 destroyers, launched between 1916 and 1917, was consequently a virtual duplication of the past. Four more classes constructed during the war were largely similar. The last of these, the S class, is representative of British destroyer design by the end of the war. The hull of a unit in this group measured 276 feet by 26 feet, 8 inches by 9 feet and displaced 1,075 tons. Mounted on the ship was an armament consisting of three 4-inch guns, quick-firing guns, one 40mm pom-pom gun, four 21-inch torpedo tubes, and depth charges. The engines could produce a maximum speed of 36 knots.

In addition to these destroyers, the British built several much larger ships known as flotilla leaders, the term *flotilla* referring to a group of destroyers. Despite the poor performance of Admiral John Fisher's *Swift* in the prewar years, the British realized the need for large destroyers of high speed that could serve as command ships. Following the purchase of the four-ship *Faulknor* class that had been under construction for Chile, the British built the *Lightfoot* class of seven ships launched between 1915 and 1916. These vessels are indicative of British flotilla leaders. The hull of *Lightfoot* measured 324 feet, 10 inches by 31 feet, 9 inches by 12 feet and displaced 1,440 tons. The larger hull stemmed partly from the need for greater crew accommodation that was necessary for a command ship. The bridge area was also more heavily built for coordination of the flotilla. Finally, *Lightfoot* carried wireless radio for communications. This innovation, first used during the 1905 Battle of Tsushima during the Russo-Japanese War, came into its own during World War I. The vessel mounted a heavier gun armament than most regular destroyers, four 4-inch guns, and a smaller torpedo battery of four 12-inch tubes. For its size, the ship's turbines were able to deliver an impressive speed of 34.5 knots. Four more classes of flotilla leaders followed, the largest being the *Scott* class that measured more than 332 feet long and displaced 1,580 tons.

Every one of the regular destroyers and flotilla leaders was eagerly accepted by the British Royal Navy in its efforts to have enough destroyers to participate in fleet actions, escort convoys, and perform the other tasks that had fallen to these vessels. In the case of destroyers that were badly damaged in battle, the British made every effort to return them to service as quickly as possible rather than declaring them constructive losses. One example is the case where two British destroyers, *Nubian* and *Zulu*, were crippled. The bow of the former broke off, while the latter lost its stern to a mine explosion. Once in dock, the remaining halves of the two ships were welded together to make a new vessel named *Zubian*.

The destroyer program of the United States, which ranked as the second largest, was, like that of Britain, a reflection of the grave need for allied destroyers. As war had raged in Europe in the years before 1917, the then-neutral United States had continued the production of destroyers built for torpedo defense. Two units of the pre-war *O'Brien* class were launched in 1915 followed by a continuation of the 1000-tonner type that numbered 12 ships in two classes. The entry of the United States into the war in April 1917 led to a significant change in the U.S. destroyer program. As a result of war and the threat posed by Germany's submarine campaign, U.S. destroyers were built increasingly for antisubmarine warfare (ASW). Construction revolved in this period around the famous flush-deckers. These vessels dispensed with the raised forecastle of earlier models, meaning that the main deck was a single, long, flat structure. This was meant to create a more seaworthy hull. The first of the flush-deckers were the six ships of the *Caldwell* class launched in the months following the U.S. entry into the war. The hull of *Caldwell* measured 315 feet, 7 inches by 30 feet, 6 inches by 8 feet, 10 inches, displaced 1,120 tons, and carried turbine engines that produced a maximum speed of 30 knots. The ship was armed with four 4-inch guns, two 1-pound AA guns, and 12 21-inch torpedo tubes. This class served as a basis for two mass-produced groups of destroyers. The *Wickes* and *Clemson* classes comprised about 300 ships, but not all of them were launched by the close of the war. Like the British, the Americans opted for producing large numbers of destroyers in the fastest time possible. The best way to accomplish this goal was the use of only a few designs.

Germany, the principal naval combatant opposing Britain and the United States, launched 11 classes of destroyers during the war that numbered some 95 vessels. The majority of these were launched before 1916, as in that year German naval construction turned to submarines. Most of these vessels possessed similar displacements that averaged between 822 and 960 tons. The last destroyers launched were the three ships of the *H.145* class. Launched in 1917 and 1918, these exhibit a German trend toward larger, more heavily armed destroyers. Even so, the Germans continued to place the highest importance on torpedo attack. The hull of *H.145* measured 277 feet, 3 inches by 27 feet, 7 inches by 11 feet, 2 inches and displaced 990 tons. The ship mounted four 4.1-inch guns, six 19.7-inch torpedo tubes, and 24 mines. Its turbines generated a maximum speed of 34 knots.

Along with the *H.145* class and its predecessors were several foreign vessels seized during the course of the war that augmented Germany's force. Like the British, the Germans were one of the leading prewar destroyer designers and builders and had contracts placed in domestic yards by other countries. On the outbreak of war, the Germans seized two classes of destroyers that each comprised four vessels. One of these groups was intended for Argentina, while the other was bound for the Netherlands. Plans existed for the production of an additional seven classes of destroyers that had led to the beginning of construction on some units, but these were incomplete at the end of the war in November 1918. An additional group that was in the planning stages was cancelled upon Germany's defeat.

The other great maritime powers of World War I also produced destroyers, but not in the numbers of the three most powerful naval combatants. Upon the outbreak of World War I, Japan was an ally of Great Britain through the 1902 Anglo-Japanese Naval Alliance. On 23 August 1914, the Japanese honored this agreement and declared war as a member of the allied powers. The Anglo-Japanese Naval Alliance had been entered into by the British so that, in the event of war against Britain, the Japanese would protect British holdings in the Pacific while the British focused their fleet strength closer to home. The Japanese deemed destroyers as absolutely necessary to fleet operations given the commitment in this alliance. The result was a construction program that continued the prior Japanese practice of building large destroyers with heavy torpedo armaments. During the war, the Japanese launched six classes of ships that totaled 28 units. The best example of the Japanese design is the two-ship *Tanikaze* class. *Tanikaze* measured 336 feet, 6 inches by 29 feet by 9 feet, 3 inches, displaced 1,300 tons, and carried turbine engines that could drive the ship at 37.5 knots. Its armament consisted of three 4.7-inch guns and six 21-inch torpedo tubes. This design would be improved upon in later years when Japan would launch some of the largest destroyers in the world.

Italy, which in 1915 became an allied power, largely neglected the construction of large warships in favor of smaller vessels needed to defend allied interests against submarines and the Austro-Hungarian fleet in the Mediterranean. The Italians pursued the construction of regular destroyers and flotilla leaders to this end. In the former category, the Italians built three classes totaling 20 ships. The *La Masa*–class vessels are indicative of Italian design during the war. Measuring 241 feet, 2 inches by 24 feet by 9 feet, 4 inches, displacing 785 tons, and capable of 30 knots, these ships were armed with six 4-inch guns and four 17.7-inch torpedo tubes. They also carried a fairly heavy AA armament of two 40mm guns and two 6.5mm machine guns. The inclusion of AA armament was a common feature in Italian destroyers of the World War I era. Finally, the vessel was also armed with 10 mines. The flotilla leaders proved to be large and fast. The Italians built 10 of these type in three classes. The *Mirabello* class proved the largest, displacing 1,784 tons.

France produced fewer than Japan and Italy. French naval construction declined rapidly as a whole due to the strain placed on the country by the war. The Western Front lay on French soil in resource-rich areas of the country. The material that was still at French disposal was directed to the army to repel the invading Germans. Plans for several large destroyers were consequently shelved, and the French were able to build only one group of destroyers to supplement their prewar fleet. Of the three *Enseigne Roux*–class ships, only two were launched. Like their predecessors, they were lightly armed. As France needed more destroyers for convoy escort duties primarily in the Mediterranean, and domestic yards could not provide the necessary ships, the French turned to other outlets. One of these was contracting for ships in Japan. This produced the 12-ship *Arabe* class whose units were all launched in 1917. *Arabe* and its sisters were built as quickly as possible to meet French needs. Otherwise unremarkable, they were equipped with triple-expansion engines rather than turbines. The rest of France's wartime destroyer production came at the expense of other powers. Four destroyers being built in France for Argentina were requisitioned, and eight Greek coastal defense destroyers were seized by French authorities.

Imperial Russia's destroyer program was also greatly affected by the war. Russia was still in the process of rearming following the Russo-Japanese War and continued upon the outbreak of World War I with its prewar program. Construction proceeded on four classes of destroyers totaling 37 ships between 1914 and 1917, but many of these, including all nine ships of one class, were never completed. Mounting economic hardship produced by the war hindered production. Ultimately, the Communist-led 1917 Russian Revolution that toppled the czarist government led to a standstill in naval construction. The last group of destroyers launched in the war, the *Kerch* class, is an example of the problem. Of the eight ships under construction, two were not launched until 1924.

The Austro-Hungarian Empire fared the worst of the naval powers in terms of destroyer output, although destroyers were important as patrolling vessels in the confines of the Adriatic Sea. Despite the need for destroyers, production lagged. The first destroyer to enter the empire's service during the war was consequently a destroyer being built for China as a prototype for a larger class of vessels. Austro-Hungarian wartime output consisted of four additional *Tatra*-class destroyers that possessed minor improvements over prewar predecessors. Plans for another four ships were under way, but these were cancelled owing to a shortage of resources that was only one facet of the decline of the empire's economy due to the pressures of war.

Regardless of the degree of success experienced by individual nations in the construction of destroyers during World War I, the destroyer was the warship built in the greatest numbers as every naval power recognized the need for such craft. When the type was first introduced in the late nineteenth century, it had been intended only for the purpose of protecting capital ships from torpedo attacks. Later, the vessel had taken on the additional duty of torpedo attack, but the roles for the destroyer were still limited to fleet operations at the dawn of war. By the end of the conflict in November 1918 with the Armistice that led to the surrender of the Central Powers, these were, despite their importance, only a few among an incredible number of roles. The vast use of destroyers in World War I is indicated by the losses experienced in the conflict: Britain lost the most with 51 ships destroyed; the German High Seas Fleet lost 48 destroyers; 14 Russian vessels were sunk; France lost 11 destroyers; three Austro-Hungarian vessels were sunk; and the United States and Japan each lost one.[12] A fitting tribute to the extensive service of these vessels was the transport of the German naval delegation to Britain in 1918 during the surrender of the German High Seas Fleet as a stipulation of the peace agreement. This diplomatic step brought to a close a devastating war. From it had emerged the destroyer as a proven, multi-role warship whose importance would not diminish in the postwar world.

ENDNOTES

1. Arthur Marder, *The Anatomy of British Sea Power: A History of British Naval Policy in the Pre-Dreadnought Era, 1880–1905* (Hamden, CT: Archon Books, 1964), p. 85.

2. Jon Tetsuro Sumida, *In Defense of Naval Supremacy: Finance, Technology, and British Naval Policy, 1889–1914* (Boston: Unwin, Hyman, 1989), p. 8.

3. Peter Charles Smith, *Hard Lying: The Birth of the Destroyer, 1893–1913* (Annapolis, MD: Naval Institute Press, 1971), p. 17.

4. James L. George, *The History of Warships: From Ancient Times to the Twenty-First Century* (Annapolis, MD: Naval Institute Press, 1998), p. 135.

5. David K. Brown, *Warrior to Dreadnought: Warship Development, 1860–1905* (London: Chatham Publishing, 1997), p. 140.

6. David Lyon, *The First Destroyers* (London: Chatham Publishing, 1996), p. 30.

7. Brown, *Warrior to Dreadnought,* p. 11.

8. George, *The History of Warships,* p. 139.

9. John Wells, *The Royal Navy: An Illustrated Social History* (Gloucestershire, UK: Alan Sutton, 1994), p. 81.

10. Ronald H. Spector, *At War at Sea: Sailors and Naval Combat in the Twentieth Century* (New York: Viking, 2001), p. 33.

11. Spencer C. Tucker, *The Great War, 1914–1918* (Bloomington: Indiana University Press, 1998), p. 113.

12. George, *The History of Warships,* p. 139.

CHAPTER 3

Advancements during the Interwar Years and World War II, 1919–1945

THE NAVAL OFFICIALS of the great powers faced a world that had been changed dramatically by World War I. The naval competition between Great Britain and Germany had ended with Germany's defeat and the surrender of the majority of its battle fleet to the victorious Allied powers. Austria-Hungary also ceased to be a maritime force, as the peace agreement with this defeated Central Power required the surrender of its fleet and deprived the empire of its ports through territorial terms that destroyed the empire itself. Finally, Russia, which had withdrawn from the war before its conclusion, was removed from the naval scene in the years immediately following 1918 because the Bolshevik revolution had toppled the government and the country was largely in chaos as imperial forces fought Communists for political control.

Destroyer construction for some years after World War I was thus in large part the product of the victorious powers. Rather than being new designs, most of the destroyers launched immediately after the war were World War I–era vessels that were in the process of completion upon the close of hostilities. Despite the fact that the destroyer had proven its importance in World War I, few politicians wished to consider the construction of new warships in the atmosphere of war-weariness that prevailed.

Great Britain, the largest producer of destroyers during World

War I, possessed a huge surplus. In addition to the 228 destroyers in operation by August 1914, the British had produced more than 300 new vessels. The British subsequently did not begin building destroyers based on new designs until the late 1920s; significant was the fact that the British economy had been severely strained by the war. Indeed, between 1919 and 1922 about 111 destroyers that were deemed unfit to serve were sold for scrap. The process of scrapping amounts to a peacetime contribution for destroyers, being ships whose roles were to this point in time solely those of war. Ships were sold by the government to private firms, where they were dismantled over the course of several months and their steel and machinery sold on the open market. The fittings of the vessels were first removed, although in the case of destroyers these were few given the relatively Spartan living conditions aboard. Their guns and superstructures were then dismantled, and scrapping crews subsequently cut down the hulls deck by deck until reaching the keel.

The process of selling ships for scrap was beneficial to governments in two respects: The government profited from the sale of the ship itself as well as through a reduction of operating costs for the fleet, as there were fewer vessels to maintain in battle readiness. This second positive aspect was important as part of British attempts to improve their battered economy by demobilizing the military. Despite the lack of new designs and the scrapping of many destroyers, the numbers of ships swelled slightly with the addition of the last of Britain's wartime construction projects. This included four flotilla leaders launched between December 1918 and September 1920. In addition to these were 32 destroyers of other classes that had been laid down during the conflict. Many of these constituted one class that had been ordered in January 1918. As a sign of the times, 38 units of the projected 53-ship group of January 1918 were cancelled in November 1918, soon after the issuance of the Armistice. Politicians in London did not consider such a large number of new destroyers in peacetime to be necessary.

The United States, like Britain, possessed a very large surplus of destroyers. Although the U.S. Navy operated only 54 destroyers in August 1914, by the end of the war U.S. shipyards had produced an additional 109. In the estimation of U.S. naval officials, there was little need to commence new designs given the size of this fleet. Indeed, some scrapping commenced immediately after the war, although the 15 ships that went to the scrap yard pales in comparison to British actions. The thinking of naval officials concerning new designs was merely reinforced by the fact that some units of the mass-produced *Wickes* class were still under construction and only 5 of the 156 *Clemson*-class destroyers were complete. Only six of this latter group were cancelled by the government. The remaining 145 ships were launched between December 1918 and early 1921, which effectively doubled the size of the destroyer fleet of the U.S. Navy. Further designs seemed an ineffective use of funds in the face of so many new ships, although their design would soon become obsolete.

The destroyer production of Japan stands in sharp contrast to that of the two leading naval powers in the immediate postwar world. The Japanese continued to pursue a program of naval expansion that placed a tremendous burden on their country given the limited resources of the home islands and the relatively poor condition of the economy. This course led to the 15 *Minekaze*-class destroyers. Launched between 1919 and 1921, these vessels were more heavily armed than their predecessors. The hull of *Minekaze* measured 336 feet, 6 inches by 29 feet, 8 inches by 9 feet, 6 inches and displaced 1,345 tons. It was armed with four 4.7-inch guns, two 7.7mm machine guns, six 21-inch torpedo tubes, and 20 mines. The vessel was capable of the very high speed of 39 knots. In addition to these vessels were the 21 *Momi*-class destroyers that were launched over the course of the first four years of peace. These mounted less armament and were viewed by most naval officials as being good only for coastal defense due to their poorer seaworthiness. Nevertheless, these vessels, combined with the *Minekaze*-class units, represented a substantial increase in Japan's destroyer fleet. The rise in numbers did not go unnoticed in the United States, where politicians were aware of guarding U.S. Pacific interests against any possible future interference by Japan. By 1922, it was clear that Japan had become a powerful naval force.

The only other naval power to launch new destroyers in the immediate postwar years was Italy. Although these 14 ships—comprising three classes that were launched between 1919 and 1923—were based on the old *Indomito,* they were important in terms of their impact on future events in the Mediterranean. These ships contributed to the growth of a new naval arms race between Italy and France for influence in the Mediterranean. Significantly for destroyer production, it would revolve primarily around the construction of smaller craft.

This arms race, however, would not occur for some years following the launch of the first new Italian destroyers. In the aftermath of World War I, France was in no condition to immediately mount a new program of naval construction. Not only were French resources drained by wartime expenditure, but the economy was badly strained by the war effort. The French did in 1920 draw up plans for 12 new destroyers, but these never materialized. These ships were sorely needed at this time, however, to replace those destroyers that were worn out by years of wartime service. Between 1919 and 1921, the French government scrapped 20 such vessels. In 1922 the government finally approved a new naval construction program that included destroyers, but it would take some years before this legislation produced new warships.

The lack of destroyer production in France was the same situation as that experienced by the other major combatants of World War I. Different factors in each country other than war-weariness or poor economic conditions were the cause. In the case of Russia, the turmoil of the Bolshevik revolution had sparked a civil war that pitted Communists against all those who were opposed to either the end of imperial Russia or the establishment of a society ruled by workers. By late 1920, the Bolsheviks under Vladimir Lenin had triumphed over their enemies. The conflict, however, had largely destroyed the Russian Navy. A large portion of the fleet had remained loyal to the czar and did not return following Lenin's victory. As a result, the new Soviet Union's navy consisted of a small collection of obsolete ships. New naval construction was not considered immediately after the civil war, as Lenin's new Soviet government turned its resources to the consolidation of power within the country. In addition, the navy was held in ill repute by the Soviets not only because of its actions in the civil war but also due to the 1921 Kronstadt mutiny in which sailors at that Baltic naval base revolted against Soviet rule. In light of these conditions, Lenin relegated the remaining naval units to control by the army and for the sole use of coastal defense. It would remain as a denuded and impotent force throughout Lenin's tenure.

Germany also experienced a massive decline in the fortunes of its navy, but this situation and the lack of destroyer production was the result of defeat in World War I rather than a revolution. As part of the Armistice that went into effect on 11 November 1918, Germany was required to surrender the bulk of its High Seas Fleet to the allied powers. The battle fleet was to be interned at the British Royal Navy base of Scapa Flow in the Orkney Islands at the extreme northern tip of the British Isles. By May 1919, the Treaty of Versailles, the formal peace treaty between the allies and Germany, was nearing completion. One clause stated that Germany would lose the bulk of its fleet to the allies as war reparations. The consequence was the German decision to scuttle its interned fleet rather than suffer this inglorious surrender. On 21 June 1919, the German warships at Scapa Flow were scuttled by their crews. Among the vessels sunk were 50 destroyers, being the largest number of warships sunk that day.

The self-destruction of the High Seas Fleet, however, was only the beginning of Germany's naval woes after the war. The Treaty of Versailles imposed restrictions on the composition of the future navy such that the force left to the new Weimar Republic was comprised of obsolete units that were good only for coastal defense. Sixteen destroyers were included as part of the new navy. Four of these had to be kept in reserve, as the treaty stipulated that a maximum of only 12 destroyers could be in service at any one time. New naval construction was limited to the replacement of vessels deemed too old and worn out to operate. Article 190 of the Treaty of Versailles set the rules for such replacement in terms of destroyers. It stated that new destroyers could be built to a maximum displacement of 800 tons and that units could not be replaced until 15 years had passed since the date of the previous ship's launch. In sum, new destroyer production lay some time away for Germany.

Whereas the Germans could at least look to future naval construction, Austria-Hungary could not. Little need be said about Austria-Hungary. Its defeat as a Central Power led to the disintegration of the empire at the Paris Peace Conference through the establishment of new states carved from its territory and the enlargement of other nations. Austria, the heart of the former empire, became a landlocked state. Units of the former Austro-Hungarian Navy were either given to the victorious powers as war reparations or transferred to Yugoslavia, being one of the new artificial states created at Austro-Hungarian expense.

New destroyer construction after 1922 took place within the context of the conditions created by World War I as war-weary powers faced another naval arms race. By 1921, the U.S. government greatly desired a conference to deal with strategic concerns that had arisen in the wake of the war. Diplomatic relations between the United States, which had become one of the most powerful navies through its construction during the war, and Great Britain, the greatest naval power since 1815, had steadily deteriorated as the two powers began to vie for naval supremacy. Neither nation, however, desired a new arms race. U.S. politicians realized that the cost would be enormous because the United States needed to maintain forces in both the Atlantic and Pacific owing to the fact that the 1902 Anglo-Japanese Alliance remained in force.

The British, by contrast, did not want to engage in a new competition given the state of their postwar economy. The result was the 1921–1922 Washington Naval Conference that included representatives of the United States, Great Britain, France, Italy, and Japan. The goal of the meeting was to prevent a future naval arms race, which was viewed by many as a cause of World War I. The resulting Washington Naval Treaty dealt primarily with the limitation of the aggregate tonnage of capital ships, being battleships and aircraft carriers, that each naval power could possess. It also stipulated restrictions on the size of new capital ships. Legislation on smaller warships like destroyers was contemplated through a U.S. proposal to extend the overall tonnage restrictions to smaller craft, but this was rejected by the French. In their view, the high cost of the French Army made destroyers, cruisers, and submarines necessary for national defense, as they were cheaper to build. As a result, the treaty signed in 1922 did not impede the construction of warships smaller than capital ships. Tonnage for capital ships was placed at 525,000 tons each for Great Britain and the United States, 315,000 tons for Japan, and 175,000 tons each for France and Italy.

Despite not having directly affected destroyer development, the Washington Naval Treaty was important for the future of the ship type. The treaty actually encouraged the production of smaller ships like destroyers to supplement battle fleets that had reached their limits in capital-ship tonnage. The numbers of destroyers subsequently built would not equal that of the pre–World War I era due to the impoverished world economy resulting from the war and economic depression in the late 1920s and early 1930s, but construction did move forward. The new destroyers that appeared after the treaty were warships that for the most part incorporated merely refined and improved versions of the technology that had either existed before the war or been produced during it. The big exception was the advent of sonar devices to detect and plot the position of enemy submarines. Although the first sonar set was produced in 1918, the system was not included in destroyers until the early 1920s.

This production took place amid a debate concerning the proper roles of destroyers that was generated by the numerous functions that the ship type had assumed in the war. The crux of the difference in the opinion among the world's naval officials was whether torpedoes or guns should be emphasized. Some naval officials advocated dispensing with torpedoes altogether given the disappointing effect of torpedo attacks at the 1916 Battle of Jutland and in the war overall. The antisubmarine role, despite the heavy use of destroyers as escorts against submarines in World War I, was generally de-emphasized. Regardless of this debate over wartime use, destroyers were seen by all naval powers as important ships of war, and construction of destroyers began in many naval powers soon after the signing of the treaty.

France was among the first to begin new construction. Although the army still received priority over the navy, the French were ready to move forward with their 1922 naval construction plan. This program was considered necessary given Italian production that threatened French power in the Mediterranean. The results fall into two different types of destroyers. The first of these were conventional destroyers. The 12-ship Bourrasque class, being the first French postwar design, was launched between 1924 and 1925, while the 14 L'Adroit-class vessels were launched from 1926 to 1929 and were merely improved versions of the first group. The hull of L'Adroit measured 351 feet, 8 inches by 32 feet, 3 inches by 14 feet, 1 inch and displaced 1,378 tons. They were more heavily armed than in the past, mounting four 5.1-inch guns, two 37mm AA weapons, two 13.2mm AA guns, and six 21.7-inch torpedo tubes. The turbine engines could produce a maximum speed of 33 knots.

The second type of destroyer marked a tendency for even larger and more heavily armed craft than either of the conventional designs. Between 1923 and 1924, the French launched the six ships of Chacal class (known also as the Jaguar class). These ships were among the superdestroyers, meaning destroyers of a particularly large size that mounted very heavy armament. The ships measured more than 415 feet long, displaced 2,126 tons, and were armed with five 5.1-inch guns and six 21.7-inch torpedo tubes. Such dimensions and armament were huge for a destroyer and were indeed unprecedented. The next group of six Guépard-class vessels were generally similar, but were the first of the French 2,400-ton designs. The last destroyers launched by the end of 1930 were the first two units of the Aigle class comprising six ships. Aigle measured 421 feet, 7 inches by 38 feet, 10 inches by 16 feet, 4 inches and displaced 2,441 tons. It was armed with five 5.5-inch guns, four 37mm and four 13.2 mm AA weapons, and six 21.7-inch torpedo tubes. The vessel was capable of a maximum speed of 36 knots.

Italy was also an early producer of destroyers after 1922 as it continued its program that had been embarked upon in the months after World War I. The country's naval rivalry with France deepened after 1922 with the rise to power of Benito Mussolini and his fascist party. One of the facets of Mussolini's plan to increase Italy's influence in the world was overseas expansion. A large navy was a necessity to further that ambition. Mussolini in the years after his rise to prominence devoted a large amount of resources to naval construction. The need for numbers led to the production between 1925 and 1927 of 16 ships in three classes that were improvements on World War I designs.

More significant was the launching between 1928 and 1929 of the 12 *Navigatori*-class destroyers. These vessels were Italy's first and only superdestroyers. *Navigatori* measured 352 feet by 33 feet, 5 inches by 11 feet, 2 inches, displaced 1,900 tons, and could steam at 38 knots. It was armed with six 4.7-inch guns and, unlike destroyers of previous eras, these were not contained in single mounts. Instead the armament was carried in three dual-piece mounts, one each being sited in the bow and the stern and the third amidships. The vessel also shipped two 40mm and four 13.2mm AA guns along with six 21-inch torpedo tubes. These vessels, with their maximum speed of 38 knots, were faster than their French equivalents and were deemed a serious threat by French naval officials. Supplementing these vessels in 1930 were the first two units of the four-ship Freccia class, which were smaller ships designed to operate with the fastest capital ships of Italy's fleet.

Japan followed closely behind France and Italy in terms of the speedy construction of destroyers after 1922. Following the end of the Anglo-Japanese Alliance in the early 1920s, the Japanese came to rely totally on their own technology and shipbuilding techniques, as they could no longer rely on British aid. Construction beginning in the mid-1920s would yield Japanese destroyers that engendered respect around the world. The Japanese plan revolved around larger destroyers, as Tokyo pursued a policy of quality over quantity in part due to Japan's more limited resources. The production of destroyers seemed a good use of naval funds given the 1922 Washington Naval Treaty. Not only was Japan at its tonnage limit in capital ships; its ceiling was less than those of the United States and Great Britain. Japanese naval officials viewed the production of powerful destroyers as a good method to supplement the power of their smaller battle fleet. In addition, destroyers were also necessary as part of Japan's strategic requirements. In February 1923, Japanese military officials had created a secret list of potential future enemies in which the United States was number one. Destroyers were envisioned as vessels that needed to be of sufficient size and endurance to operate for extended periods in the vast expanses of the Pacific in defense of Japanese interests against a potential enemy with a larger battle fleet, such as the United States.

Destroyers, in the event of war, were seen not only for battle fleet defense but also for the protection of Japanese overseas commerce and for commerce warfare. Japanese destroyers were consequently powerful. The first 12 *Mutsuki*-class ships, launched between 1925 and 1927, were merely derivatives of the preceding *Kamikaze* class, but their armament was extremely potent given the torpedoes mounted on the type. These destroyers were the first in the world to mount the 24-inch torpedo, which was pioneered by the Japanese. Known in World War II as the Long Lance, its existence at the time was a state secret. The weapon was an awesome improvement over the torpedoes of other navies. The weapon's warhead, 795 pounds of explosive, was twice that of a 21-inch torpedo. In addition, its range was greatly increased over prior models. The 21-inch torpedo could run at a maximum speed of 35 knots while reaching its maximum range of about 5,687 yards. The Long Lance could also travel at 35 knots but was capable of a maximum range of 10,936 yards. Range increased with reduction in speed. In the case of the Long Lance, the weapon could travel as far as 22,000 yards at lower velocities.

These powerful ships, however, paled in comparison to Japan's superdestroyers. These 20 ships of the *Fubuki* class were launched between 1927 and 1930 and represent a design coup for the Japanese that was acknowledged by naval officials in all other major maritime powers. The hull of *Fubuki* measured 388 feet, 6 inches by 34 feet by 10 feet, 6 inches, displaced 1,750 tons, and carried turbine engines that could produce a maximum speed of 38 knots. At the time of its launch, this ship and its sister ships were the best-armed destroyers in the world. The main gun armament of *Fubuki* consisted of six 5-inch guns that were housed in three twin-gunned turrets rather than mounts protected by gun shields. One of these turrets was located forward, while the other two were sited in the stern. This arrangement, which would be repeated in future Japanese designs, made the *Fubuki* class the first destroyers in the world to use turrets.

The turret had existed since the U.S. Civil War (1861–1865), when it was employed in the Union warship *Monitor,* but it had never been shipped on a hull as small as that of a destroyer. A turret is an enclosed gun house that protects the gun crew from enemy fire. In the case of *Fubuki*, the light armor of the gun house was strong enough to withstand splinters from explosions and worked against smoke and poison gas. This turret sat on top of a barbette, a French invention in existence since 1867. A barbette is simply a large turntable on which the guns were placed that could swivel, at this point through the use of steam or electrical power, and thus provide a large arc of fire. The barbette extended below the main deck and encased the loading machinery and magazines, the later being normally in the bottom of the ship for the sake of protection from enemy fire. Ammunition and the powder with which to fire it was passed from the lowest level of the barbette via hoists to the turret, where the crews loaded and fired the guns.

The guns of *Fubuki* were controlled from a position placed on top of the bridge that was known as director control. Pioneered by the British in the years leading up to World War I, this system was in wide use by the end of the conflict but reached destroyers later than larger ships due to the size and weight of the machinery. Director control was a range-finding center that housed electronic equipment that calculated an enemy vessel's range, course, and speed. This information was used to aim the guns, which could be fired from this location. In addition to the armament itself and the range-finding equipment that greatly increased its accuracy, later units of the *Fubuki* class were equipped with turrets that could elevate the guns up to 75 degrees in the air as opposed to the 40 degrees of prior vessels of the type. These proved to be among the world's first dual-purpose guns that were designed both to combat surface targets and to provide AA fire. Supplementing the fine gun armament of the *Fubuki* class was a torpedo armament of nine 24-inch tubes, two 13mm AA guns, and depth charges. The heavy torpedo armament was a reflection of the priority placed by the Japanese on destroyers as torpedo attack vessels.

The stir created in international circles by the heavy armament of these vessels was heightened by the fact that these ships were truly all-weather vessels that were superior to most foreign destroyers. For the first time in a destroyer, the bridge was completely enclosed to keep the bridge crew protected in rough weather and thereby increase efficiency. The *Fubuki* class was not a perfect design, however, as the addition of an enclosed bridge, director control, and turreted guns made the ship very top-heavy and unstable. Also, to save weight the hull and bridge structure were very lightly built. Indeed, the bridge was composed of aluminum rather than steel. As a result, the hull and superstructure were slightly weak, and there would be instances of plates buckling during the careers of the *Fubuki*-class ships. Nevertheless, Japan had created a ship that subsequently shaped considerations of destroyer design in many countries toward large destroyers with heavy armament.

Great Britain, among the largest naval powers in the world, was one of the last to embark on new construction in the wake of the 1922 Washington Naval Treaty. The country continued at first to rely on its surplus of World War I era destroyers while dispensing with those units considered too old to effectively function. Not until the late 1920s did the British perceive a need for appreciable numbers of new vessels. Even so, the period before this time was marked by the peacetime use of destroyers as testing platforms for new technology. The growth of the airplane as a new weapon in World War I led to experimentation that, in the case of the Royal Navy, revolved around the use of planes as scouts for battle fleets. In 1923 and 1928, the destroyers *Stronghold* and *Thanet* had their forward guns removed in lieu of the construction of aircraft catapults on their forecastles.

This era was also not wholly devoid of experimentation with destroyer design. Two destroyers, *Amazon* and *Ambuscade,* were launched in 1926 as prototypes for new ships. These led to the 19 ships of the A and B class that were launched between 1929 and 1930. These letter designations referred to ships of the same class, some bearing names beginning with "A" while others bore names beginning with "B." They were essentially enlarged and better-armed versions of the last British World War I–era designs. An A-class or B-class destroyer measured 323 feet by 32 feet, 3 inches by 12 feet, 3 inches, displaced between 1,337 and 1,360 tons, and carried turbine engines that produced a maximum speed of 35.25 knots. The heaviest pieces of their gun armament represented a technological innovation. These were four 4.7-inch quick-firing guns, these vessels being the first armed with weapons of this caliber that were quick-firers. This battery was also innovative through a design improvement based on World War I experience. The gun shields that surrounded them extended farther down toward the deck to protect the crews from splinters that could fly underneath from explosions and cut off their feet. Unlike the past, these shields also extended around the gun more fully on the sides, thus affording better protection. Although these shields were still proof only against splinters, the improvement was a sound one and was standard in most navies. In addition to this armament, the ships also carried two 40mm pom-pom guns for use against aircraft and eight 21-inch torpedo tubes. Supplementing the ships of the A and B class was one flotilla leader launched in 1929 that was essentially an enlarged ship of the same type.

The British return to destroyer production was not matched by the United States, the other large naval power, after the 1922 Washington Naval Treaty. Until 1934, U.S. politicians continued to rely on the nation's huge surplus of World War I–era destroyers despite the fact that these vessels by this date were obsolete.

This lack of destroyer production was also a continuing trend in the Soviet Union. That country was still trying to recover from the effect of the civil war, and the navy, beyond acting as a coastal defense force, was still considered a low priority. A naval program was authorized in 1926, but it called only for the construction of small coastal craft and the refurbishment of the obsolete units remaining from the old czarist fleet.

By 1930, most of the world's navies had returned to the production of destroyers. The designs were, unlike capital ships, unfettered by any treaty restrictions. Those vessels built after 1930, however, constituted a new phase in the development of destroyers where the parameters of their design were set by international law. Diplomats of the signatory powers of the Washington Treaty realized in the years after its implementation that the agreement had done little to prevent worldwide naval competition due to its exclusion of limits on smaller craft like destroyers. In 1927, plenipotentiaries of the great naval powers had met at the Geneva Conference to try and correct this problem, but the effort resulted in failure. The talks deadlocked because the United States and Great Britain could not reach agreement on the number of cruisers, which was another type of ship largely unaddressed by the Washington Treaty, that would be allowable for each navy. The next conference, however, produced compromise on this issue and also placed for the first time limits on destroyer design and the amount of destroyer tonnage allowable for each signatory country.

The London Conference, which met between 21 January and 22 April 1930, created legislation that limited the displacement and armament of destroyers as well as cruisers and submarines. The resulting London Naval Treaty stated that the majority of destroyers could be built to a maximum 1,500 tons of standard displacement—the weight of the ship fully equipped—but without fuel. A further clause stipulated that each naval power that signed the treaty could fill 16 percent of its overall destroyer tonnage with vessels that displaced up to 1,850 tons standard displacement. These destroyers, regardless of displacement, could mount a maximum caliber of 5-inch guns. In addition to these design stipulations, the talks also set the maximum tonnage of the signatory powers at 150,000 tons each for the United States and Great Britain and 105,000 tons for Japan, which translated into a 10:10:7 ratio, respectively. Notably, the French and Italians refused to sign this treaty due to the restriction on destroyers. Both powers deemed such restrictions as running counter to their naval planning, which relied heavily on the use of destroyers. Indeed, destroyers constituted the majority of the naval arms race in the Mediterranean Sea between the two powers.

The result of the London Treaty was that all of the signatory powers between 1930 and 1934 built destroyers up to the maximum of the design limitations. Great Britain is the first example of this trend, as the British produced three classes of destroyers in this period that conformed to the tonnage restrictions of the treaty. Two of these classes, the C and D class and the E and F class, were similar to one another and comprised a total of 30 warships. The first was an enlarged version of the A and B class while the second group followed from their predecessors' design. An E and an F-class vessel displaced between 1,350 tons and 1,405 tons and carried four 4.7-inch guns in single mounts protected by gun shields. These attributes were well within the stipulations of the London Treaty. The third class of two ships became the first newly designed British flotilla leaders since World War I. These vessels were merely enlarged E- and F-class boats that displaced between 1,460 tons and 1,495 tons and carried an additional 4.7-inch gun. Like the smaller destroyers, these still conformed to the lower tonnage limit of the treaty as well as the gun armament limit.

The United States, given rising concerns in Washington over Japanese imperial expansion in Asia that posed a threat to U.S. Pacific interests, returned to destroyer production with the nine *Farragut*-class ships. These vessels, being the first produced to a post–World War I design, were launched between 1934 and 1935. The hull of *Farragut* measured 341 feet, 3 inches by 34 feet, 3 inches by 11 feet, 7 inches and displaced 1,358 tons. It was armed with five 5-inch guns in single mounts. Only the two forward weapons were enclosed in gun houses. These weapons, like vessels such as *Fubuki*, were placed on dual-purpose mounts that would become a standard feature in U.S. destroyers. *Farragut* also carried four .5-inch weapons for use against enemy aircraft and eight 21-inch torpedo tubes. The vessel's turbine engines could produce a maximum speed of 36.5 knots. Like the British ships, these vessels conformed to the London Treaty. They were built for endurance to operate for extended periods in the expanses of the Pacific Ocean and thus are a reflection of the growing U.S. concern over Pacific holdings in light of the Japanese threat. The *Farragut* class proved to be the benchmark for all future U.S. destroyer designs in the years before World War II.

Japan's construction of destroyers between 1930 and 1934 took place in the context of the government's decision to pursue imperial expansion. In 1931, Japanese forces invaded and conquered the Chinese province of Manchuria. Also, plans were in existence in the early 1930s that called for the seizure of areas in Southeast Asia and the East Indies, which were rich in oil and raw materials that were necessary to sustain a Japanese economy that was increasingly devoted to the production of military equipment. A strong navy was necessary to realize the goals set forth in these plans. Destroyers constituted a large part of the subsequent construction effort.

The first new group of four *Akatsuki*-class ships was launched between 1931 and 1932 and was generally similar to *Fubuki*. A key difference was the use of electric welding to attach the hull plates to the frame rather than rivets of steel that nailed them to the beams. This method was billed as a weight-saving measure and became standard practice in subsequent decades in all the world's navies. Nevertheless, at this time the use of welding proved a problem through several instances of separations of hull plates from beams. The proceeding *Hatsuharu* class of six ships was the first built to conform to the London Treaty. *Hatsuharu's* hull measured 359 feet, 3 inches by 32 feet, 10 inches by 9 feet, 11 inches, displaced 1,490 tons, and was powered by turbines capable of 36.5 knots. The armament consisted of five 5-inch dual-purpose guns, two 13mm AA weapons, nine 24-inch torpedo tubes, and 14 depth charges.

The destroyers built in France in the wake of the London Treaty were far larger than those of the signatory powers, as the French, having refused to sign it, were unfettered by any limitation on design. As a result, France continued its program of constructing superdestroyers. Between 1931 and 1932 the French launched the six ships of the 2,441-ton *Vauquelin* class that mounted a primary armament of five 5-inch guns and seven 21.7-inch torpedo tubes. These were followed by the six *Le Fantasque*–class vessels. Launched between 1934 and 1935, these warships were some of the most impressive destroyers of their day. The hull of *Le Fantasque* measured a colossal 434 feet, 4 inches by 40 feet, 6 inches by 16 feet, 5 inches and displaced 2,569 tons. It carried five 5-inch guns in single mounts protected by gun shields, four 37mm and four 13.2mm AA weapons, nine 21.7-inch torpedo tubes, and 50 mines. Its turbine engines produced a maximum speed of 37 knots, making the vessel, as well as its sister ships, some of the fastest in the world.

Indeed, *Le Terrible* once reached a speed over 45 knots. This incredible achievement made it the fastest ship of its day and one of the quickest of all time. Due to their size, these vessels border on being light cruisers rather than destroyers.

Italy, France's chief naval rival, continued to try to equal or surpass the strength of the French fleet. The effort of the Italians, however, did not rest on building large destroyers like those of their competitor. Despite not being a signatory to the London Treaty, the Italians built smaller destroyers whose design specifications were below that of the agreement it had spurned. The four-ship *Folgore* class, launched in 1931, were units that displaced only 1,220 tons and were armed with four 4.7-inch guns housed in two twin-gunned mounts. One was located in the bow while the other was placed in the stern. They also carried six 21-inch torpedo tubes, an assortment of AA weapons, and two depth charge throwers. The follow-on four *Maestrale*-class ships were larger, similarly armed vessels.

Destroyer production between 1930 and 1934, despite being in part regulated by an international agreement designed to preserve peace, took place against the backdrop of the looming possibility of another war. By 1934, Japanese expansion had already raised concern, but a fresh challenge had also appeared by this time in Europe. In 1933, Adolf Hitler and his fascist party, the Nazi Party, had been elected to power in Germany with a platform that called for the destruction of the Treaty of Versailles as the path to a restoration of German power. Amid these tensions, the arms limitations began to fall apart. In August 1934, in keeping with their new expansionist goals in the Pacific, the Japanese announced their intention to abrogate the Washington Treaty. Although the United States and Great Britain continued to build within the guidelines of the treaty in an attempt to foster goodwill, the Japanese declaration dealt a grave blow to the spirit of arms control.

By extension, the Japanese action also threatened the framework created by the London Treaty. A subsequent attempt to further restrict naval production through the Second London Conference, which met from December 1935 to March 1936, was ultimately a failure. The Japanese, demanding parity with Great Britain and the United States in tonnage numbers of all warship types, walked out of the meeting upon being rebuffed. Their departure crippled the talks, despite some agreement by the other powers on issues other than destroyers. With the London Treaty set to expire at the end of 1936, all powers knew that the very real possibility existed of a new naval arms race.

As this sequence of events unfolded, the United States continued to produce destroyers that conformed to the London Treaty. The high number of destroyers launched between 1935 and 1939 was spurred by rising world tensions and continued to include primarily large destroyers capable of extended operations in the Pacific. The first of these were eight ships of the *Porter* class, launched between 1935 and 1936, that filled the U.S. need for flotilla leaders. These can be classed as the first U.S. superdestroyers. The hull of *Porter* measured 381 feet, 1 inch by 37 feet by 13 feet, displaced 1,834 tons, and housed engines capable of 37 knots. Its armament consisted of eight 5-inch guns in four twin-gunned mounts that were fully enclosed by gun houses. Two of these were located in the bow while the other two were sited in the stern. As a result of this armament and the ship's tonnage, *Porter* conformed to the London Treaty at a time that corresponded with the breakdown of the Second London Conference. The ship was also armed with eight 1.1-inch and two .5-inch AA guns as a reflection of the growing threat posed by the airplane. Finally, the vessel carried eight 21-inch torpedo tubes.

The *Porter* type was followed by six more classes launched up to the end of 1939 that yielded 52 new destroyers. The last of these, the *Sims* class, is an example of regular U.S. destroyer design upon the outbreak of war in Europe. The hull of *Sims* measured 348 feet, 4 inches by 36 feet by 12 feet, 10 inches and displaced 1,764 tons. It was armed with five 5-inch guns, four .5-inch AA weapons, and eight 21-inch torpedo tubes. The vessel's engines generated a maximum speed of 35 knots. In addition to ships of these general design specifications, the United States continued the production of superdestroyers. The *Somers*-class ships displaced 2,047 tons and carried an impressive primary armament of eight 5-inch guns and 12 21-inch torpedo tubes. The large displacement of these ships is evidence of the fact that by the time of their launching between 1937 and 1938 the United States had accepted the fact that the era of arms limitation was over. By this point, it was also clear to many that global conflict was once again a real possibility.

Great Britain, like the United States, continued to conform to the disarmament treaties for a few years after 1934 despite the Japanese declaration that they would abrogate the Washington Treaty. This policy of increased naval expenditure was also the result of the increasing threat posed by Hitler's Germany to peace in Europe. The first destroyers were the 24 ships of the *G*, *H*, and *I* class. These ships were launched between 1935 and 1937 and conformed to the London Treaty. They displaced 1,335–1,370 tons and were principally armed with four 4.7-inch guns in single mounts equipped with gun shields and eight 21-inch torpedo tubes. Three additional vessels were merely enlarged versions to act as flotilla leaders.

After 1936, with the expiration of the London Treaty, the numbers of British destroyers greatly increased as part of a hurried rearmament program. Britain's only superdestroyer type, the *Tribal* class, was part of this effort. The *Tribal* class was a reaction to the Japanese *Fubuki*-class destroyers, which had greatly impressed British naval officials. These ships were designed specifically to combat *Fubuki*-class vessels in the Pacific in case of war with Japan, which would threaten Britain's Eastern empire. Sixteen *Tribal*-class destroyers were launched between 1937 and 1941, the lion's share in 1937. The hull of a *Tribal*-class ship measured 377 feet by 36 feet, 6 inches by 13 feet, displaced 1,854 tons, and was powered by turbine engines that generated speeds between 36.25 and 36.5 knots. A unit of the type was armed with eight 4.7-inch guns in twin-piece mounts that were protected by gun shields. It also carried four 40mm pom-pom AA weapons and four 21-inch torpedo tubes. Ships of this design were not produced in very large numbers owing to the expense incurred in the construction of larger vessels. The result was the smaller, 24-ship *J, K,* and *N* class, of which 16 ships were ready by the opening of war in September 1939. These displaced 1,690 tons and mounted a primary armament of six 4.7-inch guns and 10 21-inch torpedo tubes.

Japan, the other signatory of the London Treaty, remained true to its stipulations on destroyers in the years between 1934 and 1936 despite the fact that the Japanese government had renounced the Washington Treaty. The embodiment of this fact is the 10-ship *Shiratsuyu* class, whose units displaced 1,685 tons and mounted five 5-inch guns. The expiration of the London Treaty in 1936, however, led the Japanese to launch ships that signaled the end of Japan's adherence to treaties concerning destroyers.

Between 1936 and 1937, the Japanese launched 10 *Asashio*-class destroyers that displaced 1,961 tons. Their gun armament was the same as the *Fubuki* class, and they also carried eight 24-inch torpedo tubes. The decision to construct a similar class of 18 *Kagero*-class ships led to the launching of 10 units of the group by the outbreak of war in Europe. All were slightly less unstable at sea than prior models in part due to the damage suffered by many destroyers of the fleet in a typhoon. In 1935, units of the Imperial Japanese Navy were caught in a storm that placed many of the earlier destroyers in danger of capsizing and led to their reconstruction between

1935 and 1937 to include more ballast to keep the vessels stable. Overall, by September 1939 the Japanese destroyer fleet was one of the most powerful in the world.

France continued its destroyer production in keeping with past programs that were never subject to the London Treaty. In the case of France, this yielded one more class of ship that was the largest superdestroyer ever built. Launched between 1936 and 1937, the two ships of the *Mogador* class displaced an incredibly large 2,884 tons each. The hull of *Mogador* measured 451 feet, 1 inch by 41 feet, 7 inches by 15 feet and contained turbine engines that could generate a maximum speed of 39 knots. The ship was armed with eight 5.5-inch guns in four twin mounts that were fully enclosed by gun houses. Two of these were located in the bow while the other two were placed in the stern. It also carried 10 21.7-inch torpedo tubes and a collection of AA armament.

Italy responded to the output of French destroyers with vessels that remained smaller than those of their Mediterranean rival. The four-ship *Oriani* class was simply a repetition of the previous type, but the final group of destroyers launched before the outbreak of war in Europe was built to a new design that became the most successful of all Italian types. In 1937 and 1938, the Italians launched 12 *Soldati*-class destroyers. *Soldati* measured 350 feet by 33 feet, 7 inches by 11 feet, 6 inches, displaced between 1,690 tons and 1,820 tons, and housed turbines that produced 38 knots. It mounted five 4.7-inch guns, six 21-feet torpedo tubes, two depth charge throwers, and 12 13.2mm AA weapons.

In addition to these conventional destroyers, the Italians in the years leading up to World War II were among the pioneers of a new type of ship that would evolve into the escort destroyer. Between 1934 and 1937, the Italians launched 37 smaller destroyers that were intended to augment the strength of the Italian Navy while at the same time not costing as much to build as regular destroyers. The final group, the *Pegaso* class, serves as an example of the type. *Pegaso* measured only 293 feet and displaced a small 840 tons. In essence, the ship was an enlarged torpedo boat. Its armament consisted of only two 3.9-inch guns, four 18-inch torpedo tubes, and eight 13.2mm AA weapons. Significantly, the ship also mounted six depth charge throwers, making it a vessel best suited for ASW. This small type of vessel, although it was not designed specifically for ASW and therefore is not considered an escort destroyer, was a portent of the future of destroyer production due to its very large ASW capability.

In addition to the destroyer production of those naval powers that represented the victors of World War I, the period between 1935 and September 1939 saw the return of two former maritime forces. The first of these, and the cause of much anxiety among other nations, was Germany. In May 1935, Hitler repudiated the Treaty of Versailles in keeping with his goal to once again make Germany a world power. This course was given legitimacy by Great Britain. Rather than enforce Versailles, in June 1935, as part of its policy of appeasement to avoid war, the British openly violated the treaty by signing a naval pact that allowed for a German fleet that was 35 percent the size of the Royal Navy. Both of these actions ultimately counted for little, because by May 1935 construction was already well under way on new destroyers that violated the peace agreement.

The first class of German destroyer built since World War I was the 1934 class that served as the blueprint of all subsequent destroyer construction for Nazi Germany. Four of these ships were launched in 1935, and each measured 391 feet, 5 inches by 37 feet by 13 feet, 1 inch, with a displacement of 1,625 tons. Unlike the German craft of the World War I era, these ships mounted a larger gun armament. A unit of the 1934 class mounted five 5-inch guns in single mounts protected by gun shields. Two each were sited on the bow and stern while the fifth was located aft amidships. The vessel also carried eight 21-inch torpedo tubes, and an assortment of AA guns. Like all subsequent destroyer types and many of those in the past, 1934-class vessels were designed to ship mines if necessary.

One drawback of this class that extended to later designs was its engines. German engineers incorporated a new high-pressure steam propulsion plant that was intended to produce greater power output. This machinery was designed to yield a maximum speed of 38.2 knots, but such velocity was rarely attained, and the plant was subject to frequent breakdowns. An additional negative aspect was the fact that these ships were rather unstable in a seaway. As a result, Germany was not the successful destroyer producer that it had been in the years before World War I. These problems were duplicated in an improved 1934 class of 12 ships that were launched between 1936 and 1937. The following class, however, was an improvement.

Although the six 1936-class ships retained the problematic high-pressure steam propulsion plant, they were designed with a new feature to help correct problems with seaworthiness. This was the clipper bow, a feature that marked some capital ships of the German Navy and had been tried by other powers. Clipper bows, named after fast sailing ships of the nineteenth century, were those where the sides of the bow flared out to better plow through the water and thereby help the ship maintain its speed in a seaway. These ships were consequently much better seafaring boats. The hull of one of these ships measured 404 feet, 2 inches by 38 feet, 8 inches by 13 feet, 1 inch and displaced 1,811 tons. Its armament and engines were virtually the same as the 1934 class, but the clipper bow enabled the possibility of a maximum 40 knots. By September 1939, the German Navy had made a relatively quick return to the family of destroyer powers. All of these vessels, which were originally known simply by their pennant numbers, were eventually named after famous German naval figures of World War I.

The Soviet Union was the other former naval power to revive its destroyer production program in the years leading up to World War II. In the late 1920s, a massive industrialization program was undertaken that proved crucial to the desire of premier Joseph Stalin, Lenin's successor, for a large battle fleet. By the early 1930s, Stalin attached importance to re-establishing his country as a naval power to expand Soviet influence. The need for a large fleet was also justified in the late 1930s by German rearmament. Included as part of the 1933 Soviet naval reconstruction program was authorization for 49 destroyers. This legislation produced three classes of destroyers by the outbreak of war.

The first of these was the one-ship *Opytnyi* class that when launched in 1935 was the first Russian destroyer design since World War I. This vessel was intended as an experimental ship, and its poor performance exhibited the fact that the ability of Russian shipyards to design destroyers had declined since the Communist takeover. Stalin consequently looked to foreign shipyards for the next class of vessels. Although the 31-ship *Gnevnyi* class was constructed entirely in Russian yards, the design was an Italian one. Between 1936 and late 1939, the Russians were able to launch 22 units of the class. The hull of *Gnevnyi* measured 370 feet, 7 inches by 22 feet, 6 inches by 13 feet, 5 inches, displaced 1,855 tons, and was powered by engines that generated 37 knots. It was armed with four 5.1-inch guns in single mounts housed in gun shields. Two each were located in the bow and stern. The ships also carried two 3-inch guns, six 21-inch torpedo tubes, two 45mm and four .5-inch guns for AA defense, and 56 mines. The latter weapon represented a continuation from czarist times of the Russian belief in destroyers serving as minelayers. Supplementing this heavily armed and numerous group were the *Storozhevoi*-class destroyers that signaled a return to wholly Russian designs. These vessels were large, displacing 2,192 tons, and possessed similar armament to the previous class. Sixteen of these ships were launched by the end of 1939. Like Germany, Russia had quickly resurrected its destroyer force.

As in the case of technology, many other aspects of the destroyers built in the prewar period were much like those of earlier days. The first example of this is the education of the crews of destroyers. The instruction of officers and men became more specialized in keeping with the trend that started at the turn of the twentieth century, but there were few radical changes in the systems that were put in place at this time. In addition, the everyday lives of the men who operated destroyers only slightly improved from the days of World War I, as the hulls of the destroyers became larger. Bathrooms complete with washbasins were a standard feature on destroyers in this period. Living quarters had expanded, as did the wardrooms where crewmen ate and spent a portion of their off-duty time. The habitability of these areas was increased not only due to the greater dimensions of these areas but also through a reduction in the pitching and rolling motion of many destroyers. Although certainly not as comfortable as capital ships of the day, the surroundings of destroyer men were certainly better than those of the pre–World War I era.

Unlike the years leading up to World War I, destroyers in the interwar years did not have the opportunity to participate in large naval actions. Their duties in this period consisted mainly of being dispatched in peacetime crisis situations. One of the early examples took place in 1922 when British destroyers were used to screen the evacuation of the Greek Army during a war that pitted Greece against Turkey. Further duties such as this one were undertaken in the late 1930s as part of the worsening situation in Europe. During the 1936–1939 Spanish civil war, British and German destroyers cruised off the Spanish coast. German destroyers were officially earmarked for patrol duties in this conflict despite the fact that Hitler was giving open aid to Spanish fascist forces under Francisco Franco. British destroyers were also not directly involved in keeping with the British government's desire to remain clear of any action that may result in war. The British vessels did, however, provide humanitarian assistance to the Spanish nationalists fighting Franco's forces and to British citizens trapped in Spain. Destroyers of the Royal Navy, sporting red, white, and blue identification bands of paint, oftentimes evacuated Spanish nationalists and British citizens to the French port of Marseilles. These destroyers were employed for two and a half years in this duty, which could pose significant danger to the ships despite Britain's neutrality.

These duties, despite their value, were not regarded as being typical for destroyers. All naval powers recognized that these ships were almost exclusively vessels of war and had built their destroyer fleets of the interwar period with this in mind. The value that naval officials attached to them is evident from the number of operational destroyers in the navies of the belligerent powers of World War II soon after the outbreak of war. By the beginning of 1940, Great Britain possessed 247 destroyers of varying age. The United States operated 149 vessels and Japan had 116 destroyers. Italy counted 90 craft in the service of its navy. France maintained 66 destroyers while the Soviet Union was close behind with 64 ships. Germany operated 37 destroyers.[1]

These numbers do not do justice to the true size of the world's destroyer fleet, as smaller naval powers are not included. Over the period between late 1918 and the beginning of 1940, other European powers had produced a significant number of destroyers. The Netherlands launched 8 vessels; Norway launched 3 small destroyers that some scholars label as frigates; Poland operated 4 destroyers; Spain counted 13 such vessels in its navy; and Sweden operated 12 destroyers. Other powers around the world also counted destroyers as a principal portion of their forces. Argentina had 12 destroyers by late 1939 while Chile operated 6 destroyers. Even the Near East country of Turkey, having been in existence only after World War I, operated four destroyers.[2]

In general, these smaller powers, with their modest financial resources, relied on destroyers due to their relatively low construction costs. Whether the destroyers were built in large naval powers or lesser maritime nations, debate had been constant over their primary purpose in the period between the end of World War I and the beginning of World War II. These duties included destroyers in their old roles of torpedo attack and defense, light gunfire support for amphibious operations, and to a lesser extent antisubmarine warfare. All of these roles were proven important once the world was plunged into a new, extremely destructive war.

Destroyers had been constructed throughout the 1930s in an atmosphere of ever-increasing world tensions created by nations that were bent on territorial expansion. In 1935, Benito Mussolini launched a war of imperial aggrandizement through the invasion of Ethiopia. Two years later Japanese imperial aggression in China that had begun in 1931 finally produced war between the Japanese and Chinese. These two conflicts, while greatly troubling to the world community, paled in comparison to the situation that subsequently developed in Europe. By 1939, Europe, after only 20 years of peace, was on the brink of all-out war. Hitler sought territorial expansion in Europe as a path to restoring Germany as a world power. The fragile peace in Europe was finally shattered on 1 September 1939, when the German Army invaded Poland. Great Britain and France, having given a guarantee to the Polish government to militarily intervene in the event of German aggression against that country, declared war on Nazi Germany.

The outbreak of hostilities once again turned the Atlantic Ocean and North Sea into the setting for a naval conflict. The nature of this conflict was dictated by the composition of the Kriegsmarine, the German Navy. Unlike World War I, the German Navy was quite small and unprepared for war. In 1939, Germany had adopted a construction program known as the Z Plan that called for a large fleet comprised primarily of 4 aircraft carriers, 8 battleships, 5 battle cruisers, 8 heavy cruisers, 13 light cruisers, and 48 destroyers. This plan, however, had been set for completion in 1948, and consequently the outbreak of war found the Kriegsmarine with only a few ships of the program ready for service. Germany possessed only 2 battle cruisers of the *Scharnhorst* class, 5 heavy cruisers of the *Deutschland* and *Hipper* classes, 6 light cruisers, and 22 destroyers, while 2 battleships of the *Bismarck* class were nearing completion. The small size of this surface fleet dictated the strategic goals of Germany in the war at sea. Hitler envisioned all German surface forces, in combination with submarines, as primarily commerce raiders to starve Great Britain of overseas supplies in much the same way as World War I. British and French efforts, until the fall of France in 1940 that removed the French Navy as a factor in the war, focused on the protection of commerce.

Although most naval powers had looked to destroyers in the interwar years as torpedo or gun craft, the antisubmarine warfare role (ASW) proved to be the role in which destroyers were most heavily employed in the Atlantic.

The Battle of the Atlantic for the Allies revolved around the protection of British commerce. Upon the Allies' reinstituting the convoy system that had proven so successful in World War I, British, Canadian, French, and later U.S. destroyers guarded against torpedo attack by German submarines, known as U-boats, that were dispatched to prey on merchant shipping. The primary weapon of destroyers versus submarines at the outbreak of war remained the depth charge. It was little changed from the model used in World War I, except that the device carried a larger explosive charge and could travel to depths of as much as 1,500 feet. The effectiveness of this weapon was greatly increased by the addition on Allied destroyers of sonar. This underwater detection device was first developed in 1918 through the Allied Submarine Detection Investigation Committee (ASDIC, the original term for the device used by the British). The United States later labeled it sonar (sound, navigation, and ranging). Although an experimental set had existed at the close of World War I, it was not until the mid-1920s that units had come into operational use. By 1940, most navies possessed the device and had installed it on their ASW warships, which were in large part destroyers. The sonar of the World War II era consisted of machinery that transmitted sound waves through the water that bounced off the hull of a submerged craft and returned to the destroyer. The operator of the set was then able to establish the range and bearing of the submarine so the commander could bring his ship to the proper position to begin a depth charge attack. This represented a great improvement over hydrophones that could not provide such data.

In addition to sonar, Allied destroyers became deadlier ASW craft with the introduction of the Hedgehog. Developed by the British and operational at sea by January 1942, the Hedgehog consisted of a launcher that was fitted forward of a destroyer's bridge. This device fired ordnance ahead of the attacking craft rather than behind in the case of depth charges. It was essentially a mortar that housed 24 bomblets in individual tubes. Each held 31 pounds of high explosives. When fired, the bombs spread out in a pattern 130 feet in diameter. These bombs fell into the water some 215 yards ahead of the attacking vessel. Only direct contact between the bomb and the hull of a submarine would cause detonation of the device. Those that missed simply sank to the ocean floor. Although the chance of sinking a U-boat with the Hedgehog was considered low, this weapon did destroy 50 submarines by the end of war and was used in tandem with depth charges.

These 50 represent only a small portion of the German submarines sunk in the war. Their loss was the result of a variety of attacks, but the destroyer was a crucial weapon that accounted for a large percentage of German losses. The sinking of so many U-boats led to the defeat of Germany in the Battle of the Atlantic. This ASW role, however, was certainly not free of danger for Allied destroyers that were subjected to the same possibility of torpedo attack as the merchantmen they escorted. An example is the case of the U.S. destroyer *Reuben James*. Although the United States was a neutral power until the attack on Pearl Harbor in late 1941, President

Franklin D. Roosevelt had authorized U.S. naval forces to escort British merchant vessels arriving and leaving the United States. *Reuben James* was an old *Clemson*-class vessel that was part of U.S. forces that escorted British convoys to Iceland, where British naval units took over the task. On 31 October 1941, *Reuben James* and four other destroyers were escorting a convoy of 44 merchant ships to Iceland when the vessel was hit by a torpedo fired from the German submarine *U-562*. The force of the explosion devastated the light hull of the ship, which broke in half following a magazine explosion. The bow section subsequently sank immediately while the aft portion foundered in about 20 minutes. Out of a crew of 160 officers and men, only 45 survived. *Reuben James* has the questionable distinction of being the first U.S. warship sunk in World War II.

The impact of destroyers as ASW craft on World War II in the Battle of the Atlantic was profound, as it enabled Britain to remain in the war against the Axis (Germany, Italy, and Japan). Ultimately, Britain would serve as the staging point for the invasion of German-controlled Western Europe in 1944 with the Normandy landings. Each vessel was vital to the effort. The actions of one destroyer while serving as a convoy escort greatly aided overall Allied victory in the Battle of the Atlantic. On 9 May 1941, the British destroyer *Bulldog* was employed, as were almost all of Britain's destroyers, in convoy protection when *U-110* launched a torpedo attack on the convoy. *Bulldog* and two other ASW vessels raced at full speed to the site where the torpedoes were probably fired; once there, a pattern of depth charges damaged the submerged German submarine and forced it to the surface. *Bulldog* subsequently opened fire with its guns; although due to inaccurate fire it caused little damage, it did induce the crew to evacuate their vessel so quickly that they did not scuttle the ship. The commander of *Bulldog* ceased fire upon seeing this event, as he sensed a great opportunity to board the U-boat. The boarding party managed to procure equipment and, significantly, the vessel's confidential code books for its Enigma code machine.

The Enigma device, created by Arthur Scherbius in the mid-1920s, encoded German communiqués. Although the British had been able to break some of the German codes thanks to research procured by the Poles before their country fell to Germany in 1939, the codes for the U-boats had been difficult to decipher. The codes seized by *Bulldog* were valid only through the month of June, but during the period between then and their seizure the British were able to conduct research using them that broke the German ciphers in general. For the remainder of the war, the Allies were able to read

Axis communiqués and thus defend against sorties of U-boats and surface raiders against merchantmen in the Battle of the Atlantic.

The ASW role of destroyers was only one of the large number of duties performed in the Atlantic Ocean and North Sea. Throughout the war at sea they also served as escorts for capital ships and various other naval forces as well as in their basic duty as surface combatants. In April 1940 the British destroyer *Glowworm*, acting as an escort for minelayers bound for Norway, encountered the German heavy cruiser *Admiral Hipper*. The subsequent action failed to produce a torpedo hit on the German vessel, and the British commander, whose destroyer was greatly outgunned by the Hipper, elected to ram. The result was the loss of the *Glowworm* from damage sustained in the collision and from enemy gunfire. Of the 149 officers and men of the British vessel, only 31 survived the action and the sinking. *Admiral Hipper* suffered a 120-foot-long hole in its side, forcing the ship to return to Germany for repairs.

The following 1940 German invasion of Norway provided several instances where destroyers were able to function in their original roles of torpedo attacks and defense as well as in general surface actions. On 10 April 1940, five British destroyers of the 2nd Destroyer Flotilla under Captain B. A. W. Warburton-Lee attacked 10 German destroyers that were taking part in the invasion and were stationed at the Norwegian port of Narvik. The ensuing battle resulted in the British sinking two of the German vessels and damaging an additional three destroyers. The high degree of loss for the Germans was due primarily to the fact that they were caught unawares. Warburton-Lee's force, however, sustained damage due to five of the German destroyers being undetected. These ships lay in wait in fjords and attacked Warburton-Lee's force from both sides as it was retiring from its initial engagement. One British destroyer was destroyed while another, Warburton-Lee's flagship, *Hardy*, was beached due to serious damage.

This first battle led to a second on 13 April as the British were determined to destroy German naval units in the Narvik area. The British battleship *Warspite*, escorted by nine destroyers, attacked the remaining German forces at the port and sunk eight more German destroyers. Only one destroyer, *Erich Giese*, survived the assault, but this vessel was critically damaged. With wounded and dying men littering its decks, the captain ordered the ship abandoned. A magazine explosion later destroyed the vessel.[3]

In events after the invasion of Norway, destroyers figured prominently. British destroyers in 1941 launched a torpedo attack on the

German battleship *Bismarck,* but without any success. German destroyers after Norway, where a large potion of their strength was lost, were used as escorts for capital ships. The most celebrated case is the 1942 Channel Dash in which the battle cruisers *Scharnhorst* and *Gniesenau* escaped from the French port of Brest and returned to Germany via the English Channel. This route ran the gauntlet of the British Royal Navy and the ships were escorted by destroyers.

Destroyers participated in surface action until the last of Germany's capital ships were driven from the sea. In 1943, British destroyers launched torpedoes against the German battle cruiser *Scharnhorst* that caused a portion of the damage that ultimately sank the vessel. This was the last surface action of the war in the Atlantic; fittingly, destroyers had played a large part in the conflict, as they had in so many other operations during the Battle of the Atlantic.

Destroyers also were called upon during war in the Atlantic theater to carry out several tertiary duties that had arisen in World War I. Rather than being employed in the ASW role, escort for capital ships, or torpedo attacks and defense, one of the first uses of destroyers in World War II was in the role of troop carrier through an evacuation. At the end of May 1940, France was reeling from the German invasion and on the point of collapse. On the beaches of Dunkirk, 250,000 men of the British Expeditionary Force were trapped and in need of transport to avert being captured. The loss of these men would have proven disastrous to the war fortunes of Great Britain and might have forced the British to negotiate for peace. In OPERATION DYNAMO, the evacuation of the BEF to Britain, destroyers were used as part of the 693-ship armada that took part in the operation. Destroyers were especially well-suited to this task as a result of their speed, which could allow for hasty trips back and forth between the French coast and Britain. By the end of the operation, the Royal Navy had lost six destroyers to air attacks by the Luftwaffe, the German Air Force.

The experience of *Keith* exhibits the nature of destroyer duties in this action. In late May, *Keith* embarked about 700 soldiers for the passage back to England.[4] Upon returning to Dunkirk on 31 May 1940, *Keith* opened fire with its guns on German troops advancing on the coast toward the evacuation point for Allied forces at Dunkirk. On 1 June, waves of German aircraft bombed the evacuation site. Two 1,000-pound bombs scored near-misses on *Keith* that stove in some of its hull plates, causing flooding, while another bomb went down the aft smoke funnel and exploded in the engine room, killing most of the engine room crew and crippling the ship.

The vessel subsequently sank. This sacrifice, however, was a small price to pay for the rescue of the BEF from France. As a result, Britain was able to remain in the war.

Germany also used its destroyers as troop carriers. In the 1940 invasion of Norway, German destroyers sortied to Norway laden with troops who were offloaded as part of the amphibious invasion before the warships assumed their stations for offensive operations. Part of these constituted another World War I role of destroyers, that of gunfire support for amphibious operations. While protecting the landing zone, Allied destroyers participated as gunfire vessels during OPERATION OVERLORD, the 1944 Allied invasion of Normandy. The warships of the Allied invasion fleet were primarily destroyers. Eighty of these craft participated along with 7 battleships and 23 cruisers.

The Battle of the Atlantic also involved destroyers in rescue operations. A celebrated case is that of the British destroyer *Kelly,* which removed the Duke and Duchess of Windsor from the French port of Le Harve in the opening days of the war to protect that royal family. *Keith,* sunk in OPERATION DYNAMO, performed the same duty on 15 May 1940 for the Dutch royal family. A rescue operation was also arguably the last battle in which destroyers were involved in the European theater of the war. On 5 May 1945, German destroyers screened the evacuation of some 45,000 refugees from East Prussia as the Soviet Red Army advanced toward Germany. The majority of rescues during the Battle of the Atlantic, however, involved aiding the survivors of sunken ships. This role was an important duty for the destroyers of all combatant navies. Due to the extreme cold and stormy conditions of the Atlantic, any surviving crewmen had to be picked out of the water as quickly as possible. Prolonged exposure to these conditions ultimately led to death.

A final role played by destroyers in the Battle of the Atlantic is indicative of their extreme importance to the Allied war effort. These ships formed the basis of one of the first wartime agreements between the United States and Great Britain. In June 1940, soon after the evacuation of Dunkirk, Britain was faced with the possibility of amphibious invasion by Germany and thus desperately needed its destroyers to act as part of a coastal defense force. In addition to this drain on resources was that posed by the German U-boat campaign against British shipping. Faced with a dearth of destroyers to cover both tasks, British Prime Minister Winston Churchill desperately appealed to U.S. President Franklin Roosevelt for aid. On 3 September 1940, the neutral United States gave Britain 50 World

War I–era destroyers in exchange for 99-year leases for British bases in Newfoundland, Bermuda, and the British Caribbean Islands. Known as the Destroyers for Bases Deal, this act was an incredible morale boost to the British people in the wake of the fall of France. It also was a further step by the United States toward outright participation in the conflict.

Destroyers proved equally as important in the Mediterranean in the same roles as those of the Battle of the Atlantic upon Italy's entry into the war on the side of Germany. Having signed the 1939 Pact of Steel with Germany and emboldened by the German conquest of France in 1940, Italian dictator Benito Mussolini declared war on Great Britain. This action opened the Mediterranean Sea as a new theater of war and consequently posed a severe strategic threat to the British. Italy's geographic position threatened British supply lanes providing oil and supplies from the eastern portion of the empire that passed through the Suez Canal into the Mediterranean and to the British home islands. The campaign in the Mediterranean quickly centered on British attempts to protect its trade and defend the island base of Malta that lay astride its shipping lanes. The Italians were conversely committed to the destruction of this valuable commerce.

Destroyers participated in almost all the major operations and engagements in the Mediterranean. These actions revolved largely around commerce war. In the context of the traditional role of protecting capital ships from torpedo attacks, the Italian Navy used its destroyers as screens for task forces of battleships and cruisers bent on the destruction of British trade.

Examples are numerous, but one of the best examples as well as one of the largest engagements in the Mediterranean was the Battle of Cape Matapan. On 28–29 March 1941, an Italian squadron comprised of 1 battleship, 8 cruisers, and 17 destroyers that was attempting to attack British convoys around Crete was intercepted by a British force of 3 battleships, 1 aircraft carrier, 4 cruisers, and 13 destroyers. The British destroyers were present in this battle, as in others in the Mediterranean, to protect their capital ships against torpedo attacks and try to launch assaults themselves; they were also among the few Allied warships that could catch the fast Italian vessels. The British detached their destroyers in an attempt to run down the Italian squadron. Although this measure failed, the destroyers did have an opportunity to later prove their worth as Italian cruisers and destroyers were sent to the aid of one crippled cruiser.

The result was a night action in which three Italian cruisers were sunk. Although the destruction was accomplished largely by gunfire from British battleships, two cruisers were finished off by torpedoes launched by British destroyers. The Allied craft were also used to attack the Italian destroyers that tried to protect the cruisers. By the end of the battle, two Italian destroyers were also sunk and the Allies had established primacy in the Mediterranean. This coup was possible in part due to the use of radar—an innovative development introduced to naval combat in World War II that the Italian Navy lacked—to pinpoint Axis vessels at night and air superiority.

Destroyers were also used for commerce warfare as escorts for merchant convoys and as commerce raiders, in which they launched torpedo attacks against merchantmen. In November 1941, an Italian convoy escorted by destroyers and bound for North Africa to resupply Axis forces was intercepted by a British squadron of cruisers and destroyers. The result was the loss of the entire Italian convoy and the destruction of two of the destroyers, one being sunk by a British submarine that arrived on the scene. The British, like the Italians, also employed destroyers as escorts. In August 1942, the desperate need to resupply the British-held island of Malta led to a convoy being dispatched in which destroyers accounted for the bulk of the covering force.

Past surface actions that arose from roles in the commerce war, destroyers were also used as resupply vessels, primarily to North Africa. The threat of attack by land-based aircraft was high in the Mediterranean due to the relatively small size of the sea in relation to the Atlantic Ocean. Destroyers were, because of their high speed, used to carry troops and supplies at night. Traveling at their maximum velocity, these ships could make a complete journey in the cover of darkness, thus greatly decreasing the chance of an air attack that could destroy not only the vessels but also the valuable cargos that they carried.

Gunfire support for amphibious invasions also became an important task for destroyers. On 8–14 November 1942, the Allies mounted an amphibious invasion to wrest control of North Africa from the Axis. Destroyers not only served as sources for covering fire while Allied troops landed on the beaches; they also guarded the unloading of supplies to the ground forces after the initial assault. The same roles were attached to the Allied destroyers in the 1943 invasion of Italy.

Finally, as in the Atlantic, destroyers were also used in evacuation and rescue operations. In April 1941, as Greece collapsed under

German invasion, Allied destroyers evacuated the king of Greece and his family. They also covered the extraction of 43,000 troops from the Balkan country. This operation resulted in the loss of 26 ships, 2 being destroyers, to German air attacks. This action is a microcosm of the enormous effort in May 1941 by British naval units to evacuate Crete in the wake of the German assault on the island. During this operation, the Royal Navy counted six destroyers sunk in addition to other warships. These vessels were destroyed by ground-based German aircraft and are examples of the fact that surface warships largely without air cover were extremely vulnerable to air attacks. (This fact became far more obvious through experience in the Pacific.) In addition to large operations such as that at Crete, destroyers were also used to retrieve the survivors of sunken vessels, one case being that of a British destroyer that picked up survivors of the Italian cruiser *Pola* following its destruction in the 1941 Battle of Cape Matapan.

As naval campaigns in the Atlantic and Mediterranean continued to unfold, in late 1941 a new theater of operations was opened that made what had been largely a European conflict a truly world war. Japan, which after September 1940 was an ally of Germany and Italy, was faced with U.S. efforts to stem imperial expansion in China through economic embargoes intended to starve the Japanese war machine of needed supplies. Tensions between Japan and the United States resulted in the Japanese attack on 7 December 1941 on the U.S. Pacific Fleet stationed at Pearl Harbor, Hawaii. This act brought the previously neutral United States into the war as an Allied power. Japan's strategy called for the conquest of Far East lands and the islands of the Pacific to supply resources for Japan's industrial base, which was dependent on overseas supplies, as the home islands possessed few raw materials. Japanese naval and military officials then envisioned a defensive war based on a perimeter of conquered Pacific possessions. They reasoned that U.S. attempts to capture these areas would prove so costly in human terms that the U.S. government would be willing to discuss peace.

The use of destroyers was crucial and consequently very high in the naval war in the Pacific. Unlike in the Atlantic, the primary task of destroyers was not ASW, despite their use in this capacity by both the United States and Japan. Indeed, the first naval shot of the Pacific War came on 7 December 1941, when the destroyer *Ward* destroyed a Japanese midget submarine that attempted to penetrate the defenses of Pearl Harbor as part of the Japanese attack. Rather, the primary use of destroyers in the Pacific was dictated by the fact that aircraft carriers were *the* capital ships of the theater. This was the duty of escort for primarily the carriers. Throughout the conflict, all navies relied on screens of destroyers to use their AA armament to intercept attacking planes before they could reach the carriers. In the case of the Japanese, the need for such protection became increasingly vital due to the loss of naval air strength that greatly reduced air cover for the surface forces of their navy. At the 23–26 October 1944 Battle of Leyte Gulf, the Japanese hoped to offset Allied air superiority through a reliance on warships such as destroyers with heavily increased AA armament. The core of the Japanese force in this operation, the Center Force under the command of Admiral Takeo Kuritia, comprised 5 battleships, 12 cruisers, and 15 destroyers serving primarily as AA screens. In total, there were 27 destroyers of the total 64 Japanese warships employed in the engagement. The United States used its destroyers in a similar fashion.

They were particularly useful in the latter stages of the war when the U.S. Navy faced attacks by kamikazes, the Japanese suicide bombers bent on the destruction of U.S. surface ships. In the April–June 1945 Allied invasion of Okinawa, kamikazes sunk 14 U.S. destroyers while the same vessels and their consorts used AA guns to defend themselves and the rest of the fleet, particularly aircraft carriers, against such attacks. U.S. destroyers were also important in the latter half of the Pacific War as radar pickets versus air attacks. In this capacity, destroyers formed a perimeter around aircraft carriers and used radar equipment to detect incoming flights of hostile planes. This ability enabled U.S. task forces some time, albeit not very much, to prepare for an assault in which the destroyers as well as other warships that formed the perimeter endeavored to shoot down as many aircraft as possible.

Amphibious assaults were also operations in which destroyers saw great use. The task of escort for landing craft was of great importance for the U.S. strategy of island-hopping across the Pacific, where select Japanese-held islands were conquered in the effort to bring Japan within the range of land-based bombers and to cut off overseas supply to the home islands. A celebrated example of this duty occurred in the 1944 Battle of Leyte Gulf at Samar. In the closing stages of the Leyte Gulf contest, the Center Force of Admiral Takeo Kurita managed to almost accomplish its goal of destroying the U.S. amphibious forces landing on the island of Leyte. As the large U.S. aircraft carriers had been drawn away from the landing zone through the lure of a decoy force comprised of Japan's last carriers, the only protections for the troops were a collection of small escort carriers, three destroyers, and four escort destroyers. These latter ships were diminutive versions of conventional destroyers.

Facing this force was Kurita's four battleships, including *Yamato*, being one of the world's largest battleships and armed with 18.1-inch guns, six heavy cruisers, and 10 destroyers. In a desperate fight, the destroyers and escort destroyers launched torpedo attacks while producing smoke screens to obscure the escort carriers, whose planes attacked the Japanese vessels. Two hours and 40 minutes later, two U.S. destroyers and one escort destroyer were sunk along with one escort carrier. The punishment they received was tremendous, as in the case of the destroyer *Hoel,* one of the lost vessels, which suffered more than 40 hits from a variety of different calibers of Japanese guns. Their action, however, unnerved Kurita, who believed that he actually was facing the planes and escort screen of a larger U.S. force. His consequent order to withdraw saved the U.S. troops on Leyte and eventually led to the successful reconquest of the Philippine Islands. This action crippled the Japanese war machine, as it cut the supply lines from the home islands to the resource-rich East Indies.

In addition to protecting landing forces, destroyers were also used as gunfire support vessels for amphibious invasions. Both the United States and Japan relied on these ships in this capacity. The United States regularly employed destroyers as gunfire ships during landings on islands on Japan's defensive perimeter. The Japanese looked to destroyers for this task during the 1942 campaign for Guadalcanal. An example is provided by action on the night of 24–25 August, when Japanese destroyers bombarded Henderson Field, a vital U.S. airfield on Guadalcanal, as a prelude for an amphibious invasion, which ultimately failed.

In connection with their roles as escorts and gunfire support vessels for amphibious operations, destroyers were also used as troop transports and resupply vessels. The best instances of this role come from the experiences of the Imperial Japanese Navy, again in the campaign for Guadalcanal. Part of the strength of the Imperial Japanese Navy involved in this struggle were destroyers under the command of Rear Admiral Raizo Tanaka. This commander, known to historians as the most accomplished Japanese destroyer leader of World War II, used the forces under his command to resupply Japanese forces on Guadalcanal. On the night of 17–18 August 1942, his squadron, known as the Tokyo Express to the Allies, conducted its first run to Guadalcanal.

Destroyers for the Japanese were well-suited to this task, as they could make a round-trip between their bases and Guadalcanal under cover of darkness thanks to their high speed. The ability to accomplish operations entirely at night was important due to Allied air superiority in the area. Daytime operations would have resulted in the destruction of the force and its supplies and troops destined for Guadalcanal. In October alone, the Tokyo Express transported 20,000 troops to Guadalcanal. During the month of November, as Japanese fortunes waned in the campaign, Tanaka's force was relied upon to get supplies to the troops by any means necessary. In one instance, the Japanese used their destroyers to drop rubberized containers into the water, which floated in the surf to land and were picked up by forces awaiting the supplies that the boxes contained. These ships were also used as troop transports. The final use of the destroyers of the Tokyo Express in the campaign for Guadalcanal came in February 1943, when they were used to evacuate the 13,000-man garrison of troops that still remained on the island.

A final duty of destroyers in the Pacific (much more prevalent than in any other theater) was the traditional role of launching torpedo attacks. Some of the earliest instances of this duty came in the wake of the Japanese attack on Pearl Harbor. Following the crippling of the U.S. Pacific Fleet as well as the destruction of a British force comprised of a battleship and a battle cruiser, the only Allied forces facing the Japanese were cruisers and destroyers. In late 1941, the United States, Great Britain, the Netherlands, and Australia formed a united command (ABDA Command) for the defense of Southeast Asia. The attempts of this force to disrupt Japanese movements led to several engagements where destroyers were heavily engaged.

The best example of destroyers as torpedo attack vessels is the 27 February 1942 Battle of the Java Sea. Five cruisers and nine destroyers of ABDA Command had sortied with the intention of intercepting a Japanese invasion force bound for Java that included 4 cruisers and 14 destroyers. In the resulting action, both sides launched torpedo attacks. Although the U.S. effort was a failure, that of the Japanese, who had always placed great emphasis on the torpedo and had meticulously trained in the execution of torpedo attacks, was successful. The devastating power of the Japanese Long Lance torpedo, as well as its superior range that allowed for the launch of an attack before Allied warships were able to do the same, exacted a heavy toll. By the end of the engagement, the Allied force had lost two cruisers and four destroyers while the Japanese vessels escaped intact. Gunfire was responsible for a large part of the destruction, but Japanese torpedoes sank one destroyer, damaged another, and were possibly responsible for the sinking of an additional destroyer. This battle decimated ABDA Command and, after one additional engagement, left Southeast Asia devoid of any significant Allied naval presence.

U.S. destroyers also claimed victories through destroyer attacks. In the 1944 Battle of Leyte Gulf, a U.S. force comprised of battleships, cruisers, and destroyers that was defending Surigao Strait annihilated the Japanese Southern Force that was attempting to steam through the strait. This night action resulted in the sinking of two Japanese battleships. One of these was sunk by torpedoes while the other was destroyed by a combination of heavy gunfire and torpedoes. Destroyers continued to the end of the war as torpedo attack vessels. As a testimony to their great service, destroyers engaged in the last naval battle in the Pacific. On 16 May 1945, the British 26th Destroyer Flotilla intercepted the Japanese heavy cruiser *Haguro*. In the ensuing engagement, the Japanese cruiser was crippled by three torpedo hits and was subsequently finished off by an additional attack.

The loss of *Haguro* provides one of many examples of destroyers being used in roles other than combat. Following the sinking of this ship, a Japanese destroyer picked up the vessel's survivors. In addition to rescuing crewmen of sunken or sinking vessels, destroyers were tasked with picking up downed pilots. Destroyers were also employed as fire-fighting ships whereby massive hoses fed by seawater would drench large vessels that were ablaze. When this measure failed or when a vessel was unsalvageable, the task of scuttling a ship to prevent its capture by the enemy fell to destroyers.

The myriad of duties performed by destroyers in all the theaters of World War II made them a vital element in the naval operations of every combatant. As a result, the destroyer was the type of warship produced in the greatest numbers during the war. The facts that they were the fastest and cheapest to build also encouraged destroyer production. Of all of the naval powers, the United States and Great Britain accounted for most of the destroyer construction of World War II. Other nations did not have the resources to produce them in very large numbers.

The United States, with its very powerful industrial base, was responsible for the greatest number of new destroyers. Like World War I, these ships represented only a handful of classes to save time on construction by eliminating the process of drawing up several different designs. As war broke out in Europe, the United States was in the process of launching the last group of its prewar destroyers. These were the 95 ships of the *Benson/Gleaves* class and were also the final ships to adhere to the stipulations of the London Treaty, despite the fact that the agreement had expired. Launched between November 1939 and February 1943, these vessels were similar to the preceding *Sims* class but with slightly greater armament. Construction increased dramatically as these ships were still in the process of building.

By June 1940 in the wake of the fall of France, U.S. politicians were aware of the possibility that the United States, although neutral, might eventually be the only power left to stand in the face of German and Japanese aggression. The result was a naval expansion program that called for a two-ocean navy to combat both threats if the need presented itself. Among the ships authorized were 115 destroyers that proved to be only part of total wartime production. Between 1940 and 1945, the United States built 470 conventional destroyers capable of fleet operations.[5]

The first of these vessels comprised the *Fletcher* class, the largest group ever produced in the world. Launched beginning in 1942, 178 ships of the class were commissioned by September 1944. The design is commonly considered one of the best in the history of the destroyer. The hull of *Fletcher* measured 376 feet, 5 inches by 39 feet, 7 inches by 13 feet, 9 inches and displaced 2,325 tons. Unlike most destroyers, the engine and machinery spaces of the hull were protected by .75-inch side armor and .5-inch deck protection. U.S. naval constructors decided to include this feature in light of British wartime experience, where even the explosions produced by ordnance that narrowly missed generated splinters that could seriously damage a destroyer's thin hull plating. The gun armament consisted of five 5-inch guns in single mounts that were completely enclosed by gun houses. Both the bow and the stern contained two each of these weapons while the fifth was sited aft just before the rear portion of the ship's superstructure, as by this time most destroyers carried auxiliary control positions in this area. In addition, *Fletcher* carried four 1.1-inch weapons and four 20mm guns for AA defense. Its torpedo weaponry consisted of 10 21-inch tubes. Finally, as with all destroyers of the age, the ship was equipped with sonar and depth charges. Powering this impressive ship were turbines that could produce a maximum speed of 38 knots.

Supplementing the ships of this type were those of the *Allen Sumner* class that comprised 59 commissioned warships by the end of 1944. These possessed slightly larger, unarmored hulls and greater armament and were also the product of wartime experience. By mid-1943, the need for AA defense was recognized by U.S. naval officials. As a result, the *Allen Sumner* class included plenty of open deck space to add additional AA guns as necessary.

The last conventional destroyer design of the war yielded 105 *Gearing*-class vessels. These were designed specifically for extended operations in the most far-flung regions of the Pacific. The hull of *Gearing* measured 390 feet, 6 inches by 40 feet, 10 inches by 14 feet, 4 inches, displaced 2,616 tons, and was powered by turbines that produced a maximum speed of 36.8 knots. This vessel was armed with six 5-inch guns in dual mounts enclosed by gun houses. Two were sited in the bow while the last was located on the stern. They also carried 10 21-inch torpedo tubes, an assortment of AA guns, and depth charges. The *Gearing*-class destroyers represent the pinnacle of conventional destroyer design in the United States.

All of these ships, as well as prewar destroyers, were continually upgraded over the course of World War II. Although some of these craft were fitted upon their construction with radar equipment, many of them had to be refitted with the device. Radar is a British invention that made its wartime debut in World War II. The U.S. Navy introduced the technology to its larger vessels in 1937, but sets small enough to fit on destroyers were not available until 1941. Radar consisted at this time of large dishes that were mounted on top of the bridge structure of warships. These transmitted ultra-high-frequency radio waves over great distances that bounced off objects such as warships. These waves then traveled back to the radar set of the tracking vessel, where machinery would reveal the position of the enemy and the distance to the target. This invention represented a great improvement over past director control systems for firing guns, as it was far more accurate. Radar also provided U.S. warships with night-fighting capability and made possible the use of destroyers as advanced warning pickets to screen aircraft carriers against air and surface attack.

Whereas only those destroyers produced before 1941 needed radar upgrades, almost all U.S. destroyers underwent refits of AA armament. The AA guns of the United States were deemed poor based on wartime experience. As a result, beginning in 1942 the standard .5-inch machine gun and the 1.1-inch type mounted on prewar destroyers and many of the wartime classes were steadily replaced by one of two new weapons. The first of these was the Oerlikon gun. This 20mm weapon was a Swiss invention and proved far better than the old type. Later, the weapon of choice became the Dutch

40mm Bofors gun. This type first went to sea in the U.S. Navy in July 1942 and was proven to be among the best AA guns. Increasingly large numbers were placed on destroyers to both replace inefficient armament and to provide the most AA defense possible. Oftentimes, the importance of the AA capability outweighed that of more traditional functions. Many U.S. destroyers had one of their aft gun mounts removed to accommodate more AA weapons.

These vessels, thanks in part to the continual refits, were the most capable destroyers produced during World War II by the United States. Ultimately, however, they did not fill the military demand for destroyers. Their numbers were large, but the myriad roles demanded of destroyers were too great to fill. The United States consequently turned to the construction of a type of destroyer that had been pioneered by the British to bridge the gap. This type was the escort destroyer.

The escort destroyer was a smaller vessel, making it faster to build, and was devoted to the performance of fewer missions than larger ships. U.S. escort destroyers were built largely for a single mission: ASW. The need for these was dire given the Battle of the Atlantic, upon which hinged the survival of Great Britain. In 1941, the British contracted with the U.S. government for vessels that could protect convoys against submarines given the fact that they could not domestically produce an adequate number of craft. Escort destroyers subsequently became important both for Great Britain and, increasingly, for the United States.

The United States built vessels comprising four escort destroyer classes over the course of the war. These vessels, influenced by the original British design, were all generally similar. The last classes, whose units were launched primarily in 1943, were the DET and FMR classes designed primarily for ASW, but also for AA defense. The hull of one of these vessels measured 306 feet by 36 feet, 7 inches by 10 feet, 5 inches and displaced 1,253 tons. Its armament consisted of three 3-inch guns in single open mounts and three 21-inch torpedo tubes. This light armament was due to the fact that the vessel carried a large ASW battery in keeping with its intended primary role. The vessel mounted one Hedgehog, eight depth charge throwers, and two depth charge racks. The small number of guns and torpedo tubes also resulted from the very large number of AA guns, being two 40mm Bofors and between 8 and 10, 20mm Oerlikons. These ships, unlike the preceding classes, were equipped with diesel-fueled engines rather than turbines. This propulsion plant was necessary because turbines took longer to build and the need for speedy production of ships was paramount. The diesel engines could generate a maximum speed of only 20.2 knots, but this was acceptable given that the role of the vessel was primarily that of protecting slow-moving convoys.

By the end of the war, the United States had commissioned 499 escorts, which eclipsed the number of conventional destroyers in service at the end of the conflict. Counted in this number, however, is a type of vessel that was designed solely for escorting merchantmen rather than being intended for both ASW and AA defense. Known as the frigate, this vessel was, like the escort destroyer, a product of British naval yards. Produced in only one type, a U.S. frigate measured 301 feet, 6 inches by 36 feet, 6 inches by 13 feet, 2 inches and displaced 1,509 tons. Its armament consisted of three 3-inch guns in single mounts, and four 40mm and nine 20mm AA guns. Most significantly, the vessel carried one Hedgehog, eight depth charge throwers, and two depth charge racks. Its engines were capable of a maximum speed of 20 knots. As with the larger escort destroyers, high speed was not considered necessary given their mission.

Great Britain also produced regular destroyers, escorts, and frigates, but in lesser numbers given that its industrial capability was not equal to that of the United States and its resources were stretched more thinly. Even so, the British commissioned 285 conventionally designed destroyers over the course of the war. Following the launch of 11 *Tribal*-class ships for the Australian and Canadian navies and 8 *J*-, *K*-, and *N*-class vessels, the British constructed the 16-ship *L* and *M* class. Launched between 1939 and 1942, these vessels were the first British wartime design and were essentially an enlargement of the preceding type with one additional 4.7-inch gun and lesser torpedo armament. The next five classes were like the *L* and *M* class in that they were generally of the same design, but with slight modifications in weaponry. The 24 units of the last of these, the *Ch, Co,* and *Cr* classes, were launched between 1944 and late 1945 and are an example of this trend. The hull of one of these vessels measured 362 feet, 9 inches by 35 feet, 8 inches by 14 feet, 5 inches, displaced between 1,710 tons and 1,730 tons, and was powered by turbines that generated 36.75 knots. The armament consisted of four 4.7-inch guns in single mounts protected by gun shields, four 21-inch torpedo tubes, and two 40mm Bofors AA weapons.

In addition to these similar classes, the British also launched three more groups of vessels that were larger than those of the past. These were intended for extended operations in the Pacific. Indicative of the larger craft are the 16 *Battle*-class destroyers. The hull of a unit in this group measured 379 feet by 40 feet, 3 inches by 15 feet, 2 inches and displaced between 2,315 and 2,325 tons. The armament consisted of four 4.5-inch guns, eight 21-inch torpedo tubes, and eight 40mm Bofors AA guns. The maximum speed of the type was 35.75 knots.

All were continually upgraded in keeping with wartime experience. The two principal improvements were refits to include radar sets and additional AA armament. Like most other navies, many destroyers finished the war lacking one or more of their primary guns in favor of more Oerlikon and Bofors AA weapons.

As in the case of the United States, the British also pursued the construction of escort destroyers for ASW and AA defense roles. These duties were deemed extremely important by British naval officials in the event of a war with Germany and had been foreseen by October 1938. Great Britain was the pioneer of the escort destroyer type through the production between 1939 and 1940 of the 23 *Hunt*-class escort destroyers. A *Hunt*-class ship measured 280 feet by 29 feet by 12 feet, 6 inches and displaced 1,000 tons. The vessel was armed with four 4-inch guns in single mounts and four 2-pounder pom-pom weapons. Most lacked any torpedo battery. This was the result of the fact that the ship was designed specifically for the protection of convoys against submarines. The *Hunt*-class units carried an impressive ASW armament that totaled between 50 and 110 depth charges. The turbine engines of one of these ships produced 28 knots. By the end of the war, the British launched three more batches of escort destroyers that were improved *Hunt*-class ships. In total, the Royal Navy operated 86 vessels of the *Hunt*-class design.

Supplementing these vessels were the frigates of the Royal Navy. Great Britain pioneered the design of frigates with the *River* class, first launched in 1942. A *River*-class vessel measured 301 feet, 4 inches by 36 feet, 8 inches by 11 feet, 10 inches and displaced between 1,310 tons and 1,460 tons. Its armament consisted of only two 4-inch guns, but it possessed a large ASW battery. This consisted of a Hedgehog and 126 depth charges mounted primarily in racks. The large amount of antisubmarine ordnance is evidence of the fact that the frigate of the Royal Navy, like that of the United States, was intended solely for use against submarines while escorting merchantmen. Great Britain built several classes following that of the original *River* type. By the end of the war, the Royal Navy operated 349 escort destroyers and frigates.

The remainder of Britain's wartime destroyers were procured rather than built. The majority of these were the 50 aging U.S. World War I–era destroyers garnered from the 1940 Destroyers for Bases Deal. The rest were, like the World War I practice, units built in British shipyards for other countries that were purchased after the outbreak of war. These were six Brazilian ships and two Turkish vessels. The vital need for destroyers made it necessary to secure them by any means necessary.

Other Allied powers produced far less than the United States and Great Britain. In June 1940, the destroyer program of France ended with its war effort upon the collapse of the country following Germany's invasion. Only four destroyers were under production at the time of France's defeat. All but one of these were subsequently scrapped. The destroyer production of the Soviet Union, which became an Allied power after Germany's June 1941 invasion, was small. Between the opening of the war in Europe in 1939 and June 1941, the Soviets were still in the process of building six *Gnevnyi*-class destroyers and three *Storozhevoi*-class vessels.

These warships were part of a Soviet commitment to the construction of naval units in the event that a defense was needed against Hitler's Germany. After the German invasion, however, the large amount of material necessary to maintain the Red Army in the face of enemy forces sapped resources from the navy. The Soviets consequently planned for only one class of destroyer. The *Ognevoi*-class destroyers were built to a prewar design. Only 10 ships were launched by the end of the war, although contracts were tendered for 16 vessels. Of these, only two were commissioned at the close of the conflict. These ships, however, are important because they shaped the immediate postwar designs of Soviet destroyers. *Ognevoi* measured 383 feet, 10 inches by 36 feet, 1 inch by 13 feet, 9 inches, displaced 2,240 tons, and could steam at a maximum speed of 37 knots. It was armed with four 5.1-inch guns in two dual mounts that were enclosed by gun houses. One each was located in the bow and stern. The vessel also carried two 3-inch guns, three 37mm AA weapons, a .5-inch machine gun for the same duty, six 21-inch torpedo tubes, and 96 mines. All told, the armament of *Ognevoi* was heavy and in keeping with past Soviet practice.

As a result of the low numbers of domestically produced destroyers, the Soviet Union depended on procuring the majority of its wartime craft from other powers. In May 1944, the British transferred eight of the World War I–era vessels garnered in the Destroyers for Bases Deal to the Soviets. These ships were of little use not only because of their age but also from the added wear of several years of World War II service. In August 1944, the Soviets further expanded their destroyer fleet when the Red Army marched into Romania, which had been a German ally. They subsequently seized four ships. Two of these had been launched in 1917 and 1918 and were, like the vessels provided by the British, of little use. The other two were of slightly greater value, as their design resembled that of the British *Shakespeare*-class flotilla leaders.

Smaller naval powers with the Allies offered what they could, but their destroyer programs during the war were on the whole minimal or nonexistent. Canada ultimately deployed a large number of destroyers and escort destroyers for use in the Battle of the Atlantic, but as Canada was a member of the British Commonwealth a large number of these ships were built in British shipyards. Some of the other vessels, notably 4 destroyers of the *Tribal*-class design and 18 frigates similar to the British *River* class, were domestically built. New Zealand and Australia, also members of the British Commonwealth, contributed a number of domestically built ships. The Netherlands managed to launch three new destroyers in late 1939 and early 1940 before being invaded and conquered by Germany in late May 1940.

Despite the collapse of France's destroyer program, the low output of Soviet shipyards, and the miniscule forces of lesser Allied navies, the forces of the United States and Great Britain dwarfed those of the Axis powers. The largest Axis program was that of Japan, which built conventional destroyers, escort destroyers, and frigates. Destroyers were the only type of warship built in any substantial quantity during the war. Japan launched 33 ships between 1941 and 1945 that were of conventional destroyer designs. The first units produced after the outbreak of war in Europe were the final six *Kagero*-class vessels. These were followed by Japan's first wartime construction, the 20 *Yugumo*-class destroyers that were generally the same as the preceding Japanese destroyers. Indeed, all Japanese destroyer classes save one were largely based on the design specifications of *Fubuki*. In 1942, *Shimakaze* was launched as an experimental one-ship class looking forward to the construction of larger destroyers. The experience gleaned from *Shimakaze* led to the launch of 12 ships of the *Akitsuki* class that were designed primarily as fast AA defense escorts for aircraft carriers. These were among the last fleet destroyers built for the Imperial Japanese Navy. The hull of *Akitsuki* measured 440 feet, 3 inches by 38 feet, 1 inch by 13 feet, 7 inches, displaced 2,701 tons, and possessed turbines that generated a maximum speed of 33 knots. Its armament consisted of eight 3.9-inch guns in dual mounts that were fully enclosed by gun houses. Two each were sited in the bow and stern. These guns, like previous Japanese destroyers, were dual-purpose weapons capable of firing on surface targets and aircraft. The vessel also carried four 24-inch torpedo tubes, four 25mm AA weapons, and 72 depth charges.

Most Japanese destroyers were refitted with additional antiair-craft guns to the extent that one of the gun houses and its armament were removed to allow the necessary space. In some cases, so many AA weapons were carried that the stability of the ship was under-mined. Japanese destroyers were also retrofitted with radar sets, but these were inferior to the equipment of the Allies.

In addition to its conventional destroyers, the Japanese mirrored the Allies with the construction of both escort destroyers and frigates. Two classes totaling 32 escort destroyers were constructed during the war. These were more heavily armed than their U.S. and British equivalents but still designed primarily for convoy escort duty. Both types were similarly armed. A unit of the *Tachibana* class measured 328 feet, 1 inch by 30 feet, 8 inches by 11 feet, 1 inch and displaced 1,289 tons. It mounted three 5-inch guns in single mounts, four 24-inch torpedo tubes, and 60 depth charges. The ves-sel's turbines were capable of 27.8 knots.

All of Japan's escort destroyers were launched between 1944 and 1945 and represent a reaction to the desperate need for commerce protection in the face of a U.S. submarine campaign that had pro-duced staggering losses in merchant shipping by this point in the war. The dearth of escorts was the result of the fact that the Japa-nese had not planned for a protracted war in which large numbers of escorts were necessary to protect the empire's commerce. The Japanese escort destroyers were an adequate design, but their small numbers were insufficient to protect against U.S. submarines. Had these been produced earlier and in greater numbers, the outcome of the U.S. submarine campaign, in which Japanese trade was deci-mated and their war effort crippled, may have been different. The majority of Japan's 264 frigates were, like the escort destroyers, launched late in the war and consequently did little to reverse the damage already done by U.S. submarines.

Germany's wartime production paled in comparison to that of Japan and consisted only of conventional destroyers. Most German vessels built during the war were variations of the 1936 type. With 19 units in three classes, they were launched between December

1939 and January 1944. The vulnerability of German shipyards to Allied strategic bombing attacks and shortages of material in the latter years of the war prevented the launch of three additional classes. Construction began on 8 of the 13 projected ships, but none ever left their shipyards. One of these classes was a design for a behemoth that incorporated armor on a hull that was 554 feet, 5 inches long and displaced 6,300 tons. It would have been armed with six 5.1-inch guns in three dual mounts enclosed by gun houses as well as 10 21-inch torpedo tubes. The last German destroyer launched was the one-ship 1942 type that resembled its 1936 predecessor, but with heavier AA armament in keeping with the trend in all of the navies of the combatants. This vessel never entered service, being bombed soon after its launch.

Despite the deterioration of Germany's destroyer program, the fleet was enlarged further through vessels seized from countries occupied during the war. One modern Dutch destroyer and a Greek vessel were taken. A French destroyer was also procured, but it was under construction at the time and never completed.

Like Germany, Italy produced few destroyers during the war. The last six units of the *Soldati* class were launched between 1941 and 1942, but these were the only ships completed by Italy during the war. Construction began on a new class comprising nine vessels, but these were never completed. In 1943, Mussolini's government collapsed after the Allied invasion of Italy. German forces seized these Italian vessels while they were still in their shipyards and scrapped them. The lion's share of Italy's wartime destroyers were consequently vessels seized from foreign powers. Three Yugoslavian vessels were procured in this fashion as well as 11 French destroyers. These latter ships were scuttled by the French at the port of Toulon in 1942 and salvaged by the Italians.

The conditions that existed aboard all of these destroyers were the same regardless of nationality. Living conditions were still harsh despite the fact that there had been improvements in the habitability of destroyers since the first ones were launched in the late nineteenth century. Nothing could be done for the fact that destroyers, despite their increase in size, were small relative to even cruisers and larger ships. Most of the room, as in the first destroyers, remained dedicated to the ship's propulsion plant, machinery, weaponry, and command centers. On some destroyers of the Royal Navy, there was not enough room to hang all of the hammocks for the men to sleep below decks. As a result, many had to sleep on the main deck exposed to the elements, when weather permitted. The continuous upgrading of the weaponry of destroyers only served to decrease the space in many of them, which exacerbated the already poor conditions. In addition, the cramped living areas were oftentimes awash with seawater that poured down from the upper decks. Amid these dank conditions was sometimes the smell of human waste from the failure of toilets and occasionally vomit from seasick crewmen.

An additional hardship was simply the product of extended operations. These vessels did not have the same storage capacity as larger ships. In escort duty in the frigid waters of the Atlantic Ocean, crews had to rely on the majority of their sustenance from canned food and hard biscuits. Most destroyers left port with fresh meat, bread, and vegetables, but these were soon exhausted. Among the commodities in short supply was water. Once the original stock ran low, many destroyer crews had to rely on water collected from the ship's evaporators contained in the engine room. Oftentimes, the small amounts gleaned from these machines was barely enough for cooking and drinking, which meant that personal hygiene suffered. Adding to the absence of creature comforts such as food and basic cleanliness was the temperature of the vessel, which could either be boiling hot in the Pacific or frigid cold in the North Atlantic. All told, the life of a destroyer man still ranked as one of the hardest in all of the world's navies.

The discomfort created by these conditions paled in comparison to the dangers faced by the officers and men of destroyers in combat. These crews, like those on other ships, were now highly trained and specialized in specific tasks to operate their vessels efficiently in combat, thereby increasing the chance of survival. The multitude of roles in which destroyers were used, however, meant that the lives of the men who crewed them were constantly threatened. Direct hits from gunfire in a surface attack could rip through the relatively light hulls of destroyers, causing massive damage and loss of life. Torpedoes and bombs launched during enemy air attacks invariably produced the same mayhem. Due to the thin hull plating, crewmen were even subject to death by shrapnel produced by explosions from near-misses. On several occasions, shrapnel ripped through hull plates, bulkheads, and the superstructures of destroyers to cut down the men inside. These steel projectiles could mangle a sailor instantaneously. Many of those who lived through shrapnel penetrating the hull lost arms or legs.

The light hulls of destroyers and their small size also meant that, in the event of the vessel being sunk, crewmen below decks had little time to escape. Destroyers on some occasions sank in only a few minutes. With the loss of power, crewmen below decks were plunged into darkness and groped for a way out. Even if they did get into the water, the chance of survival was still not great. Ordnance exploding underwater created concussions that could kill. An example is the case of the destroyer *Hammann*, which after the 1942 Battle of Midway was assigned to guard the crippled aircraft carrier *Yorktown*. A Japanese submarine was able to close within range, mortally wound the carrier, and hit the destroyer. The hull of *Hammann* consequently broke in two, and as the ship sank its depth charges reached their exploding depth and detonated, killing many of the crew in the water. Finally, if crewmen did survive the sinking of their vessel, they were still exposed to nature. Some men died of exposure, a common threat in the frigid waters of the Atlantic, while those in the Pacific faced death from shark attacks.

The forces of nature could also threaten a destroyer in the absence of combat. On 17 December 1944, the U.S. 3rd Fleet was located some 500 miles east of the island of Luzon in the Philippine Islands when it encountered a typhoon. Confronted by 70-foot waves and up to 110-knot winds, the destroyers were placed in grave danger. Many of them registered rolls of 70 degrees, and in some cases the tips of their funnels touched the water. This latter situation caused the loss of three of the destroyers of the fleet. These vessels did not right themselves and sank when water flooded down the funnels and other open vent shafts. There were few survivors of these episodes. Only 6 men survived from one destroyer; out of a crew of 18 officers and 245 men aboard another, only 7 officers and 55 men were saved.[6]

Despite all these hardships, the officers and crews of the destroyers of all nations accomplished their tasks with the same bravery and daring that had been exhibited in World War I. The myriad of tasks in which destroyers were employed and the consequent danger that the crews faced is evident in the numbers of wartime losses. Japan, whose navy was almost annihilated in the conflict, lost the most vessels, with 137 destroyers sunk. Ten escort destroyers also foundered. Close behind was Great Britain, which lost 101 destroyers and 32 escort destroyers. Italy lost 69 destroyers, the United States 68, being 56 destroyers and 12 escort destroyers. The German navy suffered the destruction of 33 destroyers of varying type and the Soviet Union lost 26 vessels. France, although it surrendered early in the conflict, lost 14 destroyers.[7]

The designation destroyer refers to those ships capable of a multitude of tasks in fleet operations, while the escort destroyer category includes not only ships of this type but also frigates. These high numbers suggest the extreme degree of their use and the vital nature of their tasks. The need for these vessels, proven in war, meant that destroyers would continue to be important in the world that emerged after World War II.

ENDNOTES

1. James L. George, *History of Warships: From Ancient Times to the Twenty-First Century* (Annapolis, MD: Naval Institute Press, 1998), p. 144.

2. Roger Chesneau, ed., *Conway's All the World's Fighting Ships, 1922–1946* (London: Conway Maritime Press, 1980). The figures used in the text are an amalgamation of different sections of this book separated by country.

3. Ian Hawkins, ed., *Destroyer: An Anthology of First-Hand Accounts of the War at Sea, 1939–1945* (London: Conway Maritime Press, 2003), p. 56.

4. Ibid., p. 78.

5. George, *History of Warships,* p. 144.

6. Norman Friedman, *U.S. Destroyers: An Illustrated Design History* (Annapolis, MD: Naval Institute Press, 1982), p. 188.

7. George, *History of Warships,* p. 144.

CHAPTER 4

The Cold War and After, 1946–2004

DESPITE THE LARGE NUMBERS of destroyers lost during World War II, it represented only a fraction of those vessels that were in service at the close of the conflict. The majority of these were U.S. and British, as their construction programs had dwarfed those of the Axis and the production of France and the Soviet Union was greatly limited. The large numbers had been necessary given the extreme importance of the ships for Allied victory. The value of destroyers had changed during the course of the conflict. The two primary roles had been to launch torpedo attacks against enemy vessels and to defend against those launched by the enemy. Of these, torpedo attack had been supplanted by two functions of even greater values: antisubmarine warfare and antiaircraft defense. The protection of capital ships and merchantmen had hinged on destroyers performing these functions given the increasing effectiveness and destructive potential of submarines and aircraft. In accordance with this change, the original mission of defending the battle fleet remained. The difference was only in the methods employed.

Construction of destroyers did not end with World War II, as the victorious powers recognized that the new mission of destroyers justified the continued production of the ship type in the years immediately after the close of the conflict. The majority of the vessels produced between 1946 and 1951, however, were units comprising wartime programs. Most of these were U.S. and British destroyers. Between August 1945 and May 1951, the United States completed

117

the last 38 destroyers of the *Gearing* class. By 1951, it also converted 18 units of the *Fletcher* class to oceangoing destroyer escorts (designation: DDE) given the perceived need for more ASW ships in the postwar world, in which tensions were rising with the Soviet Union. This process entailed the inclusion of the most advanced sonar equipment and the replacement of three 5-inch guns by two Hedgehog systems and Weapon Alpha. The development of Weapon Alpha started in 1946 with the aim of creating a rocket-boosted depth charge that could reach greater distances from a destroyer in keeping with the expanded range of the newest sonar systems. Weapon Alpha entered service in 1951 and consisted of a rocket armed with a 12.75-inch warhead that weighed 250 pounds. It was fired from an MK 108 launcher that could fire 12 rounds per minute. The maximum range of the system was 800 yards. This ASW weapon remained in service until 1969 when it was replaced by a newer model. Eleven units of the *Gearing* class received a similar conversion.

Most of the remaining postwar destroyer production directly after the war was in Great Britain, which launched 16 vessels between August 1945 and April 1951, with half the total being the units of the *Daring* class. *Daring* represented the culmination of British wartime design, although the original plan was altered in keeping with the desire, like the United States with the *Fletcher*-class conversions, to incorporate the newest technology possible. The hull of *Daring* measured 390 feet by 43 feet by 13 feet, 7 inches and displaced 2,830 tons. The vessel was armed with six 4.5-inch quick-firing guns, six 40mm Bofors weapons for antiaircraft defense, and 10 21-inch torpedo tubes. In addition, the ship mounted one Squid ASW launcher. Like the Hedgehog, this new device was designed to fire ahead of the attacking ship. The chief difference was the size of the weapon. Squid held six bombs that each weighed 300 pounds. These were fired in a sequence such that the first bomb would sink to the deepest depth setting while each subsequent bomb was set to detonate 50 feet shallower than the preceding one. Little else was changed from the original plan. The oil-fired engines of *Daring* produced a maximum speed of 34.75 knots. A crew complement of 278 officers and men operated the vessel. The other ships launched in this period were three destroyers of the *Weapon* class and five other units of varying types. The other ships of wartime construction launched directly after the war were the product of the Soviet Union. Launched in 1947, these were the remaining four units of the *Ognevoi* class.

In addition to these ships of older design were units built to post-war designs. The United States and the Soviet Union, being two powers that increasingly clashed on the world stage by the late 1940s and early 1950s, were responsible for the majority of this construction. This trend in production continued until the last decade of the twentieth century with the implosion of the former Soviet state.

Immediately postwar, the Soviet Union, although being in dire economic straits as the European portion of the country lay in ruins from the Nazi invasion, embarked on a production program of relatively cheap destroyers in keeping with Premier Joseph Stalin's desire for a large navy. As a result, the Soviet Union led the world in the early 1950s in terms of the numbers of new destroyers produced. Starting in 1950 and ending in 1951, the country launched 72 units of the *Skoriy* class. *Skoriy* measured 397 feet, 6 inches by 39 feet, 4 inches by 14 feet, 9 inches and displaced 2,240 tons. Its armament consisted of four 5.1-inch pieces in two dual-gunned gun houses. One each was located fore and aft. It also mounted an array of AA weaponry, being two 85mm pieces, seven 37mm guns, and six 25mm weapons. The vessel carried an ASW suite that consisted of two depth charge mortars and two depth charge racks housed in the stern. Finally, *Skoriy* mounted 10 21-inch torpedo tubes and was capable of shipping 50 mines. Its engines produced a maximum speed of 33.5 knots. A crew of 218 officers and seamen operated the vessel.

The design of these ships originated from that of the *Ognevoi* class and incorporated some features of German design. Being intended to meet the primary strategic requirement of coast defense for the Soviet Navy, they were not considered particularly successful, given the fact that their AA armament could not elevate enough to be truly useful against attacking aircraft. Indeed, the lack of this capability made the guns useful only for short-range surface warfare. Augmenting the size of the Soviet destroyer fleet were smaller warships also designed for coastal defense. By the end of 1951, the Soviet Union completed six *Kola*-class vessels. The hull of *Kola* measured 314 feet, 11 inches by 35 feet, 5 inches by 10 feet, 6 inches and displaced 1,900 tons. It mounted four 3.9-inch guns, four 1.5-inch weapons, three 21-inch torpedo tubes, four racks for depth charges, and two MBU-900 launchers. This latter weapon fired anti-submarine rockets and was the first Soviet postwar ASW device.

Despite the limitations of the Soviet *Skoriy* class, the number of units in the group dwarfed the production of the United States. It began construction on five new destroyers between 1949 and 1951 that were all launched by mid-1952. Like the Soviet vessels, these U.S. designs originated from experience gleaned in World War II. The first of these was *Norfolk,* originally designated as a cruiser. Some scholars continue to place this rating on the ship. In actuality, *Norfolk* was intended as a destroyer leader (designation: DL), making it the first of this type in the U.S. Navy. Essentially, the defining aspect of this type was its large size. The hull of *Norfolk* measured 540 feet by 53 feet, 6 inches by 19 feet and displaced 5,560 tons. Its armament reflected the desire of U.S. naval officials for more ships capable of ASW defense. The ship mounted eight 3-inch pieces housed in four dual-gunned gun houses. Two each were located fore and aft. *Norfolk* also carried eight 21-inch torpedo tubes as its principal ASW weaponry, being capable of firing early homing torpedoes. Finally, the ship mounted four Weapon Alpha systems. Its engines produced a maximum speed of 33 knots. A crew of 546 men manned the ship. The chief problem with *Norfolk* was the enormous cost, some $61 million for construction and weaponry.[1]

The other four units laid down by the United States before 1952 comprised the *Mitscher* class of destroyer leaders that were designed primarily for ASW operations. *Mitscher* measured 490 feet by 47 feet, 6 inches by 14 feet, 8 inches and displaced 3,642 tons. It mounted two 5-inch guns in single-piece gun houses, one each being located fore and aft. The vessel also carried four 3-inch guns, eight 20mm AA weapons, four 21-inch torpedo tubes, two Weapon Alpha ASW systems, and one depth charge rack. The vessel's engines produced a maximum speed of 36.5 knots. The *Mitscher*-class destroyers were only moderately cheaper than *Norfolk.* These ships represent the beginning of the trend toward the construction of fewer destroyers owing to their increasing cost.

The vessels of the United States and the Soviet Union represented an exception to the rule in the immediate postwar years as the victorious powers reduced the size of their navies to trim maintenance costs in a peacetime world that did not require warships in such large numbers. The United States alone had built 349 destroyers and 420 escort destroyers between the December 1941 attack on Pearl Harbor and October 1945.[2] That country slowed its production program while keeping the majority of its destroyers in service to counter the rising threat of the Soviet Union by the late 1940s. The British, due to the great financial drain of the war and the government's plan to divert what resources existed to the domestic front, viewed the reduction of the Royal Navy as a lamentable necessity. A massive program of cuts in the fleet was instituted in 1948 that led to the scrapping of primarily old cruisers. Destroyers did not receive as many cuts, partially because they were less expensive to maintain. Even so, Britain's production of new destroyers was greatly slowed given the postwar environment. France was also in poor economic condition, and new construction in the first years after the war was consequently greatly slowed. Indeed, the French possessed few vessels at all after the war, in which a large portion of their fleet was either destroyed by the British to prevent units falling into the hands of the Germans or scuttled by the French themselves to prevent the same. What few ships remained were those that had escaped to Allied ports. By 1946, the French operated only 11 destroyers. Nine of these were former German ships transferred to the French.

New destroyer construction was impossible for the defeated Axis powers in the immediate postwar years. Their economies were in ruins from the physical devastation caused to their lands during the war. Another impediment of equal importance to the development of new destroyers consisted of the peace treaties with each power that restricted the possibility of future construction even if their economies did improve. The German Kriegsmarine ceased to exist as an offensive force. Although the navy still had 15 destroyers at the close of the war, being the bulk of the Kriegsmarine by this time owing to combat losses, the British, French, and Soviets seized 13 of them after the war. The last units of the old navy formed part of a new naval organization created in the place of the Kriegsmarine. The new naval arm was primarily responsible for coastal defense and clearing minefields laid in European waters during the war.

The Imperial Japanese Navy suffered a similar fate during the general disarmament of the country. As with the German force, the majority of the surface fleet at the end of the conflict was destroyers and escort destroyers, being 25 in number. The United States, Britain, the Soviet Union, and China seized 22 of these vessels. The remaining units formed part of the new Japanese naval force. In May 1948 in place of the old navy, the Maritime Safety Agency was created and charged only with duties such as search and rescue. The only former Axis country that was allowed to retain a navy with any real surface force was Italy. It was allowed to retain four destroyers and seven escort destroyers. Nevertheless, the Italian Navy was severely restricted. Under the peace agreement with Italy, the total tonnage of Italian warships was not to exceed 67,000 tons while new construction was completely prohibited before 1 January 1950, with the exception of replacing units that were accidentally lost.

The naval restrictions placed on the former Axis countries were eased in the years following the conclusion of the peace treaties that ended World War II due to the dawn of a new conflict: the Cold War. The rise of this new struggle demonstrated the continued need for destroyers in the post–World War II world. Indeed, the new construction programs of the United States and the Soviet Union had been predicated on this fact. The worldwide conflict of the Cold War resulted from diplomatic tensions immediately after World War II that arose between the United States, its European allies, and their former Soviet ally over Soviet dealings in Eastern and Central Europe. The United States and Western European countries were alarmed at the rise of Communist governments in Eastern Europe that were allied with Moscow and that threatened the global balance of power as well as the freedoms of those under Communist systems.

In 1947, amid a Communist revolution in Greece that threatened to envelop the country, U.S. President Harry S. Truman took the first steps to check the spread of Soviet influence through the Truman Doctrine. It stated that the United States would support any free nation threatened by "outside pressures" or "armed minorities." This policy statement was clearly directed at the Soviet Union. Subsequent steps like the 1947 Marshall Plan, a massive aid program to rebuild the shattered economies of Europe in order that they might not be unstable in the face of Communist insurgency, hardened attitudes of the two sides toward one another. In 1949, as a response to the Berlin airlift crisis of the previous year and the rise of Communist China, the United States and Western European nations founded the North Atlantic Treaty Organization (NATO), a military alliance against the Soviet Union. It was initially composed of the United States, Great Britain, France, Italy, Canada, the Netherlands, Belgium, Denmark, Norway, Portugal, and Iceland.

The Soviets in turn directed their military strength against this challenge. They also employed the military power of Eastern Europe. Since the end of World War II, the Soviet Union had established control over the military forces of most of the nations of Eastern Europe. The Soviets ultimately made this arrangement official in 1955 with the creation of their own alliance, known as the Warsaw Pact. By the end of the 1940s, the world had polarized into two camps led by two superpowers, the United States and the Soviet Union, that rivaled one another around the world. This conflict, the Cold War, was one of massive military buildups. One component was a new naval arms race.

As most of the maritime powers of the world were either impoverished or devastated by World War II, the majority of the destroyer construction in this competition was U.S. and Soviet. This trend was established early during the period between 1952 and 1954 as naval powers around the world commenced destroyer production in the context of the new struggle. Dominating in terms of numbers produced was the Soviet Union, which was in the process of constructing its mammoth number of *Skoriy*-class vessels. In 1954, an enlarged and improved version of *Skoriy, Tallinn,* was completed while Soviet shipyards were also completing the first units of an additional class of destroyers, the 27-ship *Kotlin* class. The hull of *Kotlin* measured 415 feet, 1 inch by 42 feet, 8 inches by 15 feet, 1 inch and displaced 2,850 tons. The ship was armed with four 5.1-inch guns in twin-gunned, dual-purpose gun houses. One each was located fore and aft. The vessel also carried an assortment of AA weaponry, six depth charge throwers, two racks for depth charges, and 10 21-inch torpedo tubes. Propulsion was afforded by steam-powered engines that produced a maximum speed of 38 knots. It was crewed by 336 officers and men. These ships were much like the *Skoriy*-class destroyers, but upon completion of the last units in 1957 they were impressive additions to the Soviet fleet in terms of sheer numbers. Complementing these large destroyers were coastal defense units the size of escorts that were much like the previous *Kola* class. In 1952, the first of 64 ships of the *Riga* class was completed. The chief difference between the two classes was size, as *Riga*-class ships displaced almost 400 tons less than a *Kola*-class vessel.

The initial response of the United States to the rise in Soviet production of destroyers, as well as the threat of Soviet submarines, had been a program of conversions of World War II–era destroyers to include the latest ASW and AAW weaponry. The country had also commenced construction on *Norfolk* and the *Mitscher*-class ships, all being completed by mid-1954. This policy of conversions and new production was continued, and in 1952 the United States expanded its program to include the 13 ships of the *Dealey*-class destroyer escorts (designation: DE), being the first of this type launched since the end of World War II. The first was laid down in 1952 and completed in 1954, with construction on the entire group being finished in 1958. The relatively small *Dealey* measured 315 feet by 36 feet, 8 inches by 11 feet, 10 inches and displaced 1,314 tons. Its armament, like the other U.S. vessels of this era, was dedicated to ASW and consisted of four 3-inch guns and a Weapon Alpha system. The vessel's engine produced a maximum speed of 27 knots. Crew complement was 173 officers and men.

Augmenting all of these ships was a further conversion program arising from another development in the Cold War. In 1949, the Soviet Union detonated its first atomic bomb. This presented a huge threat to the United States through the possibility of airplanes armed with such weapons attacking the U.S. mainland. As a result, in 1952 the U.S. government approved the reconstruction of 12 *Gearing*-class destroyers as radar pickets. Designated DDR, these vessels proceeded an earlier failed attempt to provide ships with improved detection capabilities that could patrol off the coast of the United States and warn of incoming Soviet bombers fast enough to allow U.S. air forces to intercept them before they delivered their payloads. The radar picket ships traded some armament for vastly improved radar facilities and slightly augmented command and control equipment.

In an attempt to provide some measure of AA protection at sea against bombers detected by these radar pickets, the United States also laid down the *Forrest Sherman* class comprising 18 ships. Completed in November 1955, the hull of *Forrest Sherman* measured 418 feet, 6 inches by 44 feet, 11 inches by 15 feet and displaced 2,734 tons. The ship was armed with three 5-inch guns, four 3-inch weapons, two Hedgehog ASW launchers, four 21-inch conventional torpedo tubes, and six 12.75-inch torpedo tubes that fired ASW torpedoes. The top speed was 33 knots, and it was crewed by 324 officers and ratings. The last of these warships was completed in August 1959, by which time they were of limited use in their original configuration due to technological innovation.

The program of Great Britain, like that of the United States, rested on new construction and conversions of World War II craft. Due to the urgent need for vessels to counter what naval officials perceived as a rising Soviet submarine threat and the need for economy, the latter effort dominated the British destroyer program. The vessels that resulted were designated frigates. The term had originally been used in the Age of Fighting Sail to denote a powerful ship that was the ancestor of the cruiser. The same term was revived in 1943 by Canada to refer to vessels of lesser armament than a destroyer that were devoted to one specific task: escort. This term ultimately superseded that of destroyer escort and became commonly used in many world navies. The first of these ships for Britain were *Rocket* and *Relentless* of the World War II *R* class. In 1952, these ships were returned to service as ASW warships with a completely new superstructure made of aluminum rather than steel to save weight. This savings was partially consumed by more modern radar and sonar equipment. The weaponry of each vessel consisted of two 4-inch quick-firing guns, two 40mm AA guns, two 21-inch torpedo tubes capable of firing homing torpedoes, and two Squid ASW systems. By 1957, another 21 World War II destroyers were converted to the same specifications. An additional 10 wartime craft were converted between 1952 and 1956 with slightly reduced detection capability. The path of conversion was also initiated in 1953 for eight ships of the World War II *Ca* class. Like the other vessels, they were removed from service for a refit that included the addition of new fire control equipment and the inclusion of two Squid weapons systems. New construction was notably lacking, although the design process was under way for a return to destroyer production. In 1953, plans were drawn up to construct a new class of destroyers. The proposals called for a vessel over 450 feet long with a displacement of some 3,000 tons that was armed primarily with three 5-inch guns. This plan, however, was shelved in 1955, as the British Admiralty believed it to be an outmoded design.

The other NATO maritime powers also responded to Soviet construction through a return to destroyer production. Their numbers, however, were far lower than those of the principal combatants of the Cold War. Indeed, many of the first destroyers in the navies of the NATO powers were either vessels seized from former Axis powers or World War II ships provided by either the United States or Great Britain. France provides an example of this practice. The first additions to France's destroyer fleet after the war came in 1948 through the acquisition of the four ships of the Italian *Oriani* and *Soldati* classes. The French also received eight U.S. *Cannon*-class destroyer escorts from the United States as part of the U.S.-funded Mutual Defense Assistance Program (MDAP) established after the war. This legislation was certainly helpful for the French, as their economy suffered after the war owing partially to the fact that a great deal of fighting in the west during World War II had been on French soil and had devastated the country. France used those financial resources at its disposal to embark on a new naval policy focused on building a fleet of small escorts for NATO and a larger force based on aircraft carriers for national defense. This latter goal necessitated cruisers as part of the defense of the carriers, but also destroyers of varying types.

The destroyers of the Italian Navy between 1949 and 1955 were garnered in the same way as those in France. Although all naval restrictions placed on Italy as a result of the World War II peace treaty were rescinded upon the country's entry into NATO on 4 April

1949, the economy of the country had been damaged in the war to the extent that the Italians could not feasibly produce new destroyers. Exacerbating the problem was Italy's chronic lack of industrial raw materials needed for new construction. The Italians also had almost no vessels to convert to more modern units. Even so, the Italian Navy was tasked through NATO with the defense of Otranto Channel in the Mediterranean Sea and the protection of the Tyrrhenian Sea and the Adriatic Sea. This created an immediate need that began to be filled by U.S. aid provided through MDAP by the transfer in 1951 from the United States to Italy of two World War II destroyers, one each from the *Benson Gleaves* class. In the same year, three World War II *Cannon*-class destroyer escorts were also provided to the Italians. Although they had not been modernized, these ships were useful in the sense that the Italian Navy was somewhat strengthened and the ships served as training facilities for a new generation of Italian naval officers and men.

The Netherlands also benefited from the large wartime destroyer fleet of the United States. The invasion of Dutch possessions in the Pacific by the Japanese in World War II had led to the end of the imperial history of the Netherlands, as the former colonies were never recovered. As a result, the Dutch in 1949 devoted its navy to the defense of Europe in the context of the Cold War when they joined the NATO alliance. Specifically, the Dutch Navy became partially responsible for the protection of convoys in the area of the English Channel and North Sea. The navy became committed to ASW defense, which meant that destroyers formed a large part of their navy due to their effectiveness in this role. Between 1950 and 1951, the Netherlands acquired six U.S. *Cannon*-class destroyer escorts. Funds from MDAP also provided for frigates built in the United States. The six ships of the *Roofdier* class were completed in 1954 and relied largely on World War II technology. *Roofdier* measured 185 feet by 33 feet by 10 feet and displaced 808 tons. Its weaponry consisted of one 3-inch gun, an assortment of AA pieces, and one Hedgehog launcher.

Unlike many of the other powers, however, the postwar Dutch Navy turned to domestic production from an early stage after the war. The first new destroyers were the four ships of the *Holland* class that were specifically built for ASW defense. Laid down and completed between 1950 and 1955, a unit of this type had a hull that measured 371 feet by 37 feet by 17 feet and that displaced 2,215 tons. The destroyer was armed with four 4.7-inch weapons mounted in two dual-gunned gun houses, one each being located fore and aft. It also mounted one 40mm AA gun, two 375mm ASW mortar systems, and two depth charge racks. The engines produced a maximum speed of 32 knots. These vessels were only the first of a new program envisioned by the Netherlands that would make it an integral part of NATO defense at sea.

Potentially augmenting the destroyer force of NATO from an early period after World War II were the navies of nonaligned powers, being countries not allied with either the West or the Soviet Union, that were friendly to Western nations. Among these were Australia and New Zealand due to their past imperial connection to Great Britain. By 1951, Australia received the last of two *Battle*-class destroyers built in British shipyards. These were of an improved design over those launched for the British Royal Navy in World War II. Between 1948 and 1949, New Zealand profited from its relationship with Britain by acquiring six World War II *Loch*-class destroyer escorts, which were subsequently designated frigates. Both countries entertained more additions to their destroyer forces.

All of these nations faced primarily the Soviet Navy rather than a combined force of the entire Communist bloc. From the beginning of the Cold War, the Soviet Union had few European allies with significant naval power to aid in countering NATO forces. Few nations in the Warsaw Pact had possessed warships in the years before World War II. This development was the product either of their economies, which did not allow for a large naval armaments program, or the fact that many of the powers that became members of the Warsaw Pact were landlocked. Those powers that did have any naval force in the early 1950s garnered one from the Soviet Union. In 1949, Bulgaria received one Russian *Novik*-class destroyer, while Romania operated two obsolete destroyers that had been built in the late 1920s in Italian shipyards. The Soviets also did not have any significant naval allies outside the Warsaw Pact.

Potentially the most powerful of the Soviet Union's allies in the opening years of the Cold War was the People's Republic of China. In 1949, the Communists of China had established a Communist regime under the leadership of Mao Tse-tung. In February of the following year, a 30-year mutual assistance pact was signed with China that effectively aligned it with the Soviet Union. This agreement was extremely important for China's efforts to establish a naval force, as the country was still largely based on an agrarian rather than an industrial economy. The shipyards that had existed were in ruins due to the World War II occupations by the Japanese and the civil war between the Communists and Nationalists that had ensued at the conclusion of the war. As a result, the Chinese relied at first on Soviet help to rebuild its facilities, expand their knowledge of naval architecture, and create a navy for the new regime. This force was from its inception dedicated to coastal defense. The first units of this new navy were destroyers, being four Soviet World War II destroyers transferred between 1954 and 1955 to Chinese service. This paltry force could do little to help the Soviets versus the West.

Regardless of the number or design of destroyers in world navies in the period between 1946 and 1955, all units shared the commonality that they relied on guns and torpedoes as their primary armaments, with limited advancements in ASW and detection equipment. In the minds of naval officials in many countries by 1955, such as the British who cancelled their 1953 gun-armed destroyer design, this fact made them obsolete in the face of the advent of the missile, a new technological development that transformed naval warfare. The United States was among those nations at the forefront of this innovation, whose roots extended back to World War II. During that conflict, Nazi Germany pioneered missile technology with the development of the V-1 and V-2 rockets. U.S. naval officials sought to extend this technology to missiles aboard ships to combat a very serious strategic threat that had arisen in 1949 when the Soviet Union became an atomic power upon the detonation of its first test weapon. This development, in combination with the advent of jet power for airplanes, allowed the Soviets to attack the U.S. mainland using fast aircraft armed with weapons of mass destruction. The speed of these planes largely obviated the use of antiaircraft guns on ships that might be deployed as a defensive screen in the waters off the United States. Their rate of fire was slow, as was their aiming, which was controlled by human beings. Missiles, in contrast, could match and exceed the speed of the new jet bombers through the use of rocket technology. U.S. naval officials also believed in the need for vessels armed with missiles to protect the aircraft carriers of the fleet against assaults by enemy jets.

By the early 1950s, hurried R&D with the aid of German scientists for a missile system that could fulfill these needs bore fruit with antiaircraft missiles that became known as the "3 Ts" and were designated as surface-to-air missiles (SAMs). These were the Terrier, Talos, and Tartar missiles. They were the product of the U.S. program Bumblebee, which was begun in 1944 and was committed to the invention of SAM ordnance that possessed long range. While this long-range missile, the Talos SAM, was in the development stage, engineers built the Supersonic Test Vehicle to evaluate the performance of guidance systems for the weapon. Due to the success of this device and the fact that Talos was still years from being perfected as a viable missile, the United States decided to use the Supersonic Test Vehicle to build a SAM that possessed shorter range. Flight tests of such a weapon took place in 1951 and led to the production of the SAM-N-7, the Terrier.

The Terrier subsequently entered service in late 1955 as the first of the three U.S. SAM systems. The firing equipment consisted of two twin-armed Mark 10 launchers. Each launcher consisted of two rails, on which the missiles rested, that were positioned on either side of a swivel post that could be trained at the target. Once the missiles were fired, the rails were raised to a vertical position for reloading, where more missiles would be mounted via machinery below the main deck of a ship that raised the ordnance out of a vessel's magazine and onto the rails. Terrier missiles themselves were extremely large, being 27 feet long. The early missiles weighed 1,290 pounds, more than a 16-inch shell. They contained a 218-pound warhead and a solid-fuel rocket for launching and propulsion to the target; they could achieve a speed of Mach 1.8, about 1,337 miles per hour. The maximum range of the first Terrier missiles was 12 miles. Later versions had increased range and the ability to carry a 1-kiloton nuclear warhead. The Terrier originally used beam-riding for its guidance; machinery in the nose of the missile received targeting information from radars that were placed in the aft portion of a ship in place of the original superstructure. The fire control stations on a warship emitted a radar beam that bounced off the target and supplied the necessary data to the missile. Subsequent Terrier models incorporated technology that gave it the ability to use radar as well as beam-riding to home in on a target.

The first type of vessel chosen to ship this technological innovation in weaponry was the cruiser. The great weight and large size of the missile system necessitated the use of larger hulls. In addition, the protection of aircraft carriers against air attack was a role assigned to cruisers in World War II. The first of these cruisers, and the first surface vessels armed with missiles, were *Boston* and *Canberra*, which were two World War II–era vessels of the Baltimore class. In 1954, both ships were removed from service to reconstruct them. On 1 November 1955, *Boston* returned to service as CAG-1, a guided missile cruiser. Other conversions of cruisers followed.

Nevertheless, while the first cruisers were being converted, the United States did try to incorporate the Terrier missile system into the design of destroyers, thus ushering the vessel type into the missile age. A chief reason was the need for economy, as destroyers were both cheaper to build and maintain than cruisers and more could consequently be deployed for missile protection. This desire for experimentation led to the world's first guided missile destroyer (designation: DDG). On 1 December 1956, the *Gearing*-class destroyer *Gyatt* was recommissioned after a conversion that transformed the ship into a test bed to examine the feasibility of mounting large missile systems in relatively small ships. The hull dimensions and propulsion machinery of *Gyatt* remained unchanged, but the weaponry was substantially altered. The twin-gunned 5-inch gun house was removed as well as all of the AA weaponry in the stern. In place of the 5-inch weapons and gun house was a twin-armed Terrier missile launcher. Located just forward of the battery was loading machinery and a magazine that held 14 missiles in addition to the 2 carried on the arms of the launcher. Not only was the vessel the first destroyer to mount missiles; it was also the prototype in the U.S. Navy for the inclusion of hull stabilization equipment. The rolling and pitching motion of small hulls like those of destroyers presented a particular problem to a missile system, which needed a fair degree of stability to operate effectively. It also led to more fuel consumption for destroyers in rough seas as captains sought to maintain position in their vessels, meaning that a ship could not remain on station for as long as larger ships due to the need to refuel. As a result, *Gyatt* received the Denny-Brown Stabilization System. This technology was developed by the British and was first employed in the *Hunt*-class destroyer escorts launched between 1939 and 1940. It consisted of two 45-foot fins located below the waterline on either side of the hull. This innovation became commonplace in the destroyers of world navies. Finally, *Gyatt* received a slightly improved radar system to provide guidance for Terriers once they were in flight.

Gyatt proved that it was feasible to mount the Terrier on a vessel of destroyer size, but ultimately the test ship was unsuccessful. The lack of extensive improvement in the radar system was the result of weight restrictions arising from the small hull of the *Gearing*-class destroyer. The large radar suite mounted on the first guided missile cruisers for the Terrier system would have threatened the stability of *Gyatt* by making it too top-heavy. Without this array, the guidance system of *Gyatt* was not advanced enough to provide proper control for the Terrier missile.

Nevertheless, the United States used the experience gleaned from *Gyatt* to produce the world's first purpose-built guided missile destroyers and usher in a period of large-scale guided missile destroyer production in the U.S. Navy. Between mid-1957 and late 1961, the United States laid down and completed 10 *Coontz*-class guided missile escorts. These vessels were originally designated as frigates but became guided missile destroyers through a 1975 directive. The hull of *Coontz* measured 512 feet, 6 inches by 52 feet, 4 inches by 17 feet, 9 inches and displaced 4,167 tons. Designed for ASW and missile defense, it was armed with one Terrier SAM system mounted in the stern with a magazine capable of holding 40 missiles. It also carried six 12.75-inch torpedo tubes that fired ASW homing torpedoes, with one 5-inch gun mounted in the bow. Finally, *Coontz* was among the first vessels in the U.S. Navy to ship the ASROC (antisubmarine rocket) system. This system was first deployed by the United States in 1960. It is designed as an ASW weapon. Still in use in the U.S. Navy and those of several U.S. allies, it originally fired rockets equipped with homing torpedoes from an eight-missile box launcher that could destroy submerged targets at a range between 900 and 10,000 yards. The system was later improved through the introduction of a vertical launch system for the missile that increased its range to 15,000 yards. The vessel's steam turbine engines produced a maximum speed of 32 knots. A crew of 360 officers and men operated the warship. *Coontz* and its sister ships, thanks to their relatively large hulls, were able to mount a far better radar suite than *Gyatt* and thus obviated the drawback posed by the smaller vessel.

In addition to the *Coontz* class that shipped the Terrier missile, the United States completed the first of 23 units of the *Charles F. Adams* class that shipped a new weapon system. Completed in September 1960, *Charles F. Adams* measured 437 feet by 47 feet by 15 feet and displaced 3,250 tons and was designated a guided missile destroyer. It was armed with two 5-inch guns, one ASROC ASW system, six 12.75-inch ASW torpedo tubes, and one Tartar SAM twin-armed launcher mounted in the stern.

Research for the Tartar SAM began in early 1951, and although a prototype was produced in 1958, the weapon was not fully operational until 1962 due to testing problems. Tartar was a short-range weapon that contained a 130-pound warhead, measured 15 feet, 6 inches long, with a wingspan 24 inches across, and weighed 1,280 pounds. Its solid-fuel rocket was capable of Mach 1.8 and could propel the missile to a maximum range of about 8.5 miles. It was specifically designed to destroy any incoming aircraft that penetrated the outer screen of protection of a task force that was afforded by the Terrier and Talos missiles. This latter weapon first entered service in 1959 and possessed the longest range of the three missile types, being a maximum of 57 miles. It measured 21 feet long with a wingspan of 110 inches and weighed 3,400 pounds. A portion of this was the warhead, which weighed 300 pounds. Its ramjet engine could produce a maximum speed of Mach 2.5.

The United States was not alone in its quest to produce warships that incorporated missiles. Technological innovation in the Soviet Union challenged the missile program of the United States and was the product of a shift in the priorities of the Soviet Navy. Following World War II, Stalin had concentrated on the construction of a navy that could defend the coasts of the Soviet Union and a few large vessels that could project power further overseas. All were armed solely with guns. Upon his death in 1953, his successor, Nikita Khrushchev, turned toward the incorporation of missiles in the belief that the gun was obsolete in the face of the missile. Indeed, he believed that the sole priority of the Soviet Union should be the production of nuclear-missile technology. New warship designs were subsequently drawn up under the direction of commander-in-chief of the navy, Sergei Gorshkov, who rose to this position in 1956, that relied on the Soviet missile program for armament.

The Soviet program, like that of the United States, had begun in earnest in the months following the end of World War II with the acquisition of German rocket technology. Soviet experiments with the German equipment eventually produced missiles in the mid-1950s that alarmed the Western powers as increasingly the Soviet Navy posed a greater strategic threat through their employment. In September 1955, the Soviet Union became the first nation to fire a submarine-launched ballistic missile (SLBM), a weapon that could carry a nuclear warhead and deliver it to a target hundreds of miles away. The Soviets also produced the first conventionally powered ballistic missile submarine in 1958.

At the same time, the Soviets were in the process of developing surface ship missile systems. In the late 1950s, old warships were refitted to test the first-generation Soviet SAM missile batteries, while experiments were also under way for the world's first surface-to-surface missile (SSM) for use against enemy vessels. This latter type was the result of the need for an offensive capability against NATO aircraft carriers owing to the fact that the Soviet Union had no sea-based airpower. Soviet officials viewed Western aircraft carriers as a threat to the Soviet Union itself, as they could launch aircraft armed with nuclear weapons against Soviet military sites and cities. The Soviet Union consequently designed the world's first

SSM, the SS-N-1, in the late 1950s; it could carry either a conventional or a nuclear warhead. The missile measured 25 feet long with a wingspan of 15 feet and weighed more than 7,000 pounds. Its maximum range was 150 miles.

This innovation led to the world's first missile destroyers armed with missiles that possessed offensive capability. These were the *Kildin* class comprising four ships. All were laid down in 1957 and 1958 and were essentially modified *Kotlin*-class warships. The first of these, *Neulovimyy*, was completed in 1960 and measured 415 feet, 1 inch by 42 feet, 8 inches by 15 feet, 1 inch with a displacement of 2,850 tons. Its innovative SS-N-1 armament was comprised of a single missile launcher mounted in the stern. The magazine of this system, consisting of a hanger situated on the main deck aft, could hold four reloads. In addition to this new weapon, *Neulovimyy* also exhibited Soviet advances in ASW weaponry through the inclusion of two RBU-2500 ASW launchers. This weapon was much the same as the ASROC system of the United States. Developed in 1957 and first in service in the *Kildin*-class destroyers, it consisted of a swivel-mount launcher that held 16 barrels. Each of these contained a rocket with a 46-pound warhead that could be fired to a maximum distance of 2,730 yards against enemy submarines.[3] In addition to this weapon and the SS-N-1 launcher, *Neulovimyy* also carried 16 2.2-inch guns and four 21-inch torpedo tubes. As with the *Kotlin* class, the vessel's top speed was 38 knots. Another eight warships of the *Krupny* class were also laid down in 1958, with the first being completed some three years later. The hull of one of these warships was 452 feet, 2 inches by 48 feet, 11 inches by 10 feet, 6 inches and displaced 4,500 tons. It was armed with two SS-N-1 missile launchers, one each being located fore and aft, and carried 20 reloads. The ship's weaponry also included two RBU-2500 ASW launchers, 16 2.2-inch guns, and six 21-inch torpedo tubes. The ship's maximum speed was 36 knots, and it was crewed by 350 officers and men.

Neither *Kildin*- nor *Krupny*-class destroyers proved to be very successful designs due to the new SS-N-1 system, which had numerous drawbacks that detracted from its use. Unknown to the West, the missile was designed to release its warhead at close range to the target in order for it to submerge in the water before hitting the hull of an enemy ship. The intention was to cause damage below the waterline that would sink the target vessel. This release system was not very reliable, and consequently the probability of a hit was decreased. In addition, the Soviets lacked the electronic capability to guide the missile to targets over the horizon, which further limited the weapon's usefulness. In addition to these problems was the fact that manual labor, rather than loading machinery, was required to remove these missiles from storage and place them in the launchers. Not only was this process time-consuming; it was also extremely difficult to perform in even moderately rough seas. As the warships of the Soviet Navy operated partly in the Arctic and Atlantic Oceans, these conditions were largely the rule rather than the exception. Nevertheless, the United States and its NATO allies viewed the arrival of Soviet ships armed with SSM systems with alarm, as few of these problems were known. The Soviet Union possessed a potential offensive capability that the navies of the West lacked.

From the late 1950s forward, all of the navies of the world turned to the production of missile destroyers in light of the fact that the new weaponry had largely made warships armed primarily with guns obsolete. The United States and the Soviet Union continued to produce the majority of these warships. The destroyer program of the United States up to 1967 continued to rest on new construction and conversions/refits of older destroyers to counter the large number of Soviet destroyers, guard against incoming aircraft, and protect against the Soviet Union's ballistic missile submarine fleet.

Many of the newly constructed destroyers pressed the limits of the standard design parameters considered to be those of destroyers. The first of these was the *Leahy* class comprising nine warships that were designed primarily for AA duty. Laid down in 1959 and completed in mid-1962, the hull of the *Leahy* measured 533 feet by 53 feet, 4 inches by 19 feet and displaced 5,146 tons. It was armed with two Terrier SAM launchers, one each being located fore and aft. Each of these twin-armed launchers had a magazine that held 40 missiles. The ships also mounted one ASROC ASW system, four 3-inch guns, and six 12.75-inch torpedo tubes that fired ASW torpedoes. The ship's engines produced a maximum speed of 32 knots. Crew complement was 377 officers and men. Another nine ships of the *Belknap* class, completed between 1964 and 1967, were designed for ASW defense. As a result, they shipped only one Terrier system, albeit a modified one that could launch SAM and ASROC weapons, one 5-inch gun, two 3-inch weapons, and an array of homing torpedoes.

Also among these larger destroyers were two that signaled a new innovation in destroyer design. This was the introduction of nuclear-powered turbine engines in place of those powered by steam created by oil-fed boilers. The first use of nuclear power occurred in the late 1940s when the United States built land-based reactors. The success of these plants spurred an R&D program in the U.S. Navy for nuclear-powered propulsion in submarines and ships that was overseen by Rear Admiral Hyman Rickover. In 1954, this effort led to success when the U.S. submarine *Nautilus* was commissioned for service as the world's first nuclear-powered vessel.

The propulsion system of this submarine and all other warships that utilize nuclear power is complex. The entire plant is contained in a section of a ship known as the reactor compartment. Each nuclear reactor plant contains more than 100 tons of lead shielding to protect the crew from radiation. The reactor generates heat through the process of fission of nuclear material in water. This heat energy is transferred to a generator that produces steam that is then directed to a ship's turbine engines for propulsion. Steam is also used to power other turbines that supply electricity for shipboard operations.

There are several advantages to nuclear power. The first of these is the fact that power for the engines is available immediately upon orders being received in the engine room from the bridge. In the past, steam power had to build up gradually for a destroyer to reach its maximum speed, which took a great deal of time. In addition to this advantage is the fact that warships equipped with nuclear-powered engines are no longer hampered by the need to steam to a port and refuel. The only limiting factor to the endurance of a nuclear-powered warship is the amount of supplies that can be shipped onboard.

In 1961, the guided missile cruiser *Long Beach* became the first surface warship that went to sea with a nuclear reactor for propulsion. The ship was intended to operate with *Enterprise,* the world's first nuclear-powered aircraft carrier, completed in the same year. This innovation was extended to slightly smaller vessels than *Long Beach* out of the need for more escorts to operate with *Enterprise.*

The first of these was *Bainbridge.* Designated as a frigate, *Bainbridge* was laid down in 1959 and completed in 1962. Its hull measured 565 feet by 56 feet by 19 feet, 5 inches and displaced 7,250 tons. It was armed with two Terrier SAM systems, one each being located fore and aft, one ASROC ASW launcher, six 12.75-inch ASW torpedo tubes, and four 3-inch guns. The two turbines of the vessel were each powered by one nuclear reactor. These reactors were of the D2G model. The letters and numbers of the designation indicated the ship type for which the reactor was designed, the version of the reactor, and the designer of the plant, respectively. In the case of these reactors, the model designation indicated a second-generation reactor designed for use in ships the size of a destroyer that was manufactured by General Electric. Each reactor compartment was cylindrical, measured 37 feet high and 31 feet wide, and weighed 1,400 tons. This propulsion system generated a maximum speed of 30 knots. Crew complement was 459 officers and ratings. A larger nuclear-powered frigate, *Truxton,* was completed in 1967 and was essentially a *Belknap*-class vessel equipped with the new propulsion system.

The possibility of a failure of the engines in these two vessels as well as the other nuclear-powered warships was a constant threat. Drawbacks to this new innovation were and still are many and have had far-reaching consequences that encompass both the military and civilian sectors. Expenses to maintain the reactors of the nuclear-powered frigates were high, but they were vitally necessary. A reactor failure could lead to a nuclear meltdown that would destroy the ship and poison the entire crew with deadly radiation. In such a horrific situation, the nuclear cores would also contaminate the environment for miles around the doomed vessel. In addition, the spent fuel cores of nuclear-powered ships such as *Bainbridge* remain deadly for decades after removal from the reactors. Proper storage of such material was and still is costly and threatens the environment with radiation if the safety measures of the storage facilities fail.

Nevertheless, these ships were viewed at the time as valuable additions to the U.S. Navy. Even so, the U.S. Navy was handicapped in one respect by these vessels. A chief drawback of both the nuclear-powered and conventionally powered large frigates was their cost, which allowed for the production of only relatively small numbers. The estimated construction cost of *Truxton* was $146 million, whereas a comparably equipped conventional vessel cost an estimated $122 million. As a result, most of the destroyers produced by the United States from the early 1960s to 1967 were smaller out of the need for greater numbers.

While construction continued on the *Charles F. Adams*-class destroyers, designs were produced for still smaller vessels suited primarily for ASW duties. In 1963, both units of the *Bronstein* class, designated destroyer escorts, were completed. The hull of *Bronstein* measured 372 feet by 41 feet by 23 feet and displaced 1,882 tons. It was armed with three 3-inch guns, two 21-inch conventional torpedo tubes, six 12.75-inch homing torpedo tubes, one ASROC ASW launcher, and a new ASW system. This was the Drone Anti-Submarine Helicopter (DASH). It was designed in the late 1950s to address the limited range of ASROC in relation to the increasing detection ranges of radar and sonar devices. The system entered service in November 1962 and consisted of a small, automated helicopter armed with a homing torpedo for use against enemy submarines. It was enclosed in a heated hanger and launched from a flight deck aft. During takeoff, it was controlled from a station to the side of the hanger. Once airborne, control was passed from this location to the Combat Information Center (CIC) of the ship. Personnel in this facility guided the DASH to its target. Speed was not a consideration in the *Bronstein* class, as the propulsion system could produce only 26 knots. This fact led to the production of the larger *Garcia* and *Brooke* classes that numbered a total of 17 units. These ships mounted a slightly greater weapons array and were capable of a maximum speed of 30 knots.

Augmenting the new U.S. construction program was a massive upgrade program for elderly destroyers and destroyer escorts. In the late 1950s, U.S. naval officials realized that a large number of the destroyers built in World War II were becoming too old for service and would have to be decommissioned and sent to the scrap yards. This posed an enormous problem for the United States as hundreds of destroyers approached the end of their operational lives. The loss of so many vessels in the face of massive Soviet production of surface warships and the threat of Soviet ballistic missile submarines was deemed unacceptable by both the U.S. Navy and government. Between 1959 and 1964, consequently, the United States pursued the Fleet Rehabilitation and Modernization (FRAM) program that refitted 131 destroyers of varying World War II types. The program rested on two types of overhaul, the first being designated FRAM I, which entailed completely refurbishing the hull and machinery of a warship to extend its life by about eight years. The process also called for fitting as many modern systems—weaponry, sensory equipment, and communication equipment—on the ship that weight restrictions would allow. The cost of this endeavor averaged some $7.8 million per unit.[4] The FRAM I conversion was solely for the *Gearing*-class destroyers. A unit under this program underwent a hull refit that included hull dampening to mask the loudest noises from the old vessels that could easily be detected by Soviet warships. In most units, one of the 5-inch guns and its gun house were removed as well as all smaller weaponry. In its place was substituted one ASROC ASW system, six 12.75-inch homing torpedo tubes, and a DASH ASW system. Radar and sonar were greatly improved. The other version of the refit program, FRAM II, was designed to lengthen the operational life of a destroyer by five years. It entailed the same hull refurbishment, but with lesser weapons upgrades, and cost about $4.7 million per unit.[5] This program was employed primarily for the old *Sumner*-class destroyers. A unit under this program had the hull modernized in much the same way as FRAM I units, but it also was fitted with an entirely new bridge structure. A FRAM II conversion retained all of its 5-inch guns and mounted two Hedgehog ASW mortars, two 21-inch conventional torpedo tubes, six 12.75-inch homing torpedo tubes, and a DASH ASW system. Both these destroyers and those of the FRAM I type lacked any missile battery, which meant that they were strictly intended for the ASW role.

While the destroyer program of the United States progressed, the Soviet Union continued to build missile-armed warships. Many of these were units of the *Krupny* class of SSM armed destroyers whose first units had entered service earlier. The heart of the Soviet's program of new construction in the 1960s, however, was not SSM warships but rather vessels devoted to both AA and ASW roles. This effort began in 1960 with the conversion of a *Kotlin*-class destroyer, *Bravyy*, to carry the Soviet Union's first SAM system. This was the SA-N-1, known as Goa to the West. The SA-N-1 measured 21 feet, 7 inches with a wingspan of almost 5 feet. This 880-pound missile was capable of delivering a 132-pound warhead to a target up to 17 miles distant.

Following testing aboard *Bravyy*, the Soviet Union produced the 18-ship *Kashin*-class guided missile destroyers, being the first such group dedicated to AA defense in the Soviet Navy. The first unit entered service in 1963 with construction until 1972. The hull of a *Kashin*-class vessel measured 472 feet, 5 inches by 51 feet, 10 inches by 15 feet, 5 inches and displaced 3,750 tons. It was armed with two RBU-6000 and two RBU-1000 ASW systems, which were improvements on past models, five 21-inch torpedo tubes, and four 3-inch guns. The primary weaponry consisted of two SA-N-1 missile launchers, one each being located fore and aft. In addition to the Soviet advance of the SA-N-1 was innovation in propulsion, as the *Kashin* class was among the first equipped with gasoline-powered turbine engines. The need for boilers to produce steam is obviated in this system, as gasoline is fed directly into the engine. This propulsion plant produced a maximum speed of 37 knots. A crew of 280 officers and men operated each ship.

In addition to these larger destroyers were smaller frigates that, like the FRAM conversions of the United States, were designed primarily for the ASW role as coastal defense ships. Between 1961 and 1969, the Soviets completed 45 *Petya*-class frigates. Each unit measured 268 feet, 4 inches by 30 feet, 2 inches by 9 feet, 6 inches and displaced 950 tons. The armament consisted of four 3-inch guns, two RBU-2500 ASW launchers, five 16-inch torpedo tubes, two depth charge racks, and 22 mines. A *Petya*-class frigate could achieve a maximum speed of 32 knots. By 1966, 18 similar vessels of the *Mirka* class were completed to augment the numbers of Soviet frigates.

The remainder of the world's destroyer production in the years between 1955 and 1967 was largely the result of NATO powers seeking to augment the ability of the West to counter the Soviet Navy. The naval power with the greatest output was Great Britain. In this period, destroyers and smaller frigates came to represent the majority of the British surface fleet. This was in part due to financial restrictions, as the state of the British economy after World War II had necessitated a massive cut in the number of ships in service as well as a curtailment of new construction. Destroyers and frigates were among the cheapest to build given financial restrictions. These types of ships were also favored due to the prevailing belief in Britain, as in many other nations, that navies were largely obsolete in the age of jet bombers equipped with atomic bombs. Such a belief that emphasized airpower, however, meant that aircraft carriers still had some validity in the Royal Navy. As a result, Britain needed destroyers and frigates to serve in their AAW role to protect the carriers.

Most of the escorts Britain produced in this era were frigates rather than destroyers. The only class of destroyer produced by Great Britain in this period was the *County* class comprising eight vessels that were dedicated to the AA escort role in defense of aircraft carriers. The first six of these were completed between 1962 and 1966, while the other two were ordered in 1967 and completed three years later. The hull of the lead ship, *Devonshire,* measured 521 feet, 6 inches by 54 feet by 20 feet, 6 inches and displaced 6,200 tons. Its primary weaponry consisted of Britain's first domestically built SAM systems. The first of these was one Seaslug SAM launcher. Development for the missile had begun in 1949 and several plans had been floated for cruisers to carry the weapon, but the missile was not ready for service until 1962. By that time, Great Britain had abandoned plans for a cruiser to carry the Seaslug in preference for mounting the SAM system in cheaper destroyers. Seaslug was similar to the U.S. Terrier missile in terms of performance. It measured 16 feet, 1 inch, had a wingspan of almost 57 inches, and weighed 1,980 pounds. The original missile, the Mark I, could deliver the 200-pound warhead to a distance of 15 nautical miles at a maximum speed of Mach 1.8; the improved Mark II that entered service in 1965 could travel a distance of 35 nautical miles. The guidance of Seaslug was also much like that of Terrier—beam-riding technology. Later versions of the missile had a limited anti-ship capability. *Devonshire* carried as many as 32 reloads for this system that were located in a magazine located in the forward portion. Missiles were removed from this area and transported via a tunnel to the launcher in the stern. While en route, preflight checks were performed and fins were fitted to the ordnance. In addition to Seaslug, the *Devonshire* also mounted two Seacat SAM launchers. This missile also entered service in 1962 and was designed specifically to counter close range aircraft or missiles. A further design specification was that it had to be small and lightweight in order for frigates to mount it. As a result of these requirements, the Seacat missile measured 1.48 meters long with a wingspan of 65 centimeters and weighed 68 kilograms. Its maximum speed was Mach .9 and it could carry its payload to a range of 3 nautical miles. This missile proved successful and was adopted by several other countries. In addition to these missile systems, *Devonshire* was also armed with two 4.5-inch guns in a dual-gunned turret located in the bow, two 20mm pieces, and a helicopter for use in an ASW role. The ship's engines produced a maximum speed of 30 knots through a new propulsion system. The Combined Steam and Gas Turbine (COSAG) system employed both steam-powered turbines and new gas-powered turbines. A crew of 440 officers and ratings operated the vessel.

The *County*-class destroyers were the exception rather than the rule in terms of Britain's production of escorts between 1955 and 1967, as they were dwarfed by the number of smaller, cheaper frigates produced. During this period, Great Britain completed seven classes of frigates that totaled 58 vessels. This output made frigates the bulk of the surface fleet of the Royal Navy and signaled a decisive shift away from large-scale destroyer production for the sake of economy. It ultimately signaled the end of large-scale destroyer production in Great Britain, the country that had created the first destroyer.

The first of these ships were the six units of the *Whitby* class. Completed between 1956 and 1959, they were designed to act as ASW escorts. *Whitby* measured 370 feet by 41 feet by 17 feet, displaced 2,150 tons, and had a maximum speed of 29 knots. It was armed with two 4.5-inch guns in a single, dual-purpose turret mounted in the forward section. The frigate also shipped 12 21-inch torpedo tubes, two 40mm STAAG (Stabilized Tachymetric Anti-Aircraft Gun) pieces, and two Limbo systems. This latter device was an ASW mortar composed of three tubes that each held a bomb. Crew complement was 152 officers and ratings.

These ships did not prove very successful, as they were expensive and took a lengthy amount of time to construct. These two attributes ran counter to the reasons why the British favored frigates. Subsequent frigate designs proved more successful and were all suited for either the AAW or ASW role with the exception of the *Tribal*-class frigates that were designed as general-purpose warships. All but one of these ships relied on guns and torpedoes for offensive and defensive capabilities. The exception was a frigate of the *Salisbury* class that was launched in 1959 and equipped with a Seacat launcher.

The culmination of frigate design for Britain in this era were the *Leander*-class units, which many naval officials and scholars consider to be among the best of their type. The 16 warships of this class were completed between 1963 and 1967 and were designed for multiple roles rather than a specific one in an attempt to realize the greatest capability for the least amount of cost. *Leander* measured 372 feet by 41 feet by 18 feet, displaced 2,350 tons, and was capable of a maximum speed of 28.5 knots. It was armed with two 4.5-inch dual-purpose guns that were housed in a single turret located forward. The frigate also shipped two 40mm AA guns, one Limbo system, and one Seacat SAM launcher. Crew complement was 250 officers and ratings. These vessels proved so successful that an improved class began construction two years after the launching of the first unit of the original group.

Next to the United States and Great Britain, the NATO power with the greatest production of destroyers and frigates was France. Most of these vessels were not armed with missiles. Unlike many NATO countries, the French did not rely greatly on the United States for missile technology. Traditionally, the design of warships as well as weapons in the French Navy had been entirely domestic. French R&D in missile technology had not started until the mid-1950s and was therefore still in its infancy when France began to build its new postwar navy. This fact is evident in the design of the *Surcouf*-class destroyers, being the first built by France since World War II. The 12 ships of this group, which conformed to a design similar to those before World War II, were completed between 1955 and 1957 and were intended for the AAW role to protect aircraft carriers, which was the same driving consideration in other navies at the time. The hull of *Surcouf* measured 422 feet by 42 feet by 18 feet and displaced 2,750 tons. It was armed with six 5-inch guns, six 2.2-inch pieces, four 20mm guns, and 12 21-inch torpedo tubes. The ship's maximum speed was 34 knots and it was crewed by 347 officers and men.

Four of these ships exhibited an exception rather than the rule for France in terms of missiles when they were rearmed in the early 1960s with the U.S. Tartar SAM system. These vessels mounted two twin-armed launchers in place of their aft 5-inch guns. The next class of destroyers, the *Duperre* class, comprised of five ships and completed between 1957 and 1958, was a virtual repeat of the previous class and did not ship U.S. missiles. Augmenting these destroyers were 27 frigates of three different classes. Like the majority of their larger counterparts, these ships were armed with guns and torpedoes. Their primary roles were either AAW or ASW duty or a combination. An example is the last type of frigate produced between 1955 and 1967, being the *Commandant Riviere* class comprising nine units. *Commandant Riviere* measured 338 feet by 38 feet by 14 feet, displaced 1,750 tons, and had a maximum speed of 25 knots. The ship was designed primarily for use with NATO forces as a convoy escort. Its armament consisted of three 3.9-inch guns housed in three single-piece turrets. Two of these were located aft while the other was mounted in the forward section of the hull. The ship also carried two 30mm AA guns, one 12-inch ASW mortar, and six torpedo tubes. A crew of 180 officers and men operated the vessel.

Of these ships, the most effective were those designed for the ASW role as their armament remained effective for use against submarines. The capability of the AAW destroyers, however, was limited owing to the fact that they did not have missiles to counter jet aircraft and Soviet antiship missiles. The four modified *Surcouf*-class destroyers were exceptions, but the French insistence on the use of domestically built missiles meant that the majority were armed with World War II–era weaponry that was ill-suited to the postwar era. This problem was resolved in the early 1960s as a result of worsening diplomatic relations between France and the United States. In 1958, General Charles de Gaulle became the leader of France and subsequently criticized the command structure of the NATO alliance. In his view, France deserved greater influence in the actions of the alliance. U.S. intransigence over demands to address this issue led the French to quicken the pace of their missile R&D for the sake of lessening French dependence on the United States in terms of defense.

While France focused resources on the construction of a new SLBM, research also went forward on surface weapons. The first of the latter type to go to sea was the Malafon ASW system. The test bed for this system was *La Galissonniere,* a destroyer that had been laid down in 1958 at first as a gun-armed warship and was very similar to the design of the *Duperre* class. During its construction, the design was altered to include the Malafon. *La Galissonniere* was completed in 1962 and measured 436 feet by 42 feet, 18 inches with a displacement of 2,750 tons. It was armed with two 3.9-inch guns in single turrets located in the bow, six 21-inch torpedo tubes, one 12-inch ASW mortar, and one Malafon ASW system mounted in the stern. It was composed of a launcher that fired a single missile, which was supplied by a boxlike magazine located on the forward main deck. The ship also carried one ASW helicopter housed in a novel folding hanger that was fitted on top of the Malafon magazine. This hanger could be unfolded for use as a landing pad for the aircraft. The top speed of this vessel was 34 knots.

Months after *La Galissonniere* was completed, construction began on the first purpose-built French guided missile destroyers. These were the two units of the *Suffren* class that were designed to provide both AAW and ASW support for aircraft carriers. Laid down in 1962 and completed in 1967, *Suffren* measured 517 feet by 51 feet by 20 feet, displaced 5,335 tons, and had a maximum speed of 34 knots. Its primary armament was missiles. The ship mounted one Malafon ASW launcher amidships and a twin-armed launcher on the stern that shipped the new Mascura SAM. This system was supplied by a magazine located below decks that held up to 48 missiles. These missile systems were supported by an intricate and powerful radar set, a portion of which was located in a large dome fitted to the top of the forward superstructure. The ship was also armed with two 3.9-inch guns, two 30mm pieces, and four torpedo tubes.

Outside the United States, the destroyers and frigates of France and Great Britain constituted the majority of NATO's contribution to the Cold War. Several other European powers, however, contributed to the naval force of the alliance. One of these was the former Axis power of Italy. Italy had become a member of NATO in 1949 and was thus free of peace treaty restrictions. Plans for new warships went forward in the following years under a naval plan that rested largely on destroyers and smaller craft. Even so, actual construction was slow due to financial limitations and a lack of raw materials that continue to plague the Italian Navy. These problems served to buttress the Italian aim to construct destroyers and frigates to get the most capability at a cheap price and with the expenditure of a relatively low amount of raw material. Among the first ships of the postwar Italian Navy were the two *Impetuoso*-class destroyers. Construction began on both units in 1952, and they were completed in 1958 as vessels capable of performing both AAW and ASW roles. The hull of *Impetuoso* measured 418 feet, 9 inches by 43 feet, 2 inches by 14 feet, 9 inches and displaced 2,775 tons. It was armed with four 5-inch guns, 16 40mm AA pieces, one ASW mortar, and six 12.6-inch torpedo tubes. The top speed of the vessel was 34 knots. The proceeding two units of the *Impavido* class were largely similar to those of the *Impetuoso* type. The key difference was an example of U.S. aid to other NATO powers, being the inclusion of a Tartar SAM system aft in place of the aft 5-inch gun house.

The numbers of these two classes was eclipsed, as in many other navies, by the construction of smaller, cheaper frigates that were armed with guns and torpedoes. Italy completed two classes of this type that totaled eight ships. As in the past, the Italians showcased their flair for innovation in warship design through the *Bergamini*-class frigates. These vessels were only 308 feet, 4 inches long but shipped a landing pad aft for the operation of an ASW helicopter. This made the vessels among the smallest in the world to employ aircraft and was a considerable feat despite the fact that the design was deemed unsuccessful. The chief problem was the lack of stability possessed by the small ships that rendered very difficult the safe operation of the helicopter.

By the late 1950s, Italy was not the only former Axis power contributing naval forces to the NATO alliance. On 23 May 1949, the German Federal Republic formally came into being upon adoption of a constitution that was accepted by the former Allied powers of World War II. The need for West German participation in the Cold War increased greatly in the years after the founding of the republic. Not only was the front line of the Cold War the border between West and East Germany; NATO needed all the resources it could muster for defense against the Soviet Union. In May 1955, Germany became a member of NATO in recognition of these facts. As a result, the naval restrictions placed on West Germany after World War II were lifted and a new German Navy, the Bundesmarine, became a contributing member of the NATO force. This arrangement, however, existed in theory more than practice at first owing to the fact that the German shipbuilding industry was still in a state of reconstruction following World War II, as most of it had been destroyed in the war.

While the Germans worked to repair their facilities, they received the first units of their new surface navy from the United States and Great Britain. All of these were destroyers and frigates of the World War II era and were acquired between 1958 and 1960, being six U.S. *Fletcher*-class destroyers, three British *Hunt*-class frigates, and four British *Black Swan*–class frigates. The first domestic production of German warships after World War II was the *Koln* class comprising six frigates. The first of these was laid down in 1957 and completed in 1961; construction on the entire class was finished three years after the first unit entered operation. The hull of *Koln* measured 360 feet, 4 inches by 36 feet, 1 inch by 15 feet, 1 inch and displaced 2,090 tons. It was armed entirely with guns and torpedoes, as the Germans lacked a domestically made missile and did not garner weapons from the United States. The armament consisted of two 4-inch guns in two single-mount gun houses. One each was located fore and aft. The vessel also carried six 40mm AA guns, four 21-inch torpedo tubes, and two ASW mortars. In keeping with past German destroyers, the vessel was powered by diesel engines. These could produce a maximum speed of 32 knots. A crew of 240 officers and men operated the warship. The *Koln* class was followed by the larger *Hamburg*-class of three destroyers. The first of these units was completed in 1964 while the last entered service four years later. These ships displaced 3,340 tons and carried an additional 4-inch gun in a single-mount gun house located in the bow. Taken together, these two classes signaled the return of one of the premier destroyer powers in the world as an ally of its former enemies in the context of a new world struggle.

Between 1955 and 1967, other NATO powers also contributed to the destroyer fleet of the alliance. The total number was not insignificant, although most of them were not armed with missiles, as these nations lacked their own missile programs. As destroyers and frigates were cheaper to build in relation to other surface units, many NATO nations with economies less powerful than the large powers based their surface fleets on these warships. Canada produced 20 destroyers in four classes between 1955 and 1967 that were devoted to the AAW and ASW roles. All were gun- and torpedo-armed, but one class exhibited innovation in design. This was the *Annapolis* class of two destroyers that were completed in 1964 and incorporated a helicopter flight deck in the stern.

The production of the Netherlands was only slightly less than that of Canada, as its naval construction program continued in the context of aiding NATO in the Cold War. Between 1956 and 1958, the Netherlands completed the *Friesland* class of eight destroyers. These vessels were armed with both guns and torpedoes, as the Netherlands lacked a domestic missile program. The next surface vessels launched for the navy, however, were armed with missiles garnered from another member of the NATO alliance. Six frigates of the *Van Speijk* class were completed between 1967 and 1968 and carried the British Seacat missile.

The other NATO members that operated destroyers relied at least in part on craft sold to them by one of the larger powers of the alliance or built to one of their designs. Norway provides an example, as the country bought three old *River*-class frigates from the Canadians while also completing by 1967 the *Oslo* class of five frigates. Portugal bought or constructed 14 frigates of U.S., British, and French design. As in the Canadian and Dutch forces, these ships were armed with guns and torpedoes.

In addition to the forces of nations that were members of NATO, the West also benefited from neutral nations in the Cold War that were pro-Western. Two of these powers were Australia and New Zealand because they had been closely linked to Great Britain through their imperial past as areas of British settlement within the empire. Both powers relied on destroyers and frigates of either British or U.S. design. Australia completed three British *Daring*-class frigates between 1957 and 1959, with another unit being acquired from the British five years later. Four *Yarra*-class frigates also joined the fleet between 1961 and 1964 that were essentially designed as the British *Rothsay* class. In addition to these ships, the Australians bought three *Charles F. Adams*–class guided missile destroyers from the United States, which gave the country a limited missile capability for its surface fleet. New Zealand acquired two *Rothsay*-class frigates from Britain while also garnering one British *Leander*-class frigate.

The combined forces of these two pro-Western nations, however, paled in comparison to that of another nation that was a former World War II Axis power. Japan's navy was restricted to search-and-rescue duties and coastal defense through the Maritime Safety Agency, the organization created in 1948 that had replaced the Imperial Japanese Navy after the war. This state of affairs, however, lasted slightly less than six years due to the Cold War. Western naval officials increasingly believed that Japan needed a stronger naval defense in the face of this new struggle and also desired a friendly naval power in the Far East. As a result, in 1954 naval restrictions were lifted on the Japanese, which allowed them to create the Maritime Self-Defense Force. From its inception, the new naval force was dedicated to ASW operations. Destroyers and frigates consequently became the primary surface combatants of the new navy, as this was a specific role assigned to them. At first, the Japanese relied on U.S. ships and technology due to the state of their shipyards that had been destroyed in the war. The first units of the new Japanese force were two units each of the *Benson/Gleaves* class and *Fletcher* class acquired in 1954 and 1959, respectively, that were improved during their service in the Maritime Self-Defense Force.

In 1956, the first Japanese postwar destroyers built in domestic shipyards entered service. These were the two destroyers of the *Harukaze* class that relied on the United States for their weaponry and sensory equipment. These were followed between 1958 and 1960 by the *Ayanami* class of seven destroyers that also relied heavily on U.S. technology. Nine additional destroyers in five different classes joined the navy by 1967 that also incorporated U.S. equipment. All also shared the commonality of armament, which consisted of guns, torpedoes, and assorted ASW systems. The exception was *Amatsukaze*, the first guided missile destroyer of the new Japanese Navy. *Amatsukaze* measured 429 feet, 9 inches by 43 feet, 11 inches by 13 feet, 9 inches, displaced 3,050 tons, and was capable of a maximum speed of 33 knots. It was armed with four 3-inch guns, one Terrier SAM system mounted in the stern, one ASROC ASW launcher, two Hedgehogs, and six 12.75-inch torpedo tubes. A crew of 290 officers and men operated the warship. Augmenting the capability afforded by this ship and the others were eight frigates. By 1967, Japan was once again a naval power with a force composed almost entirely of destroyers and frigates.

Unlike the United States, the Soviet Union had few allies or friendly powers to turn to for an augmentation of its destroyer and frigate force. Few nations in the Warsaw Pact were naval powers. Economic limitations were in part responsible for the lack of construction, and only a handful of powers within the Warsaw Pact had access to the sea. The nations that did have warships relied largely on the Soviet Union for supply. Between 1956 and 1959, the German Democratic Republic, or East Germany, acquired four *Riga*-class frigates from the Soviet Union. Bulgaria by 1956 operated one *Ognevoi*-class destroyer. Only Romania operated destroyers that were not of Soviet construction, but these were two vessels built in 1917 and 1918 that were completely obsolete. Romania also possessed two Italian destroyers that were of a design produced in the late 1920s and therefore equally useless for the Cold War. By 1968, all were scrapped.

The one large power friendly to the Soviet Union in the first years of the Cold War was China, but it was not able to contribute much in the way of naval force. The Communist People's Republic of China had come into being on 1 October 1949 and had subsequently aligned itself in 1950 with the Soviet Union through a mutual assistance pact, but the country could not produce naval units. Not only was China not very industrialized; World War II and the subsequent civil war between the Communists and Nationalists had wrought destruction on existing shipyards. As a result, China relied at first on outside help for the rebuilding of its facilities and the creation of a navy whose primary purpose was coastal defense. The Soviet Union provided this aid because it courted China as a Cold War ally. This assistance took the form of destroyers and frigates to perform the mission of coastal defense. By 1959, China possessed four former Soviet destroyers and four *Riga*-class frigates whose primary armament consisted of guns and torpedoes. Such aid, however, ended in the early 1960s with the Sino-Soviet split over ideological differences concerning the nature and growth of communism in the world. The end of the relationship between China and the Soviet Union forced the Chinese to hurry a return to domestic naval production. In 1967, the first two frigates of the five-vessel *Jiangnan*-class entered service as the first warships designed and built in China in the post–World War II era. These ships were essentially *Riga*-class frigates and were very poorly armed. A great deal of work was necessary for China to approach the design and technological standards of other naval powers.

In addition to the destroyers and frigates of the different Cold War alliances and those powers associated with them, other purely neutral nations possessed craft that swelled the numbers in world service. Among these were powers whose R&D projects yielded innovation in the field of naval technology. Chief among them was Sweden, as it became the first naval power other than the Soviet Union to construct a guided missile destroyer with antiship missile capability. In 1951, Sweden laid down two destroyers of the *Halland* class based on a design that incorporated an antiship missile being developed as part of a domestic R&D program. Upon the ships' completion in 1955 and 1956, however, the missile was not ready for service. Even so, this missile, the Saab Rb08A SSM, proved a success in 1967 and was subsequently fitted to the ships. This missile measured 5.72 meters long and weighed 1,215 kilograms. It resembled a fixed-wing aircraft in shape and relied on guidance through radar enclosed in the nose cone. This system was mounted aft amidships on *Halland*'s hull, which measured 397 feet, 2 inches by 41 feet, 4 inches by 18 feet and displaced 2,630 tons. The vessel also mounted four 4.7-inch guns in two twin-piece gun houses. One each was located in the bow and stern. Additional weaponry included AA guns and assorted ASW armament. In addition to these ships, Sweden also produced four *Ostergotland*-class destroyers. They did not have antiship missile capability but were equipped in 1963 with the British Seacat SAM system.

Sweden, however, represents the exception rather than the rule for neutral nations in terms of destroyers and frigates. Most powers bought or operated vessels built by larger naval powers. Few possessed ships with any missile armament. One of the most significant contributors to the world's naval force by this manner was India through the acquisition by 1960 of 11 British frigates. All but three of these were of modern design. Other countries pursued the same course, which led to the survival of World War II destroyers into the 1980s in some instances. An example is Argentina, which bought 10 U.S. World War II destroyers.

The world's destroyers and frigates had ample opportunities to prove their continued worth in combat duty during the period between the end of World War II and the late 1960s. These operations did not involve engagements between Soviet and NATO warships, but many of them did take place in wars within the context of the Cold War. The first of these was the Korean War (1950–1953), although naval units saw very little combat. This conflict was the first hot conflict of the Cold War and had its roots in 1945 when the Korean Peninsula was occupied by Soviet troops north of the 38th Parallel and U.S. troops south at the close of World War II. Diplomats intended the dividing line between the two armies to be temporary pending reunification of Korea, but it became permanent due to the Cold War. A Communist government rose to power in the north that became militarily strong through the aid of the Soviet Union. On 25 June 1950, this new nation, the Democratic People's Republic of Korea (DPRK), invaded southern areas with the objective of unifying the peninsula under Communist rule. Both the United States and the United Nations resolved to resist the invasion with armed force.

The result was a struggle that took part largely on land, but the war effort of the United States and the United Nations Command

(UNC) depended on sea power. Destroyers and frigates were among those naval units that blockaded North Korea, provided gunfire support for troop landings, and aided in the shipment of vital overseas supplies to South Korea on which the UNC war effort depended. Destroyers and frigates were particularly useful in the role of supply as the ships performed the duty of convoy escort, which was a role assigned to them during the two world wars. In addition to these duties, destroyers and frigates exhibited the duty of protection for aircraft carriers that had been attached to their type in World War II and had been a justification for their continued existence after that war. Actual combat with enemy naval units was very limited, as the DPRK was not a naval power. The only clash occurred on 2 July 1950, when a UN naval force composed of the U.S. cruiser *Juneau*, the British cruiser *Jamaica*, and the British frigate *Black Swan* encountered six North Korean gunboats escorting 10 supply ships. In the engagement, the guns of *Black Swan* helped to sink all but two of the enemy vessels.

Destroyers and frigates also proved their worth in the Vietnam War (1964–1975). The United States became involved in the struggle following the breakdown of elections to unite Vietnam, which had been divided after World War II, owing to the fact that Washington believed that Communists in the north would win the election. The United States subsequently provided large-scale economic assistance to the Republic of Vietnam (RVN), or South Vietnam, to ward off any future seizure of South Vietnam by northern Communist forces already established in the north as the Democratic Republic of Vietnam (DRV—North Vietnam). Tensions steadily escalated and culminated in open military involvement in Vietnam against increasing Communist insurgency.

The catalyst involved destroyers through the Tonkin Gulf incidents. On 2 August 1964, three DRV torpedo boats attacked the U.S. destroyer *Maddox* as it collected intelligence data on North Vietnam while positioned in international waters. *Maddox* staved off the torpedo boats with gunfire, but the situation led to the destroyer being reinforced by an additional destroyer, *C. Turner Joy*, to guard against future attacks. On 4 August, the United States believed that another such attack had occurred during the night. Although current information supports the theory that the crews of these destroyers mistook images on their radar to be enemy torpedo boats, the situation led the United States Congress to pass the Tonkin Gulf Resolution. While Congress believed that the resolution was designed primarily to give President Lyndon Johnson the right to repel future attacks on U.S. forces with force, it also included a stipulation that the president could do whatever he deemed necessary to assist the RVN. Johnson subsequently used this resolution to justify sending U.S. military forces en masse to South Vietnam.

Over the course of the war, destroyers and frigates performed the same duties as in the Korean War, but the level of their involvement proved far greater and more dangerous. The U.S. Navy employed destroyers extensively for close-in naval bombardment that placed them at great risk to enemy shore batteries. The destroyer *Ozbourn* is an example of this peril when it was damaged by an enemy mortar while conducting shore bombardment 2 miles off the coast. Destroyers were particularly useful in the AAW role as escorts for aircraft carriers against attack by DRV aircraft while they provided air support for U.S. ground troops.

Destroyers and frigates also served in noncombat situations associated with the Cold War. The most important of these was the 1962 Cuban Missile Crisis, the event that brought the world to the brink of nuclear war. It was precipitated by a large influx of supplies to Communist Cuba from the Soviet Union that included fighters and SAM missiles. Moscow assured Washington that the nature of this aid was solely defensive, but intelligence received from Cuban refuges revealed that offensive missiles formed part of the aid sent to the island. The United States was faced with the fact that Cuba would soon have hundreds of offensive missiles only 90 miles off its shores. President John F. Kennedy, after weighing the alternatives to ending the shipments and getting the Soviet Union to withdraw its missiles, settled on a naval blockade of the island to halt the flow of weapons to Cuba. Kennedy informed Soviet premier Nikita Khrushchev that any Soviet vessel approaching the blockade that did not stop would be disabled and that any submarines approaching the island would be intercepted. In October, a force of 180 warships was deployed around Cuba that included the guided missile destroyer *Gyatt*. Destroyers and frigates were a principal part of this force, as they were used in their escort role to support the eight aircraft carriers of the blockading squadron. The U.S. Navy also intended them for use in their ASW role to detect approaching Soviet submarines. On 27 October 1962, the world waited to see if nuclear war might result from the approach of Soviet supply ships toward the blockade. These ships ultimately turned back in the face of U.S. naval forces, thus averting the crisis and leading to the Soviet withdrawal of missiles from Cuba. In addition to this famous event, destroyers on both sides of the Cold War struggle were used in noncombat roles to gather intelligence around the world on the movement of opposing forces.

Destroyers were also involved in important events outside the context of the Cold War, as they were the principal surface combatants of many smaller powers. One of the most important examples of destroyer involvement in world events separate from the Cold War took place in the aftermath of the July 1967 Arab-Israeli War that pitted Israel against Egypt and Syria. The conflict saw Israeli and Egyptian naval units go against one another and led to the sinking of two Egyptian torpedo boats by the Israeli destroyer *Eilat,* a former British World War II–era vessel and the flagship of the Israeli Navy. On 21 October 1967, in the wake of the war, *Eilat* was patrolling off Port Said, Egypt, when it was attacked by Egyptian missile boats armed with the Soviet SS-N-2 missile, which was an improvement on the first Soviet SSM model. Two of these missiles hit *Eilat* in its engine room and communications facilities, which rendered the vessel dead in the water and incapable of defending itself. Some 90 minutes later, a third SS-N-2 sank the warship, making it the first in history to be sunk by antiship missiles. This event highlighted the destructive potential of missiles when used against warships and led to continued SSM development in the Soviet Union; other nations were spurred to produce SSM technology of their own.

The aggregate effect of the many usages of destroyers at sea between 1945 and 1967 was a confirmation of their continued importance in naval operations and proof of the value of new technology such as improved radar, sonar, and, in the case of *Eilat,* offensive missiles. Between 1967 and 1982, the United States forged ahead with its destroyer and frigate programs in light of these experiences.

The largest destroyers produced were additional nuclear-powered warships that, like their predecessors, pressed the limit of the definition of a destroyer or frigate. The first of these were the two units of the *California* class completed between 1974 and 1975 as frigates. The hull of *California* measured 596 feet by 61 feet by 20 feet, 6 inches and displaced 10,150 tons. Two D2G nuclear reactors powered the vessel's turbines, which produced a maximum speed of 30 knots.

These ships represented a step forward in missile technology. In place of the older SAM batteries of the 3Ts, these vessels mounted two twin-armed Standard SAM launchers with magazines that could each hold 40 missiles. One each was located fore and aft. The Standard missile represented a great improvement over the 3Ts and is still in use in the U.S. Navy. Research and development for this weapon began in 1963 with the object of replacing the Terrier and Tartar systems. First entering service in 1967 and designated RIM-66, this missile measures 15 feet, 6 inches, weighs 1,370 pounds, and possesses a maximum range of 104 miles thanks to its solid-fuel Aerojet rocket that can produce a speed of Mach 3.5. The guidance system is greatly enhanced and allows for better accuracy through faster course corrections while in flight. As a result, it can be used against aircraft and helicopters and for defense versus cruise missiles. This latter capability was particularly important at the time given the inability of the 3T missile systems to effectively combat Soviet antiship missiles. Finally, the Standard missile can also be used against surface targets, although its destructive power in this capacity is limited.

This step forward was due in part to increased funding by Congress in the wake of the *Eilat* incident to research SSM technology and thereby address the paucity of offensive power against enemy vessels that plagued the first U.S. missile-armed warships. In addition to this system and its enhanced fire control and radar array, the *California* class also shipped an ASROC launcher and four Mark 32 torpedo launchers for ASW warfare along with a sonar system. These vessels were also armed with two 5-inch guns in single mounts for the purpose of close-range defense. Unlike guns of the past, these were fully automated, computer-controlled weapons. Each gun possessed a magazine that held 475–500 rounds and could fire 16–20 rounds per minute to a maximum range of almost 15 miles. This gun remains in use in the U.S. Navy.

Four similar warships of the *Virginia* class were completed between 1976 and 1980, the chief difference being the absence of an ASROC launcher in favor of a Standard missile system that could fire both SAM and ASROC missiles. None of the units of this latter class operated as frigates due to a change in U.S. Navy policy. In the 1970s, the United States moved increasingly toward the operation of smaller ships that were deemed equally effective as the larger ones through the scrapping of several cruisers. In 1975, as a measure to offset the reduction of cruisers, the United States chose to redesignate many of the frigates of the fleet as cruisers. The large size of the nuclear-powered frigates was one reason behind their inclusion. The move also affected the designation of the *Leahy, Bainbridge, Belknap, Truxton,* and *California* classes.

Although these vessels received a new label due primarily to their size, the first of a new class of warship entered service that was only slightly smaller, but more lightly armed. This was the destroyer

Spruance, which was the first of a class that comprised 31 vessels. These units entered service between 1975 and 1983 as warships capable of both the AAW and ASW roles. The hull of *Spruance* measures 563 feet, 4 inches by 55 feet, by 20 feet, 6 inches and displaces 5,826 tons. It is armed with two 5-inch guns in single mounts, one each being located fore and aft. In addition, the ship carries one AS-ROC ASW system, six 12.75-inch torpedo tubes that fire ASW homing torpedoes, and one helicopter that operates off a flight deck located aft amidships. Finally, the vessel is armed with one Sea Sparrow system. This consisted of an eight-cell box launcher mounted in the bow. The Sea Sparrow is a relatively small missile that can be launched as either a SAM or an SSM to a range of 8 nautical miles. Gas turbines produce a maximum speed of 30 knots.

In addition to these vessels, the United States constructed for Iran five *Kidd*-class destroyers that are virtually identical to the Spruance class. The chief difference between the two types is the inclusion of armor on the *Kidd*-class vessels, a rare feature for modern warships. This armor is a lightweight, extremely strong plastic material known as Kevlar. Although this armor, mounted on the hull over weapons and machinery spaces as well as on sensory arrays, cannot completely negate the destructive effects of larger missiles, it can localize the effects of a blast and thus decrease the damage caused by a hit. These ships also have better air-conditioning and air-filtration systems to allow them to better operate in the Middle East. The 1979 Islamic Revolution that toppled the U.S.-supported shah of Iran in favor of a fundamentalist government led the United States to cancel the transfer of the vessels. Congress subsequently purchased them, and they entered service in the U.S. Navy.

In addition to these larger vessels, the United States constructed two classes of smaller combatants. U.S. naval officials intended both to be low-cost, mass-production designs. Between 1969 and 1974, the 46 units of the *Knox* class entered service as ASW vessels with the designation destroyer escort. The hull of *Knox* measured 438 feet by 47 feet by 25 feet, displaced 3,020 tons, and was powered by a turbine that produced a maximum speed of 27 knots. Its armament consisted of one 5-inch gun, one Sea Sparrow SAM system, one ASROC ASW launcher, DASH, and four 12.75-inch torpedo tubes. Although naval officials criticized the *Knox* class as poor seafaring boats, these ships served as the foundation for the design of the next group of frigates.

This next group was the *Oliver Hazard Perry* class comprising 54 units. The first entered service in 1971; the last unit was not completed until 1989. The hull of the *Oliver Hazard Perry* measured 445 feet by 45 feet by 22 feet and displaced 2,650 tons. Warships of the class produced after 1979 had an elongated bow 10 feet longer. The original armament of *Oliver Hazard Perry* is one 3-inch gun mounted aft amidships, one Standard SAM system with a magazine that holds 40 reloads, six 12.75-inch torpedo tubes, and two helicopters. The missile launcher is capable of firing not only SAM weapons but also the Harpoon antiship missile.

Harpoon became the first true SSM in the U.S. Navy. The naval version of this missile was first deployed in the early 1980s. It is still a primary weapon of the U.S. Navy and was first deployed on the *Virginia*-class cruisers (once designated frigates) in 1982 when they were retrofitted with them. The Harpoon weighs 1,385 pounds and is 15 feet long. It carries a 488-pound warhead at a speed approaching the speed of sound and has a maximum range of almost 70 miles. The missile resembles the French Exocet, an SSM produced earlier by the French Navy. Like the Exocet, its guidance system allows it to home in on a target while skimming the surface of the ocean before striking the hull of an enemy vessel and exploding within the ship. The Harpoon greatly enhanced the offensive capability of U.S. warships through the deployment of SSM systems that were far better than the limited surface capability afforded by the Standard system, which had been originally intended for SAM defense.

During the first half of the 1980s, warships of several classes were retrofitted with the Harpoon missile as well as other innovations. In the case of Harpoons, this process normally entailed the inclusion of a box launcher that held four missiles. All former nuclear-powered frigates were slated for this upgrade as well as units of the *Farragut*, *Spruance*, and *Charles F. Adams* classes. The latter group fired Harpoons from the Tartar missile launcher rather than using the new box launcher.

Between 1967 and 1982, the Soviet Union countered the construction program of the United States with large destroyers, missile frigates, and conversions of older vessels. In 1981, two vessels entered service that, like the nuclear-powered frigates later designated as destroyers by the United States, blurred the distinction between destroyers and cruisers. One of these was *Sovremenny*, designed for anti-ship warfare that was armed with a variety of ordnance that included SSM and SAM systems. The other type was *Udaloy*, equipped for the ASW role. For purposes of comparison to the large U.S. frigates that were reclassed as cruisers, *Sovremenny* measured 511 feet, 10 inches by 56 feet, 9 inches by 21 feet, 4 inches and displaced 6,200 tons. It was armed with two SS-N-22 SSM launchers, two SA-N-7 SAM launchers, four 130mm weapons and four 30mm guns for AA defense, four 20.8-inch torpedo tubes, two RBU-1000 ASW launchers, and one helicopter. The vessel's maximum speed was 35 knots.

Ultimately, 20 units of the *Sovremenny* class and 13 vessels of the *Udaloy* class were commissioned for the Soviet Navy. The designation of these ships is a matter of debate among naval scholars. Many class them as cruisers rather than destroyers, and for purposes of this work they will be considered as cruisers. Aside from these large warships, in 1970, as construction continued on the final units of the *Kashin* class, the Soviet Union completed the first of its *Krivak*-class guided missile frigates. These were the largest of the frigates produced in this age. The hull of one of these vessels measures 405 feet, 3 inches by 46 feet, 3 inches by 15 feet, 1 inch and displaces 3,300 tons. Designed for ASW duty, the armament consists in part of one SS-N-14 ASW box launcher mounted in the bow that holds four missiles. Entering service in 1969, this missile measures 25 feet long and has a range of 30 nautical miles. It can also be used against surface ships. In addition, the ship also possesses two RBU-6000 ASW rocket launchers and eight 21-inch torpedo tubes. A *Krivak*-class warship also carries two SA-N-4 SAM launchers with 20 reloads each and four 3-inch guns mounted in dual-piece gun houses located in the stern. A subsequent version of the type, *Krivak II,* mounts two 4-inch guns in single-mount gun houses in place of the original gun armament. The top speed is 32 knots. Crew complement consists of 200 officers and men. The Soviet Union completed 33 *Krivak*-class warships between 1970 and 1982 while also producing 43 *Grisha*-class frigates designed for coastal defense. Although a unit of this class is rather small and lightly built, measuring only 234 feet, 11 inches and displacing 950 tons, it is armed with one SA-N-4 SAM launcher. This missile, like the SA-N-1, can be used against surface targets.

In addition to new construction, the Soviets augmented the overall effectiveness of their destroyer fleet by converting a large number of existing destroyers to fire missiles of varying types. Between 1967 and 1972, seven *Kotlin*-class vessels received a SA-N-1 SAM launcher in place of the aft 5.1-inch gun mount. By 1977, eight *Kanin*-class vessels had also received a SA-N-1 SAM launcher; in this instance it replaced the SS-N-1 SSM system. The Soviets also pursued conversions to SSM systems due to the continuing value attached to them by the Soviets in terms of the strategic mission of guarding against enemy aircraft carriers. In addition, the 1967 sinking of the Israeli ship *Eliat* provided reinforcement for using the SSM. Between 1973 and 1975, Soviet shipyards refitted six *Kashin*-class destroyers to include four SS-N-2C SSM launchers. Each launcher holds one missile, which is mounted aft amidship on the side of the vessel facing toward the stern. Three *Kildin*-class vessels also incorporated the SS-N-2C in the same manner as the *Kashin*-class units. By 1982, as a result of these refits as well as new construction, the Soviet Navy was capable of overseas operations to an extent that the country had not previously enjoyed.

As in the first years of the Cold War, the members of NATO, other than the United States and the pro-Western neutral powers, accounted for the majority of the rest of the world's destroyer and frigate production. One of the largest producers of destroyers between 1967 and 1982 was France, but this construction took place in an environment where France was no longer a member of NATO. Relations between France and the United States declined steadily over the issue of an increased French role in the leadership of the alliance. In 1969, the failure to resolve this standoff satisfactorily led to the French leader Charles de Gaulle's decision to withdraw France from NATO. Fortunately for the French, this action did not cripple France's ability to deploy naval missiles thanks to the fact that domestic R&D had been greatly increased in the opening stages of the diplomatic impasse with the United States.

In 1970, the French completed their second *Suffren*-class destroyer, and in 1973 they produced the ASW destroyer *Aconit* that mounted a missile armament of one Malafon ASW launcher. Far more important than this ship was the completion between 1974 and 1977 of the three *Tourville*-class destroyers whose design was descended from *Aconit*. These vessels were the first destroyers designed to ship France's new SSM missile. The Exocet was one of the first successful, purpose-built antiship missiles designed outside of the Soviet Union. It was introduced in 1968 and has proven so effective that it is still in use in more than 20 countries. Stored in a box launcher, this weapon is guided when first fired by onboard radar systems, but as it nears the target vessel it switches to internal radar control. This guidance system controls the missile in a decent to an altitude of 10–12 feet above the water to hamper detection by enemy radar devices and make it more difficult to shoot down. It can travel at a maximum velocity just below the speed of sound and delivers a 160-kilogram warhead. The missile is designed to penetrate the hull of an enemy warship before exploding to cause the maximum amount of damage.

Tourville, which measures 501 feet by 50 feet by 19 feet and displaces 4,580 tons, mounts six Exocet missiles in single-cell box launchers. It also mounts one Crotale SAM system, which was an improvement of the Mascura, shipped one Malafon ASW system that has been removed, carries two 3.9-inch guns mounted in single-piece gun houses in the bow, two torpedo tubes, and two ASW helicopters that operate off a flight deck on the stern. The vessel, crewed by 303 officers and men, is capable of 31 knots. The vessels of the *Tourville* class reflect the French intention, as in other navies in recent years, to produce destroyers capable of multiple roles out of the need for economy due to the high cost of modern warships. These vessels can perform AAW, ASW, and antiship operations. The other destroyers built in this period were intended specifically for the ASW role. Between 1979 and 1986, the French produced five *Georges Leygues*–class destroyers. These vessels mount two fewer Exocet missiles and have greater facilities for ASW helicopters. During this same period, most of the pre-existing destroyers and frigates of the French Navy were retrofitted with Exocet missiles.

Like many navies, the number of frigates constructed by France exceeded that of destroyers. French naval officials intended these ships to serve as coastal units and to show the flag overseas. Between 1976 and 1982, 13 *D'Estienne d'Orves*-class frigates entered service. These ships are rather small, being 262 feet by 34 feet by 10 feet with a displacement of 950 tons, but they are well armed for their size. *D'Estienne d'Orves* mounts two Exocet missiles, one 3.9-inch gun in a single-piece gun house mounted forward, one ASW mortar, and four torpedo tubes. Its maximum speed is only 23 knots, but this is adequate for the designed purpose of the craft.

The construction program of Great Britain mirrored that of France in the sense that the number of destroyers produced was less than that of frigates. Between 1967 and 1982, the British commissioned 12 missile destroyers. In 1973, the British completed *Bristol* as an escort for new aircraft carriers. This vessel, staffed by 300 officers and men, mounted new British missile ordnance with the Sea Dart SAM system, capable of a range of 35 miles, and the Ikara ASW system. The latter weapon was a joint effort by the British and Australians. It is an ASW torpedo affixed to a rocket. The cost of this vessel, however, led to the cancellation of further units in favor of the design of the *Sheffield*-class destroyers. This 10-ship group, completed between 1975 and 1982, were intended, like *Bristol,* as escorts. The hull of *Sheffield* measured 410 feet by 46 feet by 19 feet and displaced 3,850 tons. It was armed with one 4.5-inch gun mounted in a Mark 8 gun house located in the bow. This system resembled the U.S. model in that it was fully automated. It also carried one Sea Dart SAM system, with the launcher sited in the bow, six 12.75-inch torpedo tubes for ASW operations, and one helicopter for the same duty that operated on a flight deck located on the stern. The maximum speed of this vessel was 30 knots. These vessels have proven relatively successful, but the British did feel the need to address the size of the hull, the primary weakness of the design. The dimensions of the ship necessitated cramped living conditions for the crew as well as decreased endurance for the ship while at sea.

The British rectified this problem with the four *Manchester*-class destroyers. The first of these entered service in 1982; the other units followed three years later. The hull of *Manchester* was 53 feet longer than *Sheffield* and 3 inches wider, which allowed for better accommodation and performance at sea. It also made possible the storage of more reloads for the vessel's armament, which was the same as that of the preceding class. The difference was that while *Sheffield* held only 22 reloads, *Manchester* purportedly carries 40 missiles in its magazine.

The number of these destroyers paled in comparison to that of the cheaper frigates that Britain built in the same period. Between 1968 and 1982, 23 frigates comprising four classes entered service. The first of these were 10 improved *Leander*-class frigates completed from 1969 to 1973 that sported a hull with a wider beam, which improved endurance for extended operations at sea. Following the last of these was the frigate *Mermaid,* which represented a departure from normal British construction in the sense that it lacked missiles. President Kwame Nkrumah of Ghana ordered this ship as his presidential vessel, but a coup that toppled him led the British to commission it into the Royal Navy. The last two groups showcased the lack of a true, domestically built and designed SSM in the Royal Navy. The first was the eight-ship *Amazon* class produced between 1974 and 1978 as general purpose escorts. The hull of *Amazon* measured 384 feet by 41 feet, 9 inches by 19 feet and displaced 2,860 tons. Its armament consisted of one 4.5-inch gun in a Mark 8 gun house located in the bow, one Seacat SAM launcher, six 12.75-inch ASW torpedo tubes, and one helicopter. The vessel's maximum speed was 30 knots. Six ships of this class, the exceptions being *Amazon* and *Antelope*, were also equipped with four French Exocet SSMs in two dual-tubed launchers located on the superstructure immediately forward of the bridge.

The chief problem with these vessels was the fact that their hulls were very lightly built, which was a weakness revealed in combat. The last new frigates in service, the four *Broadsword*-class vessels, completed between 1979 and 1982, are essentially larger frigates that carry a greater AA capability through their two Sea Wolf SAM systems. The Sea Wolf missile, although smaller than the Seacat, is superior due to its speed. The Seacat traveled at a maximum velocity of Mach .6 while the Sea Wolf attains a speed of Mach 2.5. Like the Amazon class, these warships also carry four Exocet missiles. By 1982, the frigates of the *Amazon* and *Broadsword* classes were only a portion of the British vessels that carried the French weapon. Eight *Leander*-class frigates also received the Exocet through an upgrade program.

Aside from Britain and France, the majority of the destroyers and frigates constructed in Europe between 1967 and 1982 were units of the NATO nations of Italy, West Germany, and the Netherlands. Italy, in keeping with its naval construction program that rested primarily on destroyers and smaller craft, produced two *Audace*-class destroyers in 1972 that shipped an armament similar to the previous *Impavido* class. The chief difference was the inclusion of helicopters for ASW operations. The Italians also completed nine frigates. Four of these represent the *Lupo* class and are the first Italian frigates to carry an SSM system. The hull of *Lupo* measures 370 feet, 2 inches by 39 feet, 4 inches by 12 feet and displaces 2,208 tons. It is armed with one 5-inch gun in a gun house mounted in the bow, one U.S. Sea Sparrow SAM system, four 40mm AA guns, six 12.6-inch torpedo tubes, one ASW helicopter, and eight Ottomat SSM weapons. These are contained in single-cell launchers. One each is located on the sides aft amidships of the helicopter hanger. The other two are situated on either side of the forward superstructure. The current version of this weapon is a sea-skimmer like the Exocet. In 1982, the first three of eight *Maestrale*-class frigates entered service that also mount Ottomat SSM weaponry and are essentially enlarged versions of the preceding class.

The Netherlands nearly equaled the destroyer and frigate production of Italy, launching eight missile frigates. The *Kortenaer* class represents the majority of this construction. The first 6 of this 14-ship group entered service between 1978 and 1981 and are general-purpose destroyers. *Kortenaer* measures 427 feet by 47 feet by 14 feet, displaces 3,000 tons, and mounts an array of weaponry that includes one U.S. Sea Sparrow SAM launcher, eight Harpoon SSM weapons, and two helicopters. This armament reflects the Dutch decision to rely on U.S. weapons technology.

West Germany augmented its fleet with five vessels that also relied on U.S. technology. Indeed, three of these are modified U.S. *Charles F. Adams*–class destroyers. Known as the *Lutjens* class, these ships mount a modified Tartar SAM launcher that fires the Standard SAM and the Harpoon SSM. The United States completed these vessels for shipment to Germany between 1969 and 1970, making them the largest surface units of the West German Navy at that point. The Germans did not produce additional warships until 1982 with the completion of the first two units of the seven-ship *Bremen*-class frigates, which were actually a variation of the Dutch *Kortenaer* class. The hull of *Bremen* measures 420 feet by 47 feet, 10 inches by 19 feet, 9 inches and displaces 3,700 tons. The warship's armament consists of one 3-inch gun located in the bow, eight Harpoon SSMs, one Sea Sparrow SAM system, four ASW torpedo tubes, and two ASW helicopters contained in a hanger that forms the vessel's aft superstructure. The maximum speed of the ship is 30 knots.

Japan, a pro-Western nonaligned power, nearly equaled the output of all three of these European NATO powers through the construction of 18 destroyers and frigates that resoundingly signaled the return of Japan as a world naval power. These vessels continued to reflect Japan's strategic emphasis on ASW vessels and its reliance on U.S. weapons technology. Between 1967 and 1974, Japan completed 12 ASW destroyers. Among these were the last three units of the *Yamagumo* class and seven vessels of the *Takatsuki* and *Minegumo* classes that were largely similar. The other two were the innovative vessels of the *Haruna* class that revived Japan's reputation as an innovative power in destroyer design. Completed between 1973 and 1974, these destroyers were the first in the world to carry three full-sized helicopters for ASW operations. The hull of *Haruna* measures 501 feet, 11 inches by 57 feet, 5 inches by 16 feet, 8 inches, displaces 4,950 tons, and is capable of a maximum speed of 32 knots. Its armament consists of two 5-inch guns in single mounts located in the bow, one ASROC ASW system, six 12.75-inch torpedo tubes, and three helicopters that operate on a flight deck situated on the stern.

In 1980 and 1981, the Japanese constructed two additional units of the *Shirane* class that are enlarged versions of the *Haruna* design.

The addition of a Sea Sparrow SAM system to these ships increases the overall combat capability of the Japanese Navy. The Sea Sparrow was subsequently added to the *Haruna* class and was also incorporated on the *Tachikaze*-class vessels that left Japanese shipyards between 1976 and 1982. The final vessel produced, being the first of the seven-ship *Hatsuyuki* class, further increased the combat potential of the Japanese Navy through the inclusion of eight Harpoon SSMs. This ship is also testimony to the continuing reliance of Japan on U.S. weapons technology. In addition to the Harpoon, the units of the *Tachikaze* class and two of the *Takatsuki* class received Harpoons through refits in the early 1980s.

The remainder of destroyer and frigate production between 1968 and 1982 was largely the result of the other members of NATO and the pro-Western neutral powers. Within NATO, Canada completed four *Iroquois*-class destroyers in 1972 and 1973 that shipped two helicopters in keeping with the intention of producing ASW warships. New NATO powers also contributed to the alliance's naval strength. The largest contribution was that of Spain once it joined NATO in 1982; it brought 24 destroyers and frigates into the alliance. Thirteen of these were modern frigates completed between 1974 and 1982, with one class mounting the Standard SAM system while the more modern eight-ship *Descubierta* class carries the Sea Sparrow SAM.

Turkey also contributed vessels. After its entry into NATO in 1952, between 1971 and 1980 Ankara purchased nine aging U.S. *Gearing*-class destroyers that had undergone FRAM conversions. In addition to these, Turkey completed in 1972 and 1975 its first domestically built warships of any size since before World War I (these warships had been destroyers built in the last decade of the nineteenth century). These *Berk*-class frigates are small, being only 312 feet, 4 inches long, and have limited capability in the modern age, as the armament is outdated. Nevertheless, their construction gave Turkish shipyards valuable experience for use in the future. Outside the alliance, NATO felt confident that it could continue to rely on the naval forces of Australia and New Zealand in the event of a general conflict stemming from the Cold War. Between 1968 and 1982, Australia built two *Swan*-class frigates and acquired two U.S. *Oliver Hazard Perry*–class frigates. New Zealand bought two frigates of the British *Leander* type during the same period.

The world's destroyer and frigate fleet swelled additionally through the efforts of nonaligned nations other than Japan. The largest number were those of India, as the country based its navy on surface warships of destroyer and frigate size. Between 1972 and 1980, India procured three Soviet *Kashin*-class destroyers and six British *Leander*-class frigates. China continued its struggle to construct ships for a navy committed to coastal defense after the loss of Soviet financial and technical assistance. The country's efforts produced 12 *Jinan/Luta*–class destroyers that are essentially of the Soviet *Kotlin* type. China also completed 16 frigates that also reflected the country's reliance on Soviet design and weapons. The most impressive of these are the nine warships of the *Jianghu* class that are the first Chinese warships to carry SSM weaponry. The class eventually comprised 30 units. The hull of *Jianghu* measures 337 feet, 9 inches by 39 feet, 4 inches by 13 feet, 2 inches, displaces 1,800 tons, and carries four Soviet SS-N-2 SSM in two dual-cell launchers as its primary armament.

In addition, smaller neutral powers contributed through the purchase of warships from NATO and the Soviet Union. Examples are many, but among them is Argentina, with the purchase of two *Sheffield*-class destroyers, and Indonesia with the procurement of a *Claud Jones*–class frigate. World War II–era destroyers comprised a large part of the fleets of smaller nations. Among those that operated either British or U.S. destroyers in the period between 1968 and 1982 were Peru, Taiwan, South Korea, and Brazil.

All of the destroyers and frigates produced up to 1982, regardless of whether they belonged to the principal participants in the Cold War or to neutral powers, were used extensively as the surface combatants of the world's navies. A portion of the combat duty between 1968 and 1982 remained in the context of the Cold War as the Vietnam conflict remained in the balance. Destroyers and frigates of the U.S. Navy continued to act as escorts for supply convoys to Vietnam, shore bombardment vessels, and most importantly as AAW escorts. The new missile technology became extremely important in terms of this latter role. In 1972, the *Belknap*-class warships *Sterrett* and *Biddle* (designated as cruisers in 1975) shot down DRV aircraft. Both ships shot down two MiG fighters, but *Sterrett* used its missile system to also shoot down an SSM, making it the first warship in history to use a SAM missile to destroy an antiship missile.[6]

The end of the Vietnam War in 1975 did not lead to a prolonged period devoid of destroyer and frigate warfare. Indeed, the 1982 Falkland Islands War between Great Britain and Argentina led to a much higher degree of use for these vessels. The cause of the conflict was the Falkland Islands, a territorial possession of Great Britain located east of the southernmost portion of South America off the coast of Argentina. The ownership of these islands had been a source of contention since the eighteenth century. By 1982, the military junta that governed Argentina called for the acquisition of the Malvinas Islands, as the Argentines called the Falklands, in an effort to divert popular attention from poor conditions at home that included massive civil rights violations to an issue of Argentine nationalism. At this time, there were 1,800 British citizens living on the islands that wished to remain British nationals. The British government of Prime Minister Margaret Thatcher did not believe that war would occur over this issue. This view proved incorrect on 2 April 1982, when Argentina landed troops on the Falklands. The Thatcher government subsequently resolved to fight for the Falkland Islands and dispatched a task force four days later that included the aircraft carriers *Hermes* and *Invincible*. To protect these carriers against air attack and as a reflection of the fact that by this time smaller craft became the majority of the Royal Navy, the task force included 23 destroyers and frigates.[7] The British also relied on these vessels as escorts for the supply vessels that accompanied the warships.

Destroyers and frigates proved pivotal to the British war effort in the Falklands. Although the Argentine Navy remained in port following the 2 May 1982 sinking of the cruiser *General Belgrano* by a British submarine, the British had to fend off repeated attacks on the task force by the fine aircraft and pilots of the Argentine Air Force. These planes, which used French Exocet SSM weapons and bombs, exacted a heavy toll on the task force. The majority of British losses were destroyers and frigates, as they were the largest number of craft in combat and were actively engaged in the defense of the principal targets of aircraft carriers and supply vessels against Argentine air attack. On 4 May 1982, the destroyer *Sheffield* succumbed to Argentine air forces. An Exocet SSM, fired from a French-built Super Entendard fighter, caught the vessel virtually unawares, penetrated above the waterline amidships, and detonated. Among the systems damaged by the hit were the water mains used for fire-fighting, which meant that the crew had no means to fight the fires that progressively consumed the ship. *Sheffield* was abandoned and remained afloat for six days before capsizing while in tow. The attack killed 22 officers and ratings.

The *Sheffield*-class *Coventry* was also destroyed by air attack on 25 May 1982, although the method of destruction was different. Argentine aircraft bombed the vessel, hitting it three times with 1,000-pound weapons. *Coventry* was set ablaze and sank from its damage on the same day with the loss of 19 officers and ratings. In addition to these vessels, the British also suffered the destruction of the Amazon-class frigates *Ardent* and *Antelope*. In May, a rocket mortally damaged the former while bombs destroyed the latter. During the course of the conflict, Argentine aircraft damaged an additional eight British destroyers and frigates.

Nevertheless, the surface vessels of the British fleet claimed 100 Argentine planes and contributed to the British victory. On 13 June 1982, the Argentine Army on the Falklands surrendered to British troops, which brought to an end the extended conflict at sea that employed the new missile technology. Both the losses of British vessels and Argentine aircraft exhibited the value of the new weaponry. Naval officials also used the war to evaluate the performance of destroyers and frigates in the missile age and refine their design. An example is the material used to construct ships. To save weight, some naval powers in the 1970s had employed aluminum rather than steel for the construction of superstructures. The substance proved susceptible to being weakened by high-intensity heat, as in the case of *Sheffield,* and naval officials subsequently discarded it as a viable material for widespread use in warships. The dangers to the ship and crew in combat certainly did not justify the use of aluminum.

British naval officials first realized the drawbacks of aluminum construction in the years before the Falklands War when a fire in 1977 nearly destroyed the frigate *Amazon.* Unfortunately for the British, this fire was the second; in 1973 an engine room blaze nearly destroyed the destroyer *Bristol.* These events are examples of the fact that noncombat duty could prove just as dangerous being in harm's way. This fire was only one of several peacetime incidents at sea that were always possible given the extensive use of destroyers and frigates in daily fleet operations, as they formed the majority of the vessels in service for the world's navies. On 31 August 1974, the Soviets *Kashin*-class destroyer *Otvazhnyy* suffered an internal fire while on maneuvers in the Black Sea. The blaze detonated the warship's aft SA-N-1 SAM magazine. The force of the blast was so great that a large section of the vessel's deck and superstructure in the aft amidships area of the hull was blown into a position vertical to the hull. After taking this catastrophic damage, the vessel sank stern first with the loss of 200 of its crew of about 280 officers and men.

In one case, part of the crew of a frigate faced peril from a purposeful act. On 8 November 1975, the Soviet *Krivak*-class warship *Storozhevoi* lay in Riga Harbor in the Baltic with a portion of its crew ashore in celebration of the fifty-eighth anniversary of the Bolshevik takeover that ushered the Soviets to power in Russia. Some of the officers and crew used this opportunity to stage a mutiny with the object of trying to reach international waters and ultimately defect from the Soviet Union. This attempt failed, however, as Soviet jets caught and repeatedly strafed the vessel to compel the mutineers to abort their action. Soviet officials subsequently removed the entire crew, whether they had been involved in the mutiny or loyal to the government, and replaced them with a fresh complement. They also transferred *Storozhevoy* to another theater of operations.

Whether involved in combat operations or peacetime duties, destroyers and frigates were regarded around the world as indispensable vessels. Upgrades of existing units and construction continued in the context of the Cold War between 1983 and 1991, the latter date being the end of the Cold War period due to the collapse of the Soviet Union. The United States produced 26 frigates of the *Oliver Hazard Perry* class, but naval officials turned back to designs for larger craft capable of handling multiple, simultaneous threats. This move was not new by the 1980s, as many recognized in the late 1950s in the wake of the introduction of the Terrier SAM that the chief weakness of the 3-T systems was the inability to engage more than one target at a time.

This led to the Typhon program for new long- and medium-range missiles to ultimately replace the Talos and Terrier systems that would benefit from a new type of sensory array for targeting. Several proposals concerning the proper vessel to carry it led to a design for a frigate, but the extreme cost of the system and ship led to the 1963 decision to cancel the effort. Nevertheless, the concept did not die with the program in terms of an improved missile control system. This innovation, the Aegis Combat System, is designed to control and coordinate the defense of the ship that carries it, as well as to command the defense of entire task forces through the use of complex computers. First tested in 1973, the Aegis system relies on the powerful AN/SPY-1 radar that can simultaneously conduct searches and track more than 100 targets. This data is fed to the command center of a ship (the Combat Information Center), where a computer evaluates which targets pose the greatest threat to the ship or task force and uses the vessel's weapons accordingly to address the situation. At first, U.S. naval officials believed that the best warship to carry the new system was a cruiser. As a result, in 1983 the first Ticonderoga-class cruiser, equipped with the Aegis system, entered service.

In subsequent years, however, the innovation extended to destroyer design with the *Arleigh Burke* class. The lead ship, commissioned in July 1991, is one of the most advanced warships in the world. The hull of *Arleigh Burke,* which is partially armored with Kevlar, measures 504 feet, 6 inches by 66 feet, 8 inches by 32 feet, 7 inches, displaces 8,315 tons, and is powered by gas turbines that can produce a maximum speed of 32 knots. Its principal armament consists of a 29-cell vertical launch system (VLS) housed in the bow just forward of the bridge superstructure and a 61-cell VLS positioned aft. The VLS can fire Standard SAM weaponry and Tomahawk cruise missiles.

The Tomahawk was deployed in 1986 and is the most powerful offensive missile in the arsenal of the U.S. Navy. This weapon weighs 2,900 pounds, 3,500 pounds if it is equipped with a booster rocket for greater distance. It measures 18 feet, 3 inches long, but its length increases to 20 feet, 6 inches when a booster is included. The Tomahawk cruise missile can carry a 1,000-pound conventional warhead or a nuclear payload over a distance of 1,000 miles. The guidance system is extremely complex and allows for control that is largely independent of the ship that fires it. This guidance includes a targeting computer equipped with the Terrain Contour Mapping (TERCOM) system. This system uses the missile's radar to examine the topography ahead of it to match it to a three-dimensional map stored in the missile's computer memory. The computer can correct the course of the weapon based on variations between the two maps. The Tomahawk missile is also equipped with a Global Positioning System (GPS) to improve reliability of the targeting data. Finally, Tomahawks also use a system known as Digital Scene Matching Area Correlation (DSMAC) in the final stages of flight. As the missile nears its target, DSMAC uses a camera to take a picture of the target, which the computer verifies. This equipment provides for great accuracy, and the missile is extremely difficult to detect as it flies at a low altitude.

In addition to the missiles of the VLS system, the *Arleigh Burke* also ships eight Harpoon SSMs in two four-celled box launchers located aft, one 5-inch gun in an automated gun house located in the bow, six 12.75-inch torpedo tubes, one helicopter, and a Vulcan Phalanx gun. This latter armament was ready for service in 1977 and is still in use in the U.S. Navy. This weapon is a 20mm Gatling gun that is fed by a magazine that holds 1,000 rounds. It was designed as a last measure of defense to destroy incoming missiles at close range, but it can also be used against aircraft. The gun can fire at a rate of 100 rounds per second. Its computer-controlled tracking system is built into the gun mount and can direct effective fire over a range between 500 and 1,500 yards. The Aegis system coordinates the use of all of these weapons and relies on large, flat sensory panels mounted on the sides of the superstructure. All told, the *Arleigh Burke* design of multi-role destroyer is among the most advanced and powerful in the world.

The production program of the Soviet Union did not approach that of the United States. This was due to both the struggling Soviet economy by the 1980s and the coming to power in March 1985 of Mikhail Gorbachev. The new Soviet leader greatly curtailed the construction of new warships and began to lessen the extent of seaborne operations for existing units to ease some of the burden on the Soviet economy. As a result, Soviet production was a far cry from that of the first decades of the Cold War. The Soviet Union constructed nine more *Krivak*-class frigates to counter the production of the United States and its NATO allies. The majority of construction, however, centered on smaller craft designated as frigates, suitable largely for coastal defense rather than blue-water operations. Between 1986 and 1990, the Soviets commissioned 11 *Parchim*-class frigates with hulls that measure 246 feet, 8 inches by 32 feet, 2 inches by 14 feet, 5 inches and displace 769 tons. They are armed with SAM weapons and one 3-inch gun. Additional units of the *Grisha* class, a previous design intended for the same task, also left Soviet shipyards. All entered service in the Soviet Navy with an uncertain future. Owing to continually worsening economic problems and Gorbachev's policy toward the navy, many units of the Soviet fleet were already riding inactive at anchor and in a state of decay. By 1991, the problem was particularly pronounced as the Soviet Union neared collapse.

Not only did the number of new destroyers in the United States dwarf the production of the Soviet Union; so did that of the other members of the NATO alliance. Chief among these was Great Britain. Following the Falklands War, London announced plans to reverse the policy of reductions in the navy for the sake of economy that had been the hallmark of past years. This decision, although not long-lasting, resulted in the construction of two types of frigate. Between 1984 and 1990, British dockyards completed 10 *Broadsword*-class frigates in two variants of the original design. They also turned out the first three units of the *Duke* class. *Norfolk*, the lead ship, entered service in 1990 and measures 436 feet, 2 inches by 52 feet, 9 inches by 18 feet with a displacement of 3,500 tons. It is armed with eight Harpoon SSM in two four-celled launchers located in the bow, a Sea Wolf SAM system in the bow, one 4.5-inch gun, two 30mm AA guns, four torpedo tubes, and one helicopter that operates off a flight deck located on the stern. The maximum speed of the vessel is 28 knots, and the crew consists of 181 officers and ratings. Although *Norfolk* entered service, the number of total units was not determined. In 1991, London reversed its post-Falklands stance on new construction through the Option for Changes Program. This policy called for a reduction of the Royal Navy in keeping with the end of the Cold War.

Other NATO powers contributed to the destroyer and frigate fleet of the alliance, although the output steadily decreased in most nations, as in Great Britain, with the diminution of the Soviet threat. As in all other navies in Europe, frigates constituted all of the construction, as they are cheaper to build than destroyers. Germany constructed an additional five *Bremen*-class frigates by 1991, while Italy produced five units of the *Maestrale* design. Canada, out of the need for economy, relied largely in this era on refits of existing units, but it did commission the first of its *Halifax*-class frigates designed for the AAW role. In 1986, the Netherlands commissioned two *Jacob Van Heemskerck*–class vessels armed principally with eight Harpoon missiles. Two *Karel Doorman*–class frigates followed five years later. Turkey buttressed the naval force of the alliance with four *Meko*-class frigates between 1987 and 1989 that relied in part on technical assistance garnered from Germany. Spain produced the same number of ships that were launched in Spanish yards, but they are *Oliver Hazard Perry*–class vessels.

As throughout the Cold War, NATO also looked to the forces of nonaligned, pro-Western powers for aid in the event of war with the Soviet Union. The largest producer of destroyers and frigates among these powers was Japan, which added destroyers and frigates to its fleet. While units of the *Hatsuyuki* class neared completion, the Japanese also commissioned in 1986 and 1988 two *Hatakaze*-class destroyers armed with both Harpoon SSMs and Standard SAM weaponry. Closely following these vessels between 1988 and 1991 were eight *Asagiri*-class destroyers that are similarly armed. Augmenting the power of these new vessels were eight frigates. This output greatly exceeded that of France, a former NATO member that, despite its withdrawal from the alliance, was certainly still counted as a nation friendly to the organization. Between 1988 and 1991, France commissioned two more *Georges Leygues*–class vessels and two *Cassard*-class destroyers, the latter being armed with Exocet SSM and Standard SAM weapons. French shipyards also continued the *D'Estienne d'Orves*–class frigate program and launched another five such vessels.

Finally, Australia and New Zealand continued their affiliation with the West, although the latter did not build or acquire more vessels in the period from 1983 to the end of the Cold War. The former, like Spain, relied on the United States for frigates rather than producing vessels of domestic design. Between 1983 and 1992, Australia bought two *Oliver Hazard Perry*–class vessels from the United States and constructed an additional two of the same type in a domestic shipyard.

Increasingly by the end of the Cold War, the naval forces of nonaligned powers in the Cold War assumed great importance as their swelling numbers suggested the birth of new naval powers. Chief among these is India, as that country committed itself to the construction of a powerful navy with vessels that relied heavily on foreign warship design and weaponry. Between 1982 and 1988, four *Rajput*-class destroyers entered service that are a variant of the Soviet Union's *Kashin* type. They are each armed with two Soviet SA-N-1 SAM launchers and four Soviet SS-N-2C SSM weapons. These vessels joined a further unit that entered operation previously. As with these vessels, the three *Godvari*-class units are the product of foreign technology. Entering service between 1983 and 1988, their design is based on the British *Leander* class; weaponry consists of one Soviet SA-N-4 SAM launcher and four Soviet SS-N-2C SSM weapons.

Despite initial difficulties, China, like India, was in the process by 1991 of constructing a strong navy. Frigates composed part of this endeavor. By the close of the Cold War, the Chinese commissioned seven frigates built in Chinese shipyards. Some are improvements of the *Jianghu*-class design. This type of vessel established China as a world naval power through foreign demand for it. Egypt procured two such warships in 1984, and in the early 1990s Bangladesh and Thailand acquired one and four units, respectively.[8]

All nations that possessed destroyers and frigates continued to use them in fleet operations between 1983 and 1991 as the Cold War continued to unfold. There were few instances in which destroyers and frigates exhibited their roles in combat. The two conflicts of this period that did involve these warships unfolded in the Middle East in a context outside the Cold War. The first was the Iran-Iraq War (1980–1988) that pitted the two powers over control of the Shatt al-Arab waterway. This river is formed by the confluence of the Tigris and Euphrates rivers that lies in part on the border between Iran and Iraq and empties into the Arabian (Persian) Gulf. The 1975 Algerian Treaty had established joint control of the waterway between the two powers, but Iraqi dictator Saddam Hussein decided to take advantage of turmoil in Iran caused by the 1979 overthrow of the shah by Shiite forces under Ayatollah Khomeini.

In 1980, Hussein launched a large-scale offensive into western Iran. Hussein's hope for a quick victory over a disorganized enemy proved illusory as Iranian forces not only blunted the initial Iraqi assault but also launched offensives of their own. Between 1982 and 1987, the war unfolded as a stalemate. Both powers resorted to attacking shipping in the Arabian Gulf as a means to deny supply to the other. The governments of Iran and Iraq also pursued this course to damage the oil export industry of their enemy. This action drew in countries that depended in part on oil from the Arabian Gulf. Among these was the United States, which in 1987 stationed warships in the gulf to guard tankers against attack. Destroyers and frigates assumed the majority of the work in this operation as one of their primary missions was escort. On 17 May 1987, an attack on the *Oliver Hazard Perry*–class frigate *Stark* exhibited the significant risk for warships in a combat zone. The mission of *Stark* entailed showing the flag, a common practice to project a naval power's influence around the world, and to monitor ship and plane movements in the international waters of the gulf. Around 9:00 P.M. two Iraqi fighter jets took off from their airbase and one of them turned toward *Stark*. A little after 10:00 P.M., this plane approached the U.S. vessel, the captain of which being unconcerned to this point, as many Iraqi as well as Iranian jets had flown in the gulf in the past with no threat of attack on a U.S. warship.

At this point, however, the proximity of the plane led Captain Glenn Brindel to order a warning be sent to the plane to turn away from *Stark*'s position. The refusal of the pilot to do so prompted a second warning that also went unheeded. Minutes afterward, a lookout aboard *Stark* reported that a missile was approaching the vessel. This French Exocet SSM hit the unprepared ship above the waterline on the port side. Although it failed to detonate, the fuel from the ordnance created a large fire. Seconds later, a second Exocet hit and exploded in the same general area as the first. The damage was severe enough that the ship might have sunk if not for the 16-hour battle by the crew to save their vessel. Their efforts allowed *Stark* to survive the attack, but at the cost of 37 lives. The incident, although later considered inadvertent by the United States, led to an order at the time that authorized U.S. Navy warships to shoot down all aircraft that did not respond to a verbal warning to withdraw.

The plight of *Stark* was not the only instance where the destroyers and frigates of the United States were placed in harm's way during the Iran-Iraq War. A second incident involving the *Oliver Hazard Perry*–class frigate *Samuel B. Roberts* led to a U.S. response that involved frigates. On 14 April 1988, this ship was en route to port for re-supply after patrolling the gulf when a lookout spotted mines in proximity to the ship. Upon closer inspection, the captain of *Samuel B. Roberts* concluded that his warship lay in the midst of a minefield. After 21 minutes of successfully navigating the minefield, the ship struck a mine, which detonated and produced a hole 15 feet by 20 feet in a portion of the hull beneath the waterline and close to the keel. The force of the blast created a crack in the hull that held the potential of breaking the ship in half. To prevent the crack from growing larger, the crew lashed steel cables across the crack. This procedure as well as the other damage control efforts saved the vessel. The incident led three days later to an attack on Iranian oil platforms and warships. Named OPERATION PRAYING MANTIS, it involved frigates that shelled oil platforms and engaged enemy vessels.

By the close of the war in June 1988, the frigates of the United States had succeeded in protecting shipping lines for oil tankers to an extent that obviated any threat to the world economy through skyrocketing oil prices. The war, however, had left Iraq with the largest military in the Middle East with the exception of Israel. This served as a catalyst for the next conflict in the region in which destroyers and frigates participated. In August 1990, Iraqi forces, many of them being veterans of the Iran-Iraq War, invaded Kuwait in keeping with Saddam Hussein's goal of acquiring the oil reserves of the small nation. The threat posed to the stability of the region, as well as to the global economy through the disruption of oil exports from Kuwait, led to an international coalition dedicated to wresting control of Kuwait from Iraq. During the night of 16–17 January 1991, OPERATION DESERT STORM began with an air offensive conducted largely by the United States. Naval forces of several nations formed a key part of this effort as aircraft carriers conducted numerous strikes against Iraqi targets. Destroyers and frigates protected these valuable vessels from the possibility of attack. They also joined in the air offensive against Iraq through the use of their missiles.

During the operation, the *Spruance*-class destroyer *Fife* launched 58 Tomahawk missiles against Iraqi targets.[9] The destruction caused by the *Fife*, other destroyers, and larger vessels of the fleet seriously damaged Iraqi command and communication facilities. On 28 February, President George H. W. Bush declared a ceasefire after a ground war that had lasted only 100 hours. The Iraqi war effort had completely collapsed. The Gulf War became an example of the continued importance of naval units such as destroyers in joint operations with ground forces in modern warfare.

As in the past, the perceived value of destroyers and frigates in warfare partially drove their continued construction after 1991, although by the end of that year the Cold War ended with the collapse of the Soviet Union. From 1992 to the present, the United States has continued production of the *Arleigh Burke*–class Aegis destroyers and now operates an additional 48 vessels. Of these, 21 have improved helicopter facilities. These modern vessels are replacing all the destroyers of the Cold War era, as the United States no longer faces a large naval opponent such as the Soviet Union. By 2004, all of the *Spruance*-class destroyers not equipped with a VLS system, received during refits beginning in the early 1990s, had been decommissioned, as well as some of the modernized vessels, leaving only 10 of the original 31 units in service. The surviving units will eventually be removed from service as well. All of the *Kidd*-class destroyers are also laid up pending disposal while the units of the *Charles F. Adams, Farragut,* and *Forrest Sherman* classes have been scrapped. The number of frigates in the U.S. Navy is also being greatly decreased. Of the 54 units of the *Oliver Hazard Perry*–type frigate, 33 remain operational. The United States has sold many of the frigates of this class to other powers that include Turkey, Egypt, Bahrain, and Poland. As a result of cutbacks, the U.S. Navy currently maintains 38 destroyers and 33 frigates.

This force strength is on par with that of Russia since the collapse of the Soviet Union. Financial difficulties have rendered the former Soviet Navy a shadow of its former self, as there is not a great deal of money to provide for new construction. Production has not ended, and in 1993 the Russians commissioned one frigate of an improved *Krivak* design. This vessel, however, represents the only new unit in service (as of 2004) and certainly cannot make up for the losses of the fleet through financial cutbacks. Of the enormous number of destroyers and frigates produced by the Soviet Union, only 1 of the 18-ship *Kashin* class remains, and that unit is not fully operational. In addition, 15 of the 42 *Krivak*-class frigates are in service and 22 of the 43-unit *Grisha*-class frigates are operational. The frigate fleet also includes the 11 vessels of the *Parchim* class. However, the frigates are largely coastal defense vessels ill-suited to blue-water operations. In 2004, Russia operated 61 frigates of oceangoing capability and 33 smaller frigates.

In Western Europe, the principal naval powers of the post–Cold War age remain France, Great Britain, and Italy. Construction in

France since 1991 has centered on frigates. Between 1992 and 2001, France commissioned six *Floreal*-class frigates and five *Lafayette*-class vessels equipped with Exocet and SAM systems. The design of the latter generated interest abroad and has led to orders from Saudi Arabia, Taiwan, and Singapore. These new vessels joined the French Navy, which retained several of its Cold War–era destroyers and frigates. In 2004, France operated 12 destroyers: 7 *Georges Leygues*–class vessels, 2 *Cassard* class, 1 of the *Suffren* type, and 2 *Tourville*-class units. Additionally, nine of the *D'Estienne d'Orves*–class frigates remain in service. Great Britain continued its *Duke*-class frigate program and constructed 13 more of the type. The nation currently operates these new vessels as well as 11 destroyers and 4 *Broadsword*-class frigates. Italy commissioned only four frigates of the *Artigliere* class in the mid-1990s that now operate in an Italian Navy that counts four destroyers and eight other frigates as part of its strength.

Aside from these powers are other European nations whose fleets are smaller. Germany, which emerged from the Cold War as a united country through the reunification of West Germany and East Germany, has continued construction of destroyers and frigates as the core of its navy. Between 1994 and 1996, four *Brandenburg*-class frigates entered service. In 2003, the first of a new three-ship class of destroyer began its sea trials. This ship, *Sachsen*, measures 469 feet by 56 feet by 22 feet, 5 inches, displaces 5,960 tons, and is capable of a maximum speed of 29 knots. The armament includes a 32-cell VLS system and eight Harpoon missiles. When ready for service, this vessel will join seven *Bremen*-class frigates and, technically speaking, one of the old *Lutjens*-class destroyers. This latter vessel is only partially operational due to severe mechanical problems as a result of its age. The class that includes *Sachsen* is slated to replace this ship. Both the Netherlands and Spain have also augmented their fleets with new destroyers and frigates. Among the most impressive of these is the Spanish *Alvaro de Bazan* class, whose first unit is currently in service. This vessel is equipped with the Aegis system and a 48-cell VLS.

Several powers other than those of the West have also continued their destroyer and frigate programs in the wake of the Cold War. Chief among these is Japan. Between 1996 and 2002, the Japanese commissioned nine *Murasame*-class destroyers. These vessels, while a capable design, are slightly less advanced than the four *Kongo*-class destroyers that entered service between 1993 and 1998. These ships are improved *Arleigh Burke*–class destroyers that, like the U.S.

Navy design, are equipped with the Aegis system. Currently, Japan operates one of the largest naval forces in the world in terms of destroyers and frigates. In 2004, the Japanese Navy included 45 destroyers. The fleet also maintains nine frigates with two of these being built after 1991. As the Japanese Navy is dedicated to homeland defense, these ships counter the program of China, Japan's neighbor, that continues to forge ahead in destroyer and frigate production as part of its plan to extend its influence in Asia through the use of a fleet comprised of oceangoing craft. Between 1992 and 2004 the Chinese constructed 4 destroyers and 11 frigates. Currently, the Chinese operate 4 destroyers and 31 frigates. In addition to these Far East powers is India. The Indian Navy currently operates eight destroyers and four frigates. Three of the destroyers and one of the frigates represent construction since the end of the Cold War.

Added to these three powers are the host of nations around the world that base their fleets on a smaller number of destroyers and frigates that are either old units procured from other nations or new vessels purchased from foreign shipyards. Examples of the former practice include Chile, which currently operates three former British *County*-class destroyers, and Turkey, which bought eight old U.S. *Oliver Hazard Perry*–class frigates. Instances of the latter occurrence abound, as in the case of Thailand, which bought six frigates from China between 1991 and 1995.

The crews of today's modern destroyers and frigates operate in an environment where most aspects of life have changed since the dawn of the missile age. These define present-day life aboard destroyers and frigates. Education for officers and regular ratings has become much more complex as a result of the use of computers, missile systems, and nuclear power. Officers continue to receive education in naval schools, where many graduate with specialty degrees in specific systems aboard ship. These include the United States Naval Academy in Annapolis, Maryland, and the Admiral Nakhimov Naval Preparatory School in Russia. Regular ratings receive more general education both on land and through experience at sea. These sailors are currently recruited as volunteers in the case of Western nations, whereas those in the Soviet Navy, and later that of Russia after the fall of communism, are conscripts and volunteers.

In some cases, the need for efficiency has led to the abolishment of time-honored traditions that existed since the Age of Fighting Sail. One of these is the use of alcohol aboard destroyers, frigates, and warships in general. In 1970, the Royal Navy dispensed with the practice of providing rum rations to its sailors. The Soviet Navy also abolished alcohol aboard ship, but with less success. Oftentimes, Soviet sailors procured alcohol on the black market or distilled beverages from industrial alcohol used to clean machinery aboard ship. This resulted from generally poor conditions aboard Soviet, and later Russian, ships that led the crews to seek comfort through alcohol.

The greater need for well-educated and effective crews has also led to a drive in many navies to provide not only for officers and ratings but also for their families to attract people to service at sea. The Royal Navy has instituted programs in keeping with the British welfare state in which financial allowances are given to assist sailors in the purchase of housing for their families. The British also provide money for the children of sailors to attend boarding schools. The United States has also followed this course in an effort to attract people to naval service. In 1981, the pay of U.S. sailors was increased to a level that closely mirrored pay in the civilian sector to allow families to better provide for themselves.

Another change in the life of sailors is living conditions aboard ship. The crew compartments are generally more spacious, and bunks have replaced the hammocks of the past that had been shipped in the destroyers and frigates of most navies since the Age of Fighting Sail. Vessels now contain all basic amenities, such as air-conditioning, in addition to a variety of extracurricular equipment that includes Internet access and e-mail, satellite TV, and gymnasiums. Food has also improved markedly in many navies. Life aboard many of the world's destroyers and frigates, particularly those of the United States, is a much better experience today than in the past.

These living conditions have been affected in Western navies through the integration of the sexes. Although women served in Western navies during World War II, their participation was land-based rather than in combat. This situation has changed with the inclusion of women among the crews of warships. An example is the U.S. Navy. In 1976, the petitioning of women's advocacy groups and political representatives led to the acceptance of women in the United States Naval Academy in an effort to make military service open to all. By 1999, women comprised 13 percent of the U.S. Navy; of 117 combatant ships in service, 57 had integrated crews.[10]

Despite this myriad of changes, some conditions aboard destroyers and frigates remain the same and probably will never be altered. Life aboard these ships is still one that includes rigid discipline, constant drilling and training, and periods of personal hardship produced by extended deployments during which officers and sailors are separated from families. These aspects have always been present, and they still define life at sea. They are the price that the people who crew the destroyers and frigates of the world pay to fulfill the strategic requirements that are charged to the world's warships by all maritime powers.

These men and women who operate destroyers and frigates do so in an environment, despite the end of the Cold War, where duties abound. In today's world a significant duty for destroyers is the projection of power abroad. This duty reveals danger through the rising threat of global terrorism. On 12 October 2000, the *Arleigh Burke*–class destroyer *Cole* entered the port of Aden, Yemen, in the Middle East for refueling and suffered the detonation of explosives by suicide bombers aboard a small boat that was among those hired to guide the warship to its moorings. The blast blew a hole in the side of *Cole* that measured some 20 feet by 40 feet. Although the crew saved the vessel, the attack crippled it and killed 17 sailors and wounded 31 others. The attack was a serious blow to U.S. prestige in the Middle East and highlights the fact that destroyers and frigates operate in an environment of constant danger despite the fact that the Cold War has ended and the world is not in a state of general armed conflict. This situation is more apparent than ever since the terrorist attacks on 11 September 2001 that resulted in the destruction of the World Trade towers in New York City. In the unfolding war on terrorism, destroyers and frigates continue to project power overseas. As the war is primarily a land-based endeavor, direct action is limited. Even so, destroyers and frigates have participated actively in the war through the 2003 OPERATION IRAQI FREEDOM designed to topple Saddam Hussein from power. In the opening stages of this effort, the U.S. Navy counted 15 destroyers and 6 frigates in its strike force. Those destroyers equipped with Tomahawk cruise missiles were used to attack targets in advance of the ground offensive. On 20 March 2003, two *Arleigh Burke*–class destroyers joined two *Ticonderoga* class cruisers to launch 40 Tomahawk missiles at the Iraqi capital of Baghdad. On the same day, a further 50 Tomahawks were launched against other Iraqi targets by an additional *Arleigh Burke*–class vessel and American and British attack submarines.

Nevertheless, the future of destroyers is somewhat in doubt given their large construction costs versus smaller frigates, which, with the exception of the very few nations such as the United States and Japan, constitute the majority of warship construction. At present, Germany, Japan, the Netherlands, and Spain are all in the process of constructing new destroyers. In the case of Germany, these are two additional vessels of the *Sachsen* type. Japan will launch an improved *Kongo*-class destroyer in 2007 while the Netherlands is building three AAW destroyers. Spain is building an additional *Alvaro de Bazan*–class destroyer and has contracted for two more. The numbers pale in comparison to frigates.

Some of these programs are multinational to cut design costs. Among these is a frigate design, known to many as the *Horizon* class, produced from collaboration originally between France, Great Britain, and Italy, although Britain dropped out of the project. The hull of one of these vessels will measure 130 feet and mount engines that can produce a maximum speed of 27 knots. The armament of these multi-role frigates will be Exocet missiles, a SAM system, a gun, torpedoes, and a helicopter. France has contracted for 17 such ships, with 2008 being projected as the year of delivery for the first units. Italy issued orders for two of these ships, to be delivered in 2007 and 2009. Aside from joint projects, work also progresses on individual, highly advanced frigate designs in a myriad of nations around the world.

Despite the trend toward frigates, the story of the destroyer will continue for some years owing to the DD(X) program of the United States, which calls for vessels with hulls designed to mask detection by enemy sensors, a quiet electrical-drive propulsion system, and various weapons to make the warship a multirole craft. Although still in the design stage, the U.S. government projects as many as 60 orders of DD(X) vessels over the coming years. It will also endure through existing units, as all naval nations appreciate their value in a world increasingly fraught with the uncertainties of the post–Cold War age, particularly the war on global terror. Destroyers, as well as the smaller frigates, will remain at the forefront of global naval operations until unseated by still smaller, cheaper, more effective craft.

ENDNOTES

1. Norman Friedman, *U.S. Destroyers: An Illustrated Design History* (Annapolis, MD: Naval Institute Press, 1982), p. 258.

2. William G. Schofield, *Destroyers: 60 Years* (New York: Rand McNally, 1962), p. 105.

3. Norman Polmar, *Guide to the Soviet Navy* (Annapolis, MD: Naval Institute Press, 1986), p. 410.

4. Friedman, *U.S. Destroyers*, pp. 285–287.

5. Ibid.

6. Robert Gardiner, *Conway's All the World's Fighting Ships, 1947–1982—Part I: The Western Powers* (Annapolis, MD: Naval Institute Press, 1983), p. 215.

7. Max Hastings and Simon Jenkins, *The Battle for the Falklands* (New York: W. W. Norton, 1983), pp. 346–348.

8. Bernard Prézelin, *Combat Fleets of the World 1993: Their Ships, Aircraft, and Armament* (Annapolis, MD: Naval Institute Press, 1993), p. xv.

9. Ibid., p. 833.

10. Ronald Spector, *At War at Sea: Sailors and Naval Combat in the Twentieth Century* (New York: Viking, 2001), p. 394.

Destroyers and Frigates of the World

DESTROYERS, 1850s–1918

France *Durandal* Class (1899–1900)
France *Branlebas* (1907–1908)
France *Chasseur* Class (1909–1910)
Germany *D10* (1898)
Germany *S.90* (1898–1901)
Germany *S.31* Class (1913–1915)
Germany *H.145* Class (1917–1918)
Great Britain *Vesuvius* (1874)
Great Britain *Lightning* (1877)
Great Britain *Swift* (1885)
Great Britain *Rattlesnake* (1887)
Great Britain *Havock* and *Hornet* (1894)
Great Britain *Desperate* type (1897)
Great Britain *Viper* (1900)
Great Britain *River* Class (1904–1905)
Great Britain *Cricket* Class (1906–1909)
Italy *Fulmine* (1898)
Italy *Indomito* Class (1912–1913)
Japan *Shirakumo* Class (1902)
Japan *Sakura* Class (1912)
Russia *Pruitki* (1895)
Russia *Bespokoiny* Class (1913–1914)
United States *Farragut* (1899)
United States *Bainbridge* Class (1902)
United States *Paulding* Class (1909–1910)

United States *Cassin* Class (1912–1913)
United States *Clemson* Class (1918–1920)

DESTROYERS AND FRIGATES, 1919–1945

France *Chacal* Class (1923–1924)
France *Guépard* Class (1928–1930)
France *Le Fantasque* Class (1933–1934)
France *Mogador* Class (1936–1937)
Germany *1934* Class (1935)
Germany *1936* Class (1937–1938)
Great Britain *E* and *F* Classes (1934)
Great Britain *Tribal* Class (1937–1946)
Great Britain *Hunt* Class (1939–1940)
Great Britain *River* Class (1942–1944)
Great Britain *Ch*, *Co*, and *Cr* Classes (1945–1946)
Italy *Navigatori* Class (1928–1930)
Italy *Pegaso* Class (1936–1937)
Japan *Mutsuki* Class (1925–1927)
Japan *Fubuki* Class (1927–1930)
Japan *Hatsuharu* Class (1932–1934)
Japan *Kagero* Class (1938–1940)
Japan *Akitsuki* Class (1941–1944)
Soviet Union *Gnevnyi* Class (1936–1941)
Soviet Union *Storozhevoi* Class (1938–1940)
United States *Farragut* Class (1934–1935)
United States *Sims* Class (1938–1939)
United States *Benson/Gleaves* Class (1939–1943)
United States *Fletcher* Class (1942–1944)
United States *Gearing* Class (1944–1946)

DESTROYERS AND FRIGATES, 1946–2004

France *Suffren* Class (1967–1970)
France *Tourville* Class (1974–1977)
France *D'Estienne d'Orves* Class (1981–1986)
France *Lafayette* Class (2001)
Germany *Bremen* Class (1982–1990)
Great Britain *County* Class (1962–1970)

Great Britain *Leander* Class (1963–1973)
Great Britain *Amazon* Class (1974–1978)
Great Britain *Sheffield* Class (1975–1982)
Great Britain *Duke* Class (1990–2002)
Italy *Animoso* (*De La Penne*) Class (1993)
Italy *Artigliere* Class (1994–1996)
Japan *Amatsukaze* (1965)
Japan *Haruna* Class (1973–1974)
Japan *Asagiri* Class (1988–1991)
People's Republic of China *Jianghu I* Class (1975–1984)
Soviet Union *Kildin* Class (1958)
Soviet Union *Krupny* Class (1961)
Soviet Union *Kashin* Class (1963–1972)
Soviet Union *Krivak* Class (1970–1991)
Sweden *Halland* Class (1955–1956)
United States *Gyatt* (1956)
United States *Coontz* Class (1959–1961)
United States *Spruance* and *Kidd* Classes (1975–1983)
United States *Oliver Hazard Perry* Class (1977–1988)
United States *Arleigh Burke* Class (1991–)

AUTHOR NOTE

The destroyers and frigates listed above and discussed below are arranged alphabetically by country within three eras. In each country subset, the destroyers and frigates are listed chronologically according to the dates of their completion. The data concerning each vessel and class are contained in the categories described below. When referring to a class of ship, the data concerning the attributes of the type are that of the lead ship of the class.

The information and statistics included for each entry are:

Units: In the case of a class of ships, all vessels are named.
Type and Significance: A brief statement concerning the type and importance of the ship or class of vessel.
Dates of Construction: Includes the dates when construction began and the dates when a ship or class was either launched or completed.

Hull Dimensions: The measurement of a hull's length, beam, and draft (when known) in feet and inches.

Displacement: In most cases, the tonnage of the vessel is the standard displacement, meaning the weight of the ship when fully equipped but without fuel.

Armor: Side armor, deck armor, barbette armor, and turret protection are listed in measurements of inches.

Armament: The types and size of all weaponry and how the pieces were mounted.

Machinery: The propulsion plant.

Speed: Maximum speed of the ship or class.

Complement: The number of officers and sailors who crewed the vessel.

Summary: Comments on the performance and careers of the ship or class.

DESTROYERS, 1850s–1918

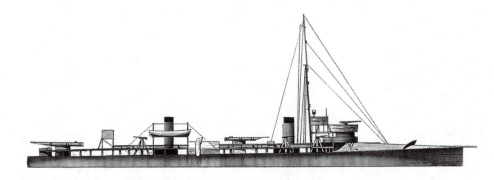

FRANCE: *DURANDAL* CLASS
Courtesy of Art-Tech/Aerospace/M.A.R.S./TRH/Navy Historical

UNITS: *Durandal, Hallebarde, Fauconneau, Espingole*

TYPE AND SIGNIFICANCE: These vessels were France's first true destroyers rather than torpedo boats.

DATES OF CONSTRUCTION: Two units launched in 1899 while another two followed in 1900.

HULL DIMENSIONS: 188'8" × 20'8" × 10'5"

DISPLACEMENT: 296 tons

ARMOR: None

ARMAMENT: One 2.5" gun, six 1.8" weapons, and two 15" torpedo tubes.

MACHINERY: Two triple-expansion engines whose power output was 4,800 horsepower that was driven by two coal-fired boilers.

SPEED: 26 knots

COMPLEMENT: 52

SUMMARY: These vessels resembled *Havock* of Great Britain. Its hull incorporated a turtleback bow intended to streamline the vessel to allow it to better cut through the water. *Espingole* was sunk in 1903 while *Durandal, Hallebarde,* and *Fauconneau* were retired from service in 1919, 1920, and 1921, respectively.

FRANCE: *BRANLEBAS* CLASS

Courtesy of Art-Tech/Aerospace/M.A.R.S./TRH/Navy Historical

UNITS: *Branlebas, Slaive, Poignard, Sabretache, Oriflamme, Étendard, Fanion, Sape, Gabion, Fanfare*

TYPE AND SIGNIFICANCE: Unlike many destroyers of this era, these ships incorporated armor into their design.

DATES OF CONSTRUCTION: Four units were launched in 1907 while construction on another five ended in 1908. The final unit was produced the next year.

HULL DIMENSIONS: 190' × 21'7" × 7'9"

DISPLACEMENT: 339 tons

ARMOR: .75" steel belt extended over the propulsion equipment.

ARMAMENT: One 2.6" gun, six 1.8" guns, and two 17.7" torpedo tubes.

MACHINERY: Two triple-expansion engines powered by two coal-fired boilers that produced 6,700 horsepower.

SPEED: 27 knots

COMPLEMENT: 60

SUMMARY: The incorporation of armor into the design showcased the French penchant for innovation in warship design. All of these warships were operational in World War I. *Branlebas* was sunk in 1915 while *Étendard* was destroyed in 1917. The other units of the class were gradually retired over the interwar years as they became obsolete. The last vessel, *Slaive*, went to the breakers in 1932.

FRANCE: *CHASSEUR* CLASS
Courtesy of Walker Archive

UNITS: *Chasseur, Fantassin, Janissaire, Cavalier*

TYPE AND SIGNIFICANCE: The first turbine-powered and oil-fueled destroyers of the French Navy.

DATES OF CONSTRUCTION: *Chasseur* and *Fantassin* were launched in 1909; the other two units followed the next year.

HULL DIMENSIONS: 210'8" × 21'4" × 16'2" (These dimensions for the *Chasseur* only. Other units differed slightly in length and beam.)

DISPLACEMENT: 450 tons

ARMOR: None

ARMAMENT: Six 2.5" guns and three 17.7" torpedo tubes

MACHINERY: Turbines powered by four oil-fired boilers with the exception of the *Chasseur*, which had coal-fired boilers. The maximum power output was 7,200 shaft horsepower.

SPEED: 28 knots

COMPLEMENT: 79

SUMMARY: Not only were these ships the first French destroyers fitted with turbines and oil-fired boilers; they were also the first warships overall in the French Navy to incorporate oil-fired boilers into their design. Although the machinery of the vessels suffered frequent breakdowns, all served extensively in World War I primarily in the Mediterranean theater of operations. *Fantassin* was wrecked in 1916 through a collision with the French destroyer *Mameluk*. The other units survived the conflict, with *Chassuer* and *Janissaire* being removed from service in 1919 and 1920, respectively. *Cavalier* followed in 1927 after being used as a target ship.

GERMANY: *D10*

Courtesy of Naval Historical Foundation

TYPE AND SIGNIFICANCE: Germany's first destroyer.

DATES OF CONSTRUCTION: Launched in 1898.

HULL DIMENSIONS: 217' × 19'6" × 7'9"

DISPLACEMENT: 365 tons

ARMOR: None

ARMAMENT: Five 2" guns and three 17.7" torpedo tubes

MACHINERY: Two triple-expansion engines driven by coal-fired boilers that produced a maximum power output of 5,600 horsepower.

SPEED: 27 knots

COMPLEMENT: 47

SUMMARY: This vessel was not an indigenous design, being built by Britain's Thornycroft shipbuilding company. As a result, it resembled British vessels built by the same organization. By the opening of World War I, *D10* was aged to the point that the majority of its wartime career was in coastal defense duties. It was scrapped in 1922.

GERMANY: *S.90* CLASS
Courtesy of Naval Historical Foundation

UNITS: *S.90–S.101*

TYPE AND SIGNIFICANCE: These were Germany's first domestically designed and constructed destroyers. They are among the first that incorporated a raised forecastle into their design.

DATES OF CONSTRUCTION: Launched between 1898 and 1901.

HULL DIMENSIONS: 206'10" × 22'11" × 9'4"

DISPLACEMENT: 388 tons

ARMOR: None

ARMAMENT: Three 1.9" guns and three 17.7" torpedo tubes.

MACHINERY: Two triple-expansion engines powered by coal-fired boilers that generated 3,900 horsepower.

SPEED: 26.5 knots

COMPLEMENT: 55

SUMMARY: The hull of *S.90*-class units incorporated a raised forecastle rather than the turtleback bow of destroyers in other navies. Developed in Germany at the same time as the United States, the raised forecastle made ships of this class much more seaworthy than those equipped with turtleback bows. Some speed was sacrificed, making these ships slower than destroyers in some other nations. This reduction, however, was offset by the increase in their capabilities that was afforded by the new hull design. The other naval powers of the world eventually adopted the feature of the raised forecastle.

All of these craft save one were scrapped by the early 1920s. The exception was the *S.90*, which sank on 17 October 1914, after running aground during the siege of Tsingtao, China, in World War I.

GERMANY: *S.31* CLASS
Courtesy of Wüerttembergische Landesbibliothek

UNITS: *S.31–S.36*

TYPE AND SIGNIFICANCE: The last German destroyers launched before World War I and the first to incorporate solely oil-fired boilers into their design.

DATES OF CONSTRUCTION: All units were launched between 1913 and 1915.

HULL DIMENSIONS: 261'2" × 27'4" × 9'2"

DISPLACEMENT: 802 tons

ARMOR: None

ARMAMENT: Three 3.45" guns, six 19.7" torpedo tubes, and 24 mines.

MACHINERY: Turbines powered by three oil-fired boilers that produced 23,516 shaft horsepower.

SPEED: 33.5 knots

COMPLEMENT: 83

SUMMARY: These vessels are indicative of German design in the years leading up to World War I in that they generally mounted fewer, slightly smaller guns than their British counterparts, a reflection of the continued German belief in the primary role of destroyers being torpedo attack. The use of mines represents the German belief before World War I that destroyers could assume the role of minelayer in addition to their primary mission. Although their oil-fired boilers made them the first German destroyers equipped with that innovation, they also had the unusual feature of a second auxiliary rudder placed beneath the bow in case the other was rendered inoperable in combat.

All served extensively in World War I. *S.31* and *S.34* were sunk in 1915 and 1918, respectively, by mines. A British submarine torpedoed and sunk S.33 in 1918, while S.35 was sunk by heavy gunfire from British battleships in the 1916 Battle of Jutland. The crews of S.32 and S.36 scuttled their vessels in 1919 at the British naval base of Scapa Flow while the Imperial German Navy lay there pending the conclusion of the Paris Peace Conference that ended World War I. These latter two units were raised in 1925 and scrapped.

GERMANY: *H.145* CLASS

Courtesy of Wüerttembergische Landesbibliothek

UNITS: *H.145–H.147*

TYPE AND SIGNIFICANCE: The last destroyers built for the Imperial German Navy in World War I.

DATES OF CONSTRUCTION: *H.145* was launched in 1917, while the other two units were launched in early 1918.

HULL DIMENSIONS: 277'3" × 27'7" × 11'2"

DISPLACEMENT: 990 tons

ARMOR: None

ARMAMENT: Four 4.1" guns, six 19.7" torpedo tubes, and 24 mines.

MACHINERY: Turbines powered by three oil-fired boilers that generated 23,849 shaft horsepower.

SPEED: 34 knots

COMPLEMENT: 105

SUMMARY: These destroyers represent a shift in German design from vessels whose armament emphasized the torpedo to larger, more heavy-gunned warships. Even so, the primary mission of these ships, as those in the past for Germany, was torpedo attack. None of these craft had time to justify their existence in World War I, as they were launched at the close of the conflict. *H.145* was scuttled in 1919 at the British naval base of Scapa Flow while the Imperial German Navy lay there pending the conclusion of the peace conference in Paris that ended World War I. France received both *H.146* and *H.147* at the end of the war as reparations from Germany. *H.147* was scrapped in 1933, while *H.146* followed two years later after service in the French Navy.

GREAT BRITAIN: *VESUVIUS*
Courtesy of Art-Tech/Aerospace/M.A.R.S./TRH/Navy Historical

TYPE AND SIGNIFICANCE: The first British warship designed specifically for torpedo attack.

DATES OF CONSTRUCTION: Construction on *Vesuvius* began in 1873 and was completed in 1874.

HULL DIMENSIONS: 90' × 22' × 8'6"

DISPLACEMENT: 245 tons

ARMOR: None

ARMAMENT: One 16" torpedo tube mounted in the bow.

MACHINERY: A compound engine driven by coal-fired boilers capable of producing 350 horsepower.

SPEED: 9.7 knots

COMPLEMENT: 15

SUMMARY: This ship represents an early design step forward toward the destroyer. It proved an unsuccessful design as the relatively deep draft for the size of the hull produced an inordinately high amount of drag in a seaway, which greatly affected the speed of the vessel. As a result, most battleships, the principal prey of a ship like *Vesuvius*, were faster than the torpedo craft and could outrun it. The design problem of *Vesuvius* led quickly to the vessel being removed from active service in favor of use as an experimental craft. The vessel went to the scrap yard in 1924.

GREAT BRITAIN: *LIGHTNING*
Courtesy of Art-Tech/Aerospace/M.A.R.S./TRH/Navy Historical

TYPE AND SIGNIFICANCE: Britain's first torpedo boat.

DATES OF CONSTRUCTION: Construction commenced in 1876 and was completed the following year.

HULL DIMENSIONS: 87' × 10'8" × 5'2

DISPLACEMENT: 32.5 tons

ARMOR: None

ARMAMENT: The original armament consisted of two torpedo cages that could be lowered into the water on either side of the craft. These proved impractical and were replaced by a torpedo tube in the bow.

MACHINERY: A compound engine driven by coal-fired boilers that produced a maximum of 460 horsepower.

SPEED: 19 knots

COMPLEMENT: 15

SUMMARY: This very tiny craft was intended to fire torpedoes after steering the ship directly at the target to offer the smallest silhouette and thus make it harder for the enemy's gunners to hit it. The small size essentially dictated its use in coastal defense operations rather than blue-water duties. Even so, all naval powers recognized the value of torpedo boats as these cheap craft could destroy expensive battleships with their torpedoes. The potential threat posed by *Lightning* ultimately led to ships designed to hunt them down and prevent their torpedo attacks. These vessels would be destroyers.

The hull of *Lightning*, like all torpedo boats and many destroyers, was not very strong as a heavy hull would impede the vessel's speed. Consequently, in 1896 *Lightning* went to the breakers with a highly degraded hull.

GREAT BRITAIN: *SWIFT*
Courtesy of Wüerttembergische Landesbibliothek

TYPE AND SIGNIFICANCE: British warship designed as a torpedo boat catcher that proved to be an antecedent toward the production of the first true destroyer.

DATES OF CONSTRUCTION: Laid down in 1884 and launched in 1885.

HULL DIMENSIONS: 153'8" × 17'6" × 9'6"

DISPLACEMENT: 137 tons

ARMOR: None

ARMAMENT: Four 3-pounder guns and three 14" torpedo tubes.

MACHINERY: Engines that produced a maximum output of 1,330 horsepower

SPEED: 24 knots

COMPLEMENT: 25

SUMMARY: This vessel was classed as a torpedo boat but was larger and more heavily armed than preceding warships. The reason for this was that the designers intended the vessel to protect the capital ships of the battle fleet against torpedo boat attack. As such, *Swift* was an early prototype of the destroyer.

Swift enjoyed a long career that included service in World War I when the British fitted hydrophones and depth charges to the vessel for ASW. *Swift* was scrapped in 1921.

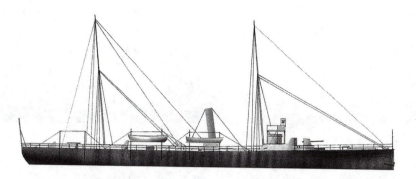

GREAT BRITAIN: *RATTLESNAKE* CLASS
Courtesy of Art-Tech/Aerospace/M.A.R.S./TRH/Navy Historical

UNITS: *Rattlesnake, Grasshopper, Sandfly, Spider*

TYPE AND SIGNIFICANCE: These vessels were improved torpedo boat catchers and another design step toward the destroyer.

DATES OF CONSTRUCTION: *Rattlesnake* was laid down in 1885 and completed in 1887; the other units were launched in 1888.

HULL DIMENSIONS: 200'(pp) × 23' × 10'4"

DISPLACEMENT: 550 tons (*Rattlesnake*) while the other units displaced 526 tons.

ARMOR: A .75" protective deck over the machinery and engines.

ARMAMENT: One 5" gun, six 3-pound pieces, and four 14" torpedo tubes.

MACHINERY: Two triple-expansion engines driven by coal-fired boilers that rendered 2,700 horsepower.

SPEED: 19.25 knots

COMPLEMENT: 66

SUMMARY: These vessels were enlarged versions of *Swift* and resulted from the continuing quest by the British for a torpedo boat catcher to counter the threat of small torpedo boats versus battleships. Labeled by the British as torpedo gunboats (TGBs), the warships of the *Rattlesnake* class were not the ultimate solution to the threat posed by the torpedo boat. They were capable of more operations at sea rather than just coastal defense owing to the incorporation of the triple-expansion engine in their design, which consumed less coal, but their top speed was a glaring problem, as it was not high enough to permit the ships to overtake the fast torpedo boats that they were intended to destroy. They also were not very seaworthy and limited in range due to their relatively small size. All four vessels were sold to scrap yards between 1903 and 1910.

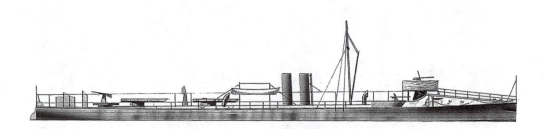

GREAT BRITAIN: *HAVOCK* AND *HORNET*
Courtesy of Art-Tech/Aerospace/M.A.R.S./TRH/Navy Historical

UNITS: *Havock, Hornet*

TYPE AND SIGNIFICANCE: Generally regarded as the world's first destroyers.

DATES OF CONSTRUCTION: Construction on both *Havock* and *Hornet* commenced in 1892 and ended in 1894.

HULL DIMENSIONS: 185' × 18'6" × 7'3"

DISPLACEMENT: 275 tons

ARMOR: None

ARMAMENT: One 12-pound quick-firing gun, three 6-pound quick-firing weapons, and three 18" torpedo tubes.

MACHINERY: Triple expansion engines that, in the case of *Havock,* were powered by coal-fired, locomotive style boilers. New water-tube boilers drove the engines of the Hornet.

SPEED: 27 knots

COMPLEMENT: 42

SUMMARY: These ships were the first to truly pose a viable solution to the torpedo boat, as their top speed allowed them to run down their opponents. Their high speed was partially the result of the turtleback bow. These ships suffered from poor seaworthiness that resulted from their lightly built hulls and machinery breakdowns caused by the strain put on the engines to attain their top speed. *Hornet* was broken up for scrap in 1909; *Havock* followed in 1912.

GREAT BRITAIN: *DESPERATE*-TYPE
Courtesy of Art-Tech/Aerospace/M.A.R.S./TRH/Navy Historical

UNITS: *Desperate, Fame, Foam, Mallard*

TYPE AND SIGNIFICANCE: These vessels are among the first of the British 30-knotters that dominated construction in the country in the last decade of the nineteenth century.

DATES OF CONSTRUCTION: All units were laid down in 1895 and completed in 1897.

HULL DIMENSIONS: 210' × 19'6" × 7'

DISPLACEMENT: 310 tons

ARMOR: None

ARMAMENT: One 12-pounder quick-firing gun, five 6-pounder quick-firing weapons, and two 18" torpedo tubes.

MACHINERY: Triple expansion engines powered by coal-fired boilers that produced a maximum power output of 5,700 horsepower.

SPEED: 30 knots

COMPLEMENT: 63

SUMMARY: These ships were the product of the British desire by the turn of the twentieth century for destroyers of the greatest speed possible. The 30-knotters, of which these ships were a part, were completed between 1896 and 1902 and possessed larger hulls to house the more powerful machinery needed to attain the extra knots sought by the British Admiralty. Meeting the Admiralty requirement came at the cost of reliability and sea-keeping. Due to the great emphasis on speed, these vessels were lightly built and their engines strained to generate their maximum output. Oftentimes the engines broke down or their vibration led to stress on the hull that could warp it or crack the plating, thus causing leaks that endangered the ships.

Their small hulls, like so many destroyers at the time, were also too small to carry the fuel and supplies necessary for extended operations.

The problems with the machinery and structural weakness led to the scrapping of *Foam* in 1914, but the other units served in World War I. *Desperate* and *Mallard* went to the breakers in 1920; *Fame* followed a year later.

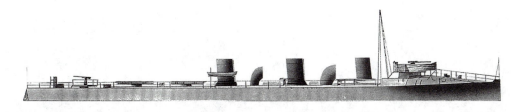

GREAT BRITAIN: *VIPER*

Courtesy of Art-Tech/Aerospace/M.A.R.S./TRH/Navy Historical

TYPE AND SIGNIFICANCE: A destroyer, *Viper* was the first warship in the world equipped with turbine engines.

DATES OF CONSTRUCTION: *Viper* was laid down in 1898 and completed in 1900.

HULL DIMENSIONS: 210'3.5" (pp) × 21'

DISPLACEMENT: 344 tons

ARMOR: None

ARMAMENT: One 12-pounder quick-firing gun, five 6-pounder quick-firing weapons, and two 18" torpedo tubes.

MACHINERY: Turbines supplied by coal-fired boilers.

SPEED: 33.75 knots

COMPLEMENT: 70

SUMMARY: The 1897 debut of the turbine-powered vessel *Turbina* designed by Charles Parson led the British Admiralty to commission private shipyards to produce turbine-powered destroyers. *Viper* was the first to enter service, but the vessel did not yield much experience with turbines in warships due to its being wrecked in the English Channel in 1901.

GREAT BRITAIN: *RIVER* CLASS
Courtesy of Art-Tech/Aerospace/M.A.R.S./TRH/Navy Historical

UNITS: *Erne, Ettrick, Exe, Kennet, Jed, Derwent, Eden, Foyle, Itchen, Ribble, Teviot, Usk, Welland, Cherwell, Dee, Waveney, Arun, Blackwater, Chelmer, Colne, Gala, Garry, Swale, Ure, Wear, Ness, Nith, Liffey, Moy, Ouse, Boyne, Doon, Kale, Rother*

TYPE AND SIGNIFICANCE: Destroyers that are generally regarded as the world's first oceangoing destroyers.

DATES OF CONSTRUCTION: Completed between 1904 and 1905.

HULL DIMENSIONS: 233'6" × 23'6" × 9'9" (*Erne*)

DISPLACEMENT: 550 tons (*Erne*)

ARMOR: None

ARMAMENT: One 12-pound quick-firing gun, five 6-pound quick-firing guns, and two 18" torpedo tubes.

MACHINERY: Triple expansion engines or turbines powered by coal-fired boilers that produced a maximum output

between 7,000 and 7,500 horsepower.

SPEED: 26 knots

COMPLEMENT: 70

SUMMARY: Several different private firms built these vessels to Britush Admiralty specifications. These ships are considered by most scholars as the world's first oceangoing destroyers, as the German *S.90* class and the U.S. *Bainbridge* class that preceded the British ships and were similar in design proved to be less seaworthy and of lesser endurance. Despite their reduced speed in comparison to the British 30-knotters, the reduction was acceptable given the advantages that it presented. These ships, with their raised forecastles, had better sea-keeping abilities than past British destroyers. In addition, the surrender of some power decreased mechanical breakdowns through lessened wear on the engines. Finally, the raised forecastle and internal arrangement of the hulls of the *River*-class units allowed for shipping more coal and thus improving their cruising radius. The advantages of the *River* class led all other naval powers to incorporate features of their design into their own vessels.

Gala and *Blackwater* were lost in collision in 1908 and 1909, respectively, while *Cherwell* and *Dee* were scrapped months after completion in 1904. The other units served in World War I. *Eden, Derwent, Kale, Itchen,* and *Foyle* were destroyed in the conflict. The surviving units were broken up between 1919 and 1920.

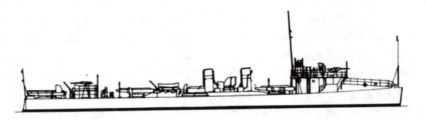

GREAT BRITAIN: *CRICKET* CLASS
Courtesy of Art-Tech/Aerospace/M.A.R.S./TRH/Navy Historical

UNITS: *Cricket, Dragonfly, Firefly, Sandfly, Spider, Gadfly, Glowworm, Gnat, Grasshopper, Greenfly, Mayfly, Moth, TB13–TB36*

TYPE AND SIGNIFICANCE: The units of the *Cricket* class were the first in the world to use oil-fired boilers rather than coal-fired ones.

DATES OF CONSTRUCTION: Launched over a period between 1906 and 1909.

HULL DIMENSIONS: 180' × 17'6" × 6'

DISPLACEMENT: 225 tons

ARMOR: None

ARMAMENT: Two 12-pounder quick-firing guns and three 18" torpedo tubes.

MACHINERY: Turbines powered by oil-fueled boilers that generated 3,750 horsepower.

SPEED: 26 knots

COMPLEMENT: 35

SUMMARY: The British intended these destroyers for only coastal duties owing to the nature of their relatively small hulls. Nevertheless, they proved unseaworthy in general and are important only for their use of oil fuel. All units were involved in World War I with *Grasshopper, TB13,* and *TB24* being sunk in collisions. Mines destroyed *Greenfly* and *Moth.* The surviving units were sold for scrap between 1919 and 1922.

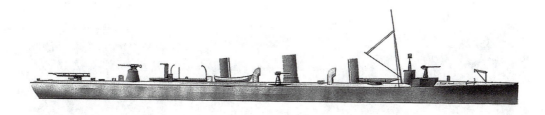

ITALY: *FULMINE*

Courtesy of Art-Tech/Aerospace/M.A.R.S./TRH/Navy Historical

TYPE AND SIGNIFICANCE: *Fulmine* was Italy's first domestically produced destroyer.

DATES OF CONSTRUCTION: Laid down in 1897 and completed the following year.

HULL DIMENSIONS: 203'11.5" × 21' × 7'6.5"

DISPLACEMENT: 293 tons

ARMOR: None

ARMAMENT: The original armament consisted of five 2.2" guns and three 14" torpedo tubes. In 1901, this was altered to one 3" gun, three 2.2" pieces, and two 14" torpedo tubes.

MACHINERY: Triple expansion engines powered by four coal-fired boilers that produced a maximum power output of 4,729 horsepower.

SPEED: 24 knots

COMPLEMENT: 50

SUMMARY: Although being a step forward for Italy in terms of domestic warship production, Italian naval officials considered *Fulmine* an unsuccessful design. As a result, the vessel's only value was to act as an experimental craft to yield information for future construction. The vessel went to the scrap yard in 1921.

ITALY: *INDOMITO* CLASS
Courtesy of Walker Archive

UNITS: *Indomito, Intrepido, Irrequieto, Impavido, Impetuoso, Insidioso*

TYPE AND SIGNIFICANCE: These vessels were the first Italian destroyers to mount turbines driven by oil-fueled boilers.

DATES OF CONSTRUCTION: *Indomito, Intrepido,* and *Irrequieto* were launched in 1912 while the other three units followed the next year.

HULL DIMENSIONS: 239'6" × 24' × 7'11"

DISPLACEMENT: 672 tons

ARMOR: None

ARMAMENT: One 4.7" gun, four 3" pieces, and two 17.7" torpedo tubes.

MACHINERY: Turbines driven by four oil-fired boilers that produced a maximum of 17,620 horsepower.

SPEED: 30 knots

COMPLEMENT: 80

SUMMARY: These vessels were both the first Italian destroyers to mount turbines and the first large destroyers built for the Italian Navy. All served in World War I, in which *Intrepido* and *Impetuoso* were sunk. The Italians scrapped three of the units in 1937; the last, *Insidioso,* served in World War II. The Germans seized the vessel in late 1943 for use in their navy, but in August 1944 a U.S. torpedo plane sank the ship.

JAPAN: *SHIRAKUMO* CLASS

Courtesy of Art-Tech/Aerospace/M.A.R.S./TRH/Navy Historical

UNITS: *Shirakumo, Asashio*

TYPE AND SIGNIFICANCE: These vessels are examples of early Japanese destroyers.

DATES OF CONSTRUCTION: Construction on both units began in 1901 and ended in 1902.

HULL DIMENSIONS: 216' × 20'9" × 6'

DISPLACEMENT: 342 tons

ARMOR: None

ARMAMENT: Two 12-pound guns, four 6-pound pieces, and two 18" torpedo tubes.

MACHINERY: Triple expansion engines that generated 6,000 horsepower.

SPEED: 29 knots

COMPLEMENT: 59

SUMMARY: These vessels are indicative of Japanese destroyers of the early twentieth century in that they are British designs rather than domestic ones as Japan continued to develop its shipbuilding capacity. Both units served in World War I and were scrapped in 1923.

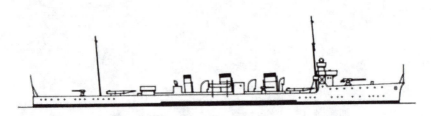

JAPAN: *SAKURA* CLASS

Courtesy of Art-Tech/Aerospace/M.A.R.S./TRH/Navy Historical

UNITS: *Sakura, Tachibana*

TYPE AND SIGNIFICANCE: These were the first destroyers built in Japanese shipyards to a domestic design.

DATES OF CONSTRUCTION: *Sakura* was laid down in 1911; *Tachibana* followed in the next year. In 1912, both units entered service.

HULL DIMENSIONS: 274' × 24' × 7'3"

DISPLACEMENT: 605 tons

ARMOR: None

ARMAMENT: One 4.7" gun, four 3.1" pieces, and four 18" torpedo tubes.

MACHINERY: Triple expansion engines powered by five boilers that produced 9,500 horsepower.

SPEED: 30 knots

COMPLEMENT: 95

SUMMARY: These ships represented a milestone for the Japanese shipbuilding industry, being the first destroyers launched in a Japanese yard to a domestic design. Although the ships were of limited value as they were primarily designed for coastal defense, the Japanese garnered valuable experience through the construction of the *Sakura* class. Both vessels went to the scrap yards in 1933 after extensive service that included World War I.

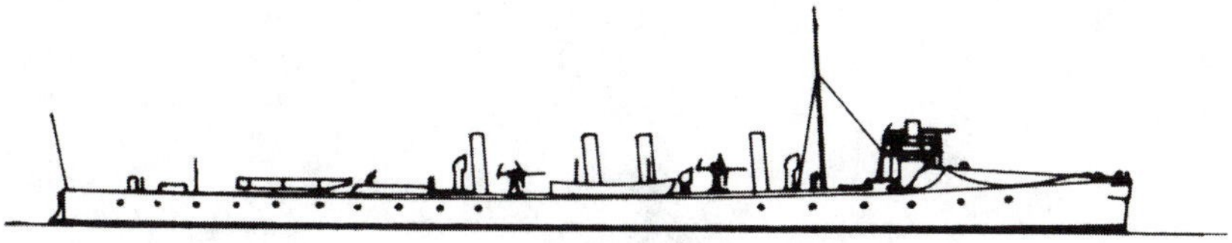

RUSSIA: *PRUITKI*

Courtesy of Art-Tech/Aerospace/M.A.R.S./TRH/Navy Historical

TYPE AND SIGNIFICANCE: *Pruitki* was one of the fastest of the world's early destroyers.

DATES OF CONSTRUCTION: Construction of *Pruitki* began in 1894 and concluded the following year.

HULL DIMENSIONS: 190' × 18'6" × 7'6"

DISPLACEMENT: 220 tons

ARMOR: None

ARMAMENT: The original armament consisted of one 11-pounder, three 3-pound guns, and two 15" torpedo tubes. Alterations later in the vessel's career led to an armament comprised of two 11-pound guns, two 15" torpedo tubes, and 10 mines.

MACHINERY: Triple expansion engines powered by eight coal-fired boilers that produced 3,800 horsepower.

SPEED: 30.2 knots

COMPLEMENT: 54

SUMMARY: *Pruitki*, known by most of the world as *Sokol*, generated a great deal of interest among naval officials outside of Russia due to its speed. After serving as a minelayer in World War I, the craft went to the breakers in 1922.

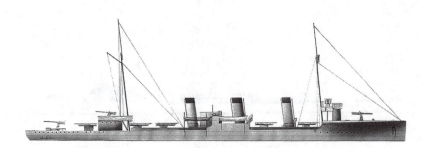

RUSSIA: *BESPOKOINY* CLASS

Courtesy of Art-Tech/Aerospace/M.A.R.S./TRH/Navy Historical

UNITS: *Bespokoiny, Gnevy, Gromki, Derzki, Pronzitelny, Bystry, Pospeshny, Pylki, Schastlivy*

TYPE AND SIGNIFICANCE: The Russian destroyers were among the early craft that mounted weaponry for use against aircraft.

DATES OF CONSTRUCTION: All units entered service between 1913 and 1914.

HULL DIMENSIONS: 321'6" × 30'6" × 10'6"

DISPLACEMENT: 1,100 tons

ARMOR: None

ARMAMENT: Three 4" guns, two 1.8" pieces, four machine guns, 10 18" torpedo tubes, and 80 mines.

MACHINERY: Turbines powered by five oil-fired boilers that generated 25,500 horsepower.

SPEED: 34 knots

COMPLEMENT: 125

SUMMARY: Russian naval officials appreciated the potential of the airplane in naval warfare and the danger it posed to surface vessels. The Russians consequently intended the 1.8" guns and the machine guns of the *Bespokoiny* class for use versus enemy aircraft. All units served in World War I, in which the Russians scuttled *Pronzitelny* and *Gromki* in June 1918; in October 1918 *Schastlivy* was wrecked. The Russians sold the surviving units for scrap in 1924 with the exception of *Bystry,* which was destroyed in 1941.

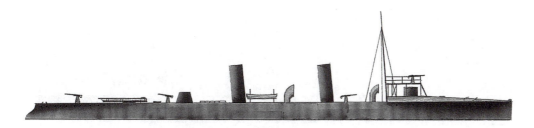

UNITED STATES: *FARRAGUT*

Courtesy of Art-Tech/Aerospace/M.A.R.S./TRH/Navy Historical

TYPE AND SIGNIFICANCE: *Farragut* was the first destroyer of the U.S. Navy.

DATES OF CONSTRUCTION: Construction began in 1897, and in 1899 the vessel was commissioned into the navy.

HULL DIMENSIONS: 214' × 20'8" × 6'

DISPLACEMENT: 279 tons

ARMOR: None

ARMAMENT: Four six-pound guns and two 18" torpedo tubes.

MACHINERY: Two triple-expansion engines powered by three coal-fired boilers that generated 5,888 horsepower.

SPEED: 30 knots

COMPLEMENT: 66

SUMMARY: Although officially classed as a torpedo boat, *Farragut* was in actuality a destroyer. In 1919, the U.S. Navy sold the ship for scrap.

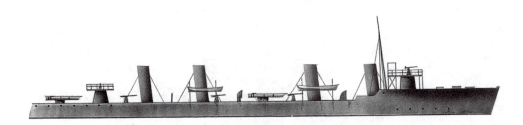

UNITED STATES: *BAINBRIDGE* CLASS
Courtesy of Art-Tech/Aerospace/M.A.R.S./TRH/Navy Historical

UNITS: *Bainbridge, Barry, Chauncey, Dale, Decatur*

TYPE AND SIGNIFICANCE: The *Bainbridge* class was the first multiple-unit class of destroyer in the U.S. Navy.

DATES OF CONSTRUCTION: All units were laid down in 1899 and completed in 1902.

HULL DIMENSIONS: 250' × 23'7" × 6'6"

DISPLACEMENT: 420 tons

ARMOR: None

ARMAMENT: Two 3" guns in single mounts, five 6-pounders, and two 18" torpedo tubes.

MACHINERY: Triple expansion engines powered by four coal-fired boilers that produced a maximum power output of 8,000 horsepower.

SPEED: 29 knots

COMPLEMENT: 73

SUMMARY: These vessels signaled the beginning of a construction plan in the United States that centered on destroyers as protection against enemy torpedo vessels. They were not extremely seaworthy vessels despite the incorporation of a raised forecastle rather than a turtleback bow. All units served in World War I, in which *Chauncey* was lost in 1917 after a collision with another vessel. The other units were sold for scrap in 1920.

UNITED STATES: *PAULDING* CLASS
Courtesy of Art-Tech/Aerospace/M.A.R.S./TRH/Navy Historical

UNITS: *Roe, Terry, Paulding, Drayton, Perkins, Sterrett, McCall, Warrington, Burrows, Mayrant*

TYPE AND SIGNIFICANCE: These vessels were the first destroyers in the U.S. Navy to use oil rather than coal for fuel.

DATES OF CONSTRUCTION: *Roe* and *Terry* were launched in 1909; the other units followed in the next year.

HULL DIMENSIONS: 293' × 26'3" × 8'

DISPLACEMENT: 742 tons

ARMOR: None

ARMAMENT: Five 3" guns in single mounts and six 18" torpedo tubes.

MACHINERY: Turbines fed by four oil-fired boilers that produced 12,000 shaft horsepower

SPEED: 29.5 knots

COMPLEMENT: 86

SUMMARY: All vessels enjoyed lengthy service and were scrapped between 1934 and 1935.

UNITED STATES: *CASSIN* CLASS
Courtesy of Art-Tech/Aerospace/M.A.R.S./TRH/Navy Historical

UNITS: *Aylwin, Balch, Parker, Benham, Cassin, Cummings, Duncan, Downs*

TYPE AND SIGNIFICANCE: These destroyers were the first of the U.S. 1,000-tonners.

DATES OF CONSTRUCTION: All units launched between 1912 and 1913.

HULL DIMENSIONS: 305'5" × 30'2"

DISPLACEMENT: 1,010 tons

ARMOR: None

ARMAMENT: Four 4" guns in single mounts and eight 18" torpedo tubes.

MACHINERY: Turbines and reciprocating engines powered by four boilers that generated 16,000 shaft horsepower.

SPEED: 29 knots

COMPLEMENT: 98

SUMMARY: These ships represent the culmination of U.S. destroyer design in the era before World War I. All participated in World War I and served well into the interwar period, being broken up between 1934 and 1935.

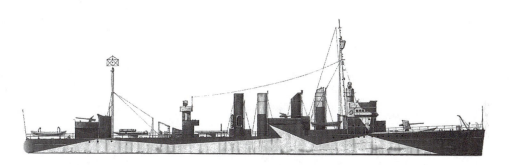

UNITED STATES: *CLEMSON* CLASS

Courtesy of Art-Tech/Aerospace/M.A.R.S./TRH/Navy Historical

UNITS: This class comprised 161 units.

TYPE AND SIGNIFICANCE: The *Clemson*-class destroyers represent one of two mass-produced groups of craft to meet the needs of World War I.

DATES OF CONSTRUCTION: Construction took place between 1918 and 1920.

HULL DIMENSIONS: 314'4" × 30'10" × 9'10"

DISPLACEMENT: 1,190 tons

ARMOR: None

ARMAMENT: Four 4" guns in single mounts, one 3" gun, and 12 21" torpedo tubes.

MACHINERY: Turbines powered by four oil-fired boilers that produced a maximum power output of 27,000 shaft horsepower.

SPEED: 35 knots

COMPLEMENT: 114

SUMMARY: Almost all of these flush-decked ships were still under construction at the close of World War I. Several went to the scrap yards in the early 1930s, but some units served in World War II, in which various causes led to the destruction of 15 units. Among these was *Reuben James,* torpedoed and sunk by a German submarine on 31 October 1941. This vessel was the first U.S. warship sunk in World War II. Following World War II, the United States transferred some units to the British Royal Navy and the Royal Canadian Navy. The remaining ships were all scrapped by 1946.

DESTROYERS AND FRIGATES,

1919–1945

FRANCE: *CHACAL* CLASS

Courtesy of Art-Tech/Aerospace/M.A.R.S./TRH/Navy Historical

UNITS: *Jaguar, Lynx, Tigre, Chacal, Léopard, Panthère*

TYPE AND SIGNIFICANCE: These vessels were among the first known as superdestroyers.

DATES OF CONSTRUCTION: Construction on *Jaguar* came to an end in 1923; the other units were launched the following year.

HULL DIMENSIONS: 415'11" × 37'2" × 13'5"

DISPLACEMENT: 2,126 tons

ARMOR: None

ARMAMENT: Five 5.1" guns in single mounts protected by gun shields, two 3" pieces, and six 21.7" torpedo tubes. In 1939, eight 13.2mm AA guns replaced one of the aft 5.1" pieces.

MACHINERY: Turbines fed by five oil-fired boilers that produced 50,000 shaft horsepower.

SPEED: 35 knots

COMPLEMENT: 195

SUMMARY: *Chacal* and its sister ships were designated by world naval officials as superdestroyers due to their large size and powerful armament relative to the type of ship. This class fared poorly in World War II, which claimed most of the units. *Jaguar* was sunk on 23 May 1940 by a German torpedo boat attack; *Chacal* was sunk the next day by aircraft. *Lynx* was scuttled in 1942; the Italians seized *Panthère* and scuttled it the following year. *Léopard* was wrecked off the coast of Tobruk. Only *Tigre* survived, being scrapped in 1954.

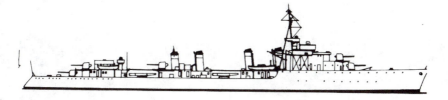

FRANCE: *GUÉPARD* CLASS
Courtesy of Art-Tech/Aerospace/M.A.R.S./TRH/Navy Historical

UNITS: *Guépard, Valmy, Verdun, Bison, Lion, Vauban*

TYPE AND SIGNIFICANCE: The first French superdestroyers that displaced over 2,400 tons.

DATES OF CONSTRUCTION: *Guépard, Valmy, Verdun,* and *Bison* were launched in 1928; *Lion* was completed in 1929 with *Vauban* following the next year.

HULL DIMENSIONS: 427'2" × 38'7" × 15'4"

DISPLACEMENT: 2,436 tons

ARMOR: None

ARMAMENT: Five 5.5" guns in single mounts protected by gun shields, four 37mm pieces and four 13.2mm guns for AA defense, and six 21.7" torpedo tubes.

MACHINERY: Turbines powered by four oil-fired boilers that generated 64,000 horsepower.

SPEED: 35.5 knots

COMPLEMENT: 230

SUMMARY: These superdestroyers were larger, faster, and more heavily armed than the preceding *Chacal* class. None survived World War II. In 1940, *Bison* was bombed and sunk off the coast of Norway. On 27 November 1942, the crews of the *Guépard, Valmy, Verdun, Lion,* and *Vauban* scuttled their vessels at the French naval base of Toulon. The Axis, however, raised *Guépard, Valmy, Verdun,* and *Lion. Lion* and *Valmy* were scuttled by the Italians in 1943 and 1945, respectively, while *Guépard* was destroyed by bombs in March 1944. *Verdun,* despite being raised, was never repaired.

FRANCE: *LE FANTASQUE* CLASS
Courtesy of Art-Tech/Aerospace/M.A.R.S./TRH/Navy Historical

UNITS: *Le Malin, Le Terrible, L'Indomptable, L'Audacieux, Le Fantasque, Le Triomphant*

TYPE AND SIGNIFICANCE: Contemporary naval officials viewed the super-destroyers of the *Le Fantasque* class as some of the most impressive destroyers of their era. Additionally, *Le Terrible* remains one of the fastest vessels in modern naval history.

DATES OF CONSTRUCTION: *Le Malin, Le Terrible,* and *L'Indomptable* were launched in 1933; the others followed in the next year.

HULL DIMENSIONS: 434'4" × 40'6" × 16'5"

DISPLACEMENT: 2,569 tons

ARMOR: None

ARMAMENT: Five 5.5" guns in single mounts protected by gun shields, four 37mm guns and four 13.2mm pieces for AA defense, nine 21.7" torpedo tubes, and 50 mines. Between 1943 and 1944, refits on surviving units altered the AA armament to eight 40mm guns and 10 20mm weapons. The only exception is *Le Triomphant*, which shipped only six 40mm guns.

MACHINERY: Turbines powered by four oil-fired boilers that generated 74,000 shaft horsepower.

SPEED: 37 knots

COMPLEMENT: 210

SUMMARY: These destroyers were extremely powerful and fast in terms of their type. *Le Terrible* achieved a maximum speed of 45 knots, which remains an enviable record in the modern age. All units served in World War II. *L'Indomptable* was scuttled in 1942; *L'Audacieux* was destroyed by bombing in May 1943. The other units served well past the end of the war. *Le Triomphant* was removed from service in 1954; *Le Fantasque* followed in 1957. *Le Terrible* and *Le Malin* went to the breakers in 1962 and 1964, respectively.

FRANCE: *MOGADOR* CLASS
Courtesy of Art-Tech/Aerospace/M.A.R.S./TRH/Navy Historical

UNITS: *Volta, Mogador*

TYPE AND SIGNIFICANCE: These two vessels were the largest superdestroyers ever built.

DATES OF CONSTRUCTION: French shipbuilders completed construction of *Volta* in 1936; *Mogador* was launched the following year.

HULL DIMENSIONS: 451'1" × 41'7" × 15'

DISPLACEMENT: 2,884 tons

ARMOR: None

ARMAMENT: Eight 5.5" guns in dual-piece mounts protected by gun houses. Two each were mounted in the bow and stern. The remainder of the armament comprised four 37mm guns and four 13.2mm weapons for AA defense, 10 21.7" torpedo tubes, and 40 mines.

MACHINERY: Turbines powered by four oil-fired boilers that yielded 92,000 shaft horsepower.

SPEED: 39 knots

COMPLEMENT: 264

SUMMARY: Both conducted operations in World War II. Neither unit survived the war, as they were scuttled on 27 November 1942 at the French naval base of Toulon. They were raised the next year and scrapped.

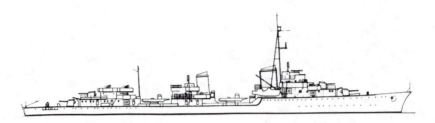

GERMANY: *1934* CLASS

Courtesy of Art-Tech/Aerospace/M.A.R.S./TRH/Navy Historical

UNITS: Z1 (*Leberecht Maas*), Z2 (*Georg Thiele*), Z3 (*Max Schultz*), Z4 (*Richard Beitzen*)

TYPE AND SIGNIFICANCE: Germany's first class of destroyer built in the period after World War I.

DATES OF CONSTRUCTION: All units were launched in 1935.

HULL DIMENSIONS: 391'5" × 37' × 13'1"

DISPLACEMENT: 1,625 tons

ARMOR: None

ARMAMENT: Five 5" guns in single mounts protected by gun shields, four 37mm pieces and four 20mm weapons for AA defense, and eight 21" torpedo tubes.

MACHINERY: Turbines powered by six oil-fired boilers that generated 70,000 shaft horsepower.

SPEED: 38.2 knots

COMPLEMENT: 315

SUMMARY: These vessels signaled Germany's return to destroyer production after World War I, but they were not considered extremely successful owing to design limitations. The engines were a high-pressure type intended to produce a great deal of energy for propulsion, but they frequently broke down. Indeed, these vessels were rarely able to maintain their maximum speed. In addition, the ships were not very seaworthy.

All units served in World War II. On 22 February 1940, German aircraft sunk both Z1 (*Leberecht Maas*) and Z3 (*Max Schultz*) when the pilots mistakenly dropped their bombs. Z2 (*Georg Thiele*) was sunk the same year by British destroyers. The British seized Z4 (*Richard Beitzen*) as a war reparation at the end of the conflict. They subsequently scrapped the ship in 1947.

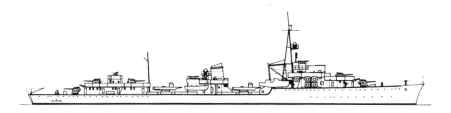

GERMANY: *1936* CLASS

Courtesy of Art-Tech/Aerospace/M.A.R.S./TRH/Navy Historical

UNITS: Z17 (*Diether von Roeder*), Z18 (*Hans Lüdemann*), Z19 (*Hermann Künne*), Z20 (*Karl Galster*), Z21 (*Wilhelm Hiedkamp*), Z22 (*Anton Schmitt*)

TYPE AND SIGNIFICANCE: These ships were among the last destroyers to enter service in Germany before World War II.

DATES OF CONSTRUCTION: All units were launched between 1937 and 1938.

HULL DIMENSIONS: 404'2" × 38'8" × 13'1"

DISPLACEMENT: 1,811 tons

ARMOR: None

ARMAMENT: Five 5" guns in single mounts protected by gun shields, four 37mm pieces and seven 20mm weapons for AA defense, and eight 21" torpedo tubes.

MACHINERY: Turbines powered by six oil-fired boilers that generated 70,000 shaft horsepower.

SPEED: 40 knots

COMPLEMENT: 313

SUMMARY: Although these vessels retained the problematic high-pressure steam plant of the 1934 class, the incorporation of a clipper bow made them more seaworthy. All but one vessel was destroyed in World War II during the 1940 German invasion of Norway. On 10 April 1940, British destroyers sunk Z21 (*Wilhelm Hiedkamp*) and Z22 (*Anton Schmitt*); three days later Z17 (*Diether von Roeder*), Z18 (*Hans Lüdemann*), and Z19 (*Hermann Künne*) engaged British destroyers, with the former being sunk. The crews of the other two ships, after exhausting their supply of ammunition, scuttled their vessels. The Soviets seized Z20 (*Karl Galster*) as a war reparation in 1946 and subsequently scrapped it around 1961.

GREAT BRITAIN: *E* AND *F* CLASS

Courtesy of Art-Tech/Aerospace/M.A.R.S./TRH/Navy Historical

UNITS: *Echo, Eclipse, Electra, Encounter, Escapade, Escort, Esk, Express, Fame, Fearless, Firedrake, Forester, Foresight, Fortune, Foxhound, Fury*

TYPE AND SIGNIFICANCE: The units of this destroyer class are examples of vessels built to the stipulations of the 1930 London Treaty.

DATES OF CONSTRUCTION: Construction was completed on all of these vessels in 1934.

HULL DIMENSIONS: 329' × 33'3" × 12'6"

DISPLACEMENT: 1,350–1,405 tons

ARMOR: None

ARMAMENT: The original armament consisted of four 4.7" quick-firing guns in single mounts protected by gun shields and eight 21" torpedo tubes. A refit removed four torpedo tubes in favor of one 3" gun and 1–4 20mm weapons for the purpose of AA defense. By the end of World War II, several vessels had undergone a further refit that converted them into escort destroyers that shipped three 4.7" guns, six 20mm weapons, four 21" torpedo tubes, 125 depth charges, and a Hedgehog ASW launcher. Still other units were refitted for mine laying.

MACHINERY: Turbines powered by three oil-fired boilers that generated 36,000 shaft horsepower.

SPEED: 36 knots

COMPLEMENT: 145

SUMMARY: This class conformed to the tonnage restrictions of the 1930 London Treaty, the international agreement crafted for the purpose of arms limitation. All of these units served in World War II, with *Eclipse, Electra, Encounter, Escort, Esk, Fearless, Firedrake,* and *Foresight* being sunk from various causes. *Fury* stayed afloat after suffering heavy damage from a mine in 1944, only to be declared beyond repair. After the war, the British sold *Echo* and *Fame* to Greece and the Dominican Republic, respectively. The former power broke up *Echo* in 1956, while the latter nation scrapped *Fame* in 1968. All the other units remaining in British service save *Express* were scrapped between 1946 and 1948. *Express* followed in 1956.

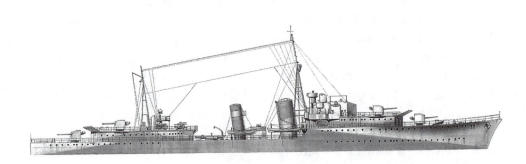

GREAT BRITAIN: *TRIBAL* CLASS

Courtesy of Art-Tech/Aerospace/M.A.R.S./TRH/Navy Historical

UNITS: *Afridi, Ashanti, Bedouin, Cossack, Eskimo, Gurkha, Maori, Mashona, Matabele, Mohawk, Nubian, Punjabi, Sikh, Somali, Tartar, Zulu, Arunta, Bataan, Warramunga, Athabaskan (I), Haida, Huron, Iroquois, Athabaskan (II), Cayuga, Micmac, Nootka*

TYPE AND SIGNIFICANCE: These ships were Great Britain's only super-destroyers.

DATES OF CONSTRUCTION: All units were launched between 1937 and 1946.

HULL DIMENSIONS: 377' × 36'6" (37'6" in the Canadian version) × 13'

DISPLACEMENT: 1,854 tons

ARMOR: None

ARMAMENT: Eight 4.7" guns placed in four dual-gunned mounts protected by gun shields with two each being located fore and aft, four 2-pound pom-pom AA guns, four 21" torpedo tubes, and 30–45 depth charges. During World War II, two 40mm guns and as many as 12 20mm guns were added for AA defense.

MACHINERY: Turbines supplied by three oil-fired boilers that produced 44,000 shaft horsepower.

SPEED: 36.25–36.5 knots

COMPLEMENT: 190–250

SUMMARY: These vessels constitute a British reaction to the Japanese *Fubuki*-class destroyer and were intended primarily to engage vessels of similar design. Although a British design, the Canadians and Australians built some of the units. Of those vessels that served in World War II, a total of 13 were sunk from various causes during the war. The British, Canadians, and Australians scrapped the others between 1948 and 1966, with the exception of one. *Haida*, a Canadian warship, was preserved for the nation in 1964 and is now a museum ship anchored at Hamilton, Ontario.

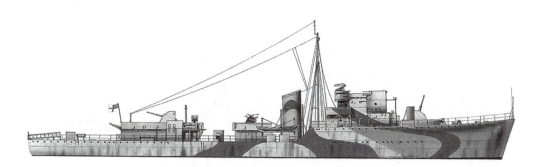

GREAT BRITAIN: *HUNT* CLASS

Courtesy of Art-Tech/Aerospace/M.A.R.S./TRH/Navy Historical

UNITS: *Atherstone, Berkeley, Blencathra, Brocklesby, Cattistock, Cleveland, Cotswold, Cottesmore, Eglinton, Exmoor, Fernie, Garth, Hambledon, Liddesdale, Mendip, Meynell, Pytchley, Quantock, Quorn, Southdown, Tynedale, Whaddon*

TYPE AND SIGNIFICANCE: The units of this class were the world's first escort destroyers.

DATES OF CONSTRUCTION: All of the vessels were launched between 1939 and 1940.

HULL DIMENSIONS: 280' × 29' × 12'6"

DISPLACEMENT: 1,000 tons

ARMOR: None

ARMAMENT: Four 4" guns in two dual-gunned mounts protected by gun houses, four 2-pounder pom-pom AA weapons, and 50–110 depth charges.

MACHINERY: Turbines powered by three oil-fired boilers that generated 19,000 shaft horsepower.

SPEED: 28 knots

COMPLEMENT: 147

SUMMARY: The design of the *Hunt* class was intended primarily for ASW warfare to protect convoys against enemy submarines, which is why they became known as escort destroyers. All of them operated in World War II. *Berkeley, Exmoor, Quorn,* and *Tyndale* were destroyed in the conflict by either bombs or torpedoes. The British retained the surviving units after the war and sold *Mendip* to China in 1948, *Cottesmore* to Egypt in 1950, and *Meynell* and *Quantock* to Ecuador in 1954. China returned *Mendip* in 1949, which the British subsequently scrapped. Egypt operated its vessel into the 1980s; Ecuador discarded its warships in 1978. The 14 units that remained in British service were scrapped between 1948 and 1968.

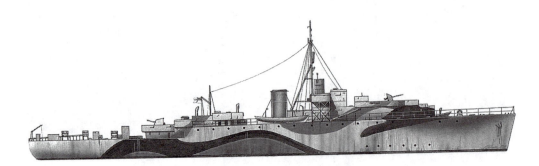

GREAT BRITAIN: *RIVER* CLASS

Courtesy of Art-Tech/Aerospace/M.A.R.S./TRH/Navy Historical

UNITS: This class comprised 139 units.

TYPE AND SIGNIFICANCE: These vessels were the first frigates in the world.

DATES OF CONSTRUCTION: All units were launched between 1942 and 1944.

HULL DIMENSIONS: 301'4" × 36'8" × 11'10"

DISPLACEMENT: 1,310–1,460 tons

ARMOR: None

ARMAMENT: Two 4" guns in single mounts, one being located fore and aft, 126–150 depth charges, and one Hedgehog ASW launcher.

MACHINERY: Triple expansion engines powered by three oil-fired boilers that produced 6,500 shaft horsepower.

SPEED: 20 knots

COMPLEMENT: 140

SUMMARY: The British intended this type for accelerated mass production to counter the dire threat of German submarines to British commerce in World War II. Although the British produced this design, the Canadians and Australians built a substantial amount of the overall number. These vessels, known as frigates, were totally devoted to convoy escort, which is evident given the small number of guns and low speed that rendered them incapable of fleet operations.

Only six of these craft were destroyed in World War II. Most of the others remained in service in the British Royal Navy, Royal Canadian Navy, and Royal Australian Navy; some were sold to a variety of nations. The majority of the *River* class was scrapped by the mid-1960s.

GREAT BRITAIN: *CH, CO, CR* CLASSES
Courtesy of Art-Tech/Aerospace/M.A.R.S./TRH/Navy Historical

UNITS: *Chaplet, Charity, Chequers, Cheviot, Chevron, Chieftain, Childers, Chivalrous, Cockade, Comet, Comus, Concord, Consort, Constance, Contest, Cossack, Creole, Crescent, Crispin, Cromwell, Crown, Croziers, Crusader, Crystal*

TYPE AND SIGNIFICANCE: This class was among the last built in Great Britain during World War II.

DATES OF CONSTRUCTION: All units were launched between 1944 and 1945 and completed between 1945 and 1946.

HULL DIMENSIONS: 362'9" × 35'8" × 14'3"

DISPLACEMENT: 1,710–1,730 tons

ARMOR: None

ARMAMENT: The original armament consisted of four 4.5" guns in single mounts protected by gun shields, two 40mm Bofors AA guns, and four 21" torpedo tubes. They also shipped a depth charge armament of up to 108 depth charges. During World War II, all units received additional AA weapons, normally being 20mm guns.

MACHINERY: Turbines driven by three oil-fired boilers that produced 40,000 shaft horsepower.

SPEED: 36.75 knots

COMPLEMENT: 186–211

SUMMARY: These vessels did not enter service in time to participate in World War II. The British scrapped 16 of them between 1960 and 1971 and sold the others to foreign powers. Pakistan acquired four and Norway bought another four. The first power operated three of its ships into the 1980s; the latter nation scrapped its vessels between 1966 and 1967.

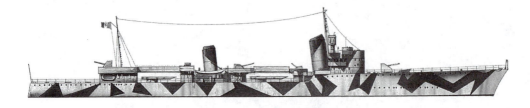

ITALY: *NAVIGATORI* CLASS

Courtesy of Art-Tech/Aerospace/M.A.R.S./TRH/Navy Historical

UNITS: *Nicolo Zeno, Luca Tarigo, Ugolini Vivaldi, Alvise da Mosto, Antonio da Noli, Nicoloso da Recco, Giovanni di Varrazzano, Lanzerotto Malocello, Leone Pancaldo, Emanuele Pessagno, Antonio Pigafetta, Antoniotto Usodimare*

TYPE AND SIGNIFICANCE: These vessels comprised Italy's first and only class of superdestroyers.

DATES OF CONSTRUCTION: The ships were launched between 1928 and 1930.

HULL DIMENSIONS: 352' × 33'5" × 11'2"

DISPLACEMENT: 1,900 tons

ARMOR: None

ARMAMENT: Six 4.7" guns placed in three dual-piece mounts, one each being sited in the bow and the stern while the third was located amidships. In addition, two 40mm guns and four 13.2mm for AA defense and six 21" torpedo tubes.

MACHINERY: Turbines powered by four oil-fired boilers that generated 50,000 horsepower.

SPEED: 38 knots

COMPLEMENT: 224

SUMMARY: Italy constructed these vessels to counter the superdestroyers of France, its primary naval rival. The ships were slightly unstable in a seaway, but the relatively calm waters of the Mediterranean Sea, their principal theater of operation, obviated any potential problem. All units served in World War II. Only *Nicoloso da Recco* survived the war and served until 1954, when the Italians scrapped the ship.

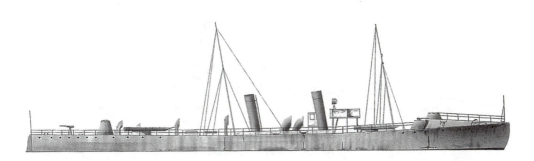

ITALY: *PEGASO* CLASS
Courtesy of Art-Tech/Aerospace/M.A.R.S./TRH/Navy Historical

UNITS: *Pegaso, Procione, Orsa, Orione*

TYPE AND SIGNIFICANCE: These small vessels represent the Italian trend of building smaller destroyers for the sake of quick construction.

DATES OF CONSTRUCTION: *Pegaso* was launched in 1936; the other three units followed the next year.

HULL DIMENSIONS: 293' × 31'9" × 12'3"

DISPLACEMENT: 840 tons

ARMOR: None

ARMAMENT: Two 3.9" guns in single mounts protected by small gun shields, four 18" torpedo tubes, eight 13.2mm AA weapons, and six depth charge throwers.

MACHINERY: Turbines powered by two oil-fired boilers that generated 16,000 horsepower.

SPEED: 28 knots

COMPLEMENT: 168

SUMMARY: Although the Italians did not specifically design these ships as escort destroyers, their rather heavy ASW armament made them best suited for the role. As a result, this design was a step toward the purpose-built escort destroyer. All units served in World War II, with *Pegaso* and *Procione* being scuttled in 1943. The Italians removed *Orsa* and *Orione* from service in 1964 and 1965, respectively.

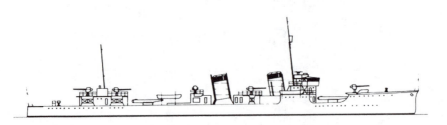

JAPAN: *MUTSUKI* CLASS

Courtesy of Art-Tech/Aerospace/M.A.R.S./TRH/Navy Historical

UNITS: *Mutsuki, Kisaragi, Yayoi, Udzuki, Satsuki, Minadsuki, Fumidsuki, Nagatsuki, Kirudsuki, Mikadsuki, Mochidsuki, Yudsuki*

TYPE AND SIGNIFICANCE: These destroyers were the first in the world to carry the 24" torpedo, known as the Long Lance.

DATES OF CONSTRUCTION: All units were launched between 1925 and 1927.

HULL DIMENSIONS: 320'(pp) × 20' × 9'9"

DISPLACEMENT: 1,315 tons

ARMOR: None

ARMAMENT: Four 4.7" dual-purpose guns in single, unprotected mounts, two 7.7mm weapons, six 24" torpedo tubes, and 18 depth charges.

MACHINERY: Turbines powered by four oil-fired boilers that yielded 38,500 shaft horsepower.

SPEED: 37.2 knots

COMPLEMENT: 150

SUMMARY: The Japanese attached great value to the use of destroyers in their role of torpedo attack. The units of the *Mutsuki* class, with their 24" Long Lance torpedo tubes, exhibited this emphasis. All warships of the class were sunk in World War II. *Minadsuki* was destroyed by a U.S. submarine; the others were sunk by Allied aircraft.

JAPAN: *FUBUKI* CLASS

Courtesy of Naval Historical Foundation

UNITS: *Fubuki, Shinonome, Isonami, Usugumo, Shirakumo, Shirayuki, Hatsuyuki, Miyuki, Murakumo, Uranami, Shikinami, Ayanami, Asagiri, Sagiri, Yugiri, Amagiri, Oboro, Akebono, Sazanami, Ushio*

TYPE AND SIGNIFICANCE: At the time of their launch, the units of the *Fubuki* class were the best-armed destroyers in the world.

DATES OF CONSTRUCTION: *Fubuki* was launched in 1927 and followed by the other units between 1927 and 1930.

HULL DIMENSIONS: 388'6" × 34' × 10'6"

DISPLACEMENT: 1,750 tons

ARMOR: Light armor on turrets

ARMAMENT: Six 5" guns housed in three, twin-gunned turrets. One of these was located in the bow while the other two were placed in the stern. In addition, two 13mm guns for AA defense, nine 24" torpedo tubes, and 18 depth charges.

MACHINERY: Turbines powered by four oil-fired boilers that produced 50,000 shaft horsepower.

SPEED: 38 knots

COMPLEMENT: 197

SUMMARY: The *Fubuki*-class destroyers set a design trend for heavily armed destroyers in many other naval powers. Their design caused a great stir in naval circles due to their many innovations. These vessels were the first destroyers to mount their guns in turrets and these were armored to prevent damage from splinters. The inclusion of director control for aiming greatly increased the effectiveness of the guns. Later units of the class also incorporated the innovation of dual-purpose weapons, being guns that could either fire at surface targets or aircraft. A further improvement in destroyer design that the Japanese incorporated in the *Fubuki* class was a totally enclosed bridge to protect the crew from the elements. This made the *Fubuki* class the first in the world with this feature.

The main design weakness was stability at sea, as the weight of the turrets, director, and bridge made the units of the *Fubuki* class top-heavy. All but one, *Miyuki*, which was sunk in 1934 by a collision with another vessel, served in World War II. Only *Ushio* survived the conflict. It was scrapped in 1948.

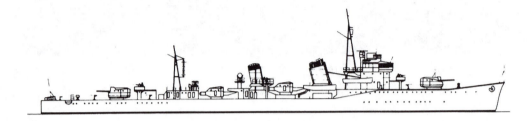

JAPAN: *HATSUHARU* CLASS
Courtesy of Art-Tech/Aerospace/M.A.R.S./TRH/Navy Historical

UNITS: *Nenohi, Hatsuharu, Hatsushimo, Wakaba, Yugure, Ariake*

TYPE AND SIGNIFICANCE: These destroyers were the first in Japan designed to conform to the stipulations of the 1930 London Treaty.

DATES OF CONSTRUCTION: *Nenohi* was launched in 1932; the other units followed in 1933 and 1934.

HULL DIMENSIONS: 359'3" × 32'10" × 9'11"

DISPLACEMENT: 1,490 tons

ARMOR: None

ARMAMENT: Five 5" dual-purpose guns, two 13mm AA weapons, nine 24" torpedo tubes, and 14 depth charges.

MACHINERY: Turbines powered by three oil-fired boilers that generated 42,000 shaft horsepower.

SPEED: 36.5 knots

COMPLEMENT: 200

SUMMARY: Following Japan's signing of the 1930 London Treaty that limited the displacement of destroyers to 1,500 tons and the size of the armament to 5" guns, the Japanese sought to incorporate the greatest amount of armament into a ship that conformed to the displacement stipulation. All operated in World War II, during which all were lost.

JAPAN: *KAGERO* CLASS
Courtesy of Art-Tech/Aerospace/M.A.R.S./TRH/Navy Historical

UNITS: *Kagero, Kuroshio, Oyahio, Hatsukaze, Natsushio, Yukikaze, Hayashio, Maikaze, Isokaze, Shiranui, Amatsukaze, Tokitsukaze, Urakaze, Hamakaze, Nowaki, Arashi, Hagikaze, Tanikaze*

TYPE AND SIGNIFICANCE: This design was the last produced by Japan before the outbreak of World War II.

DATES OF CONSTRUCTION: Construction of the class took place between 1938 and 1940.

HULL DIMENSIONS: 388'9" × 35'5" × 12'4"

DISPLACEMENT: 2,033 tons

ARMOR: None

ARMAMENT: The armament consisted originally of six 5" dual-purpose guns, four 25mm AA weapons, eight 24" torpedo tubes, and 16 depth charges.

During World War II, the Japanese altered the armament in favor of a greater AA capacity. This arrangement consisted of four 5" dual-purpose guns, 14 25mm AA weapons, and 36 depth charges. Subsequent refits increased this new armament to as many as 24 25mm AA guns.

MACHINERY: Turbines powered by three oil-fired boilers that produced 52,000 shaft horsepower.

SPEED: 35 knots

COMPLEMENT: 240

SUMMARY: All but one was lost in World War II to a variety of causes that included Allied air attack and surface action. The survivor, *Yukikaze*, was transferred to China in 1947 and then Taiwan in 1949. The Taiwanese scrapped the vessel in 1971.

JAPAN: *AKITSUKI* CLASS

Courtesy of Art-Tech/Aerospace/M.A.R.S./TRH/Navy Historical

UNITS: *Akitsuki, Terutsuki, Suzutsuki, Hatsusuki, Niitsuki, Wakatsuki, Shimotsuki, Fuyutsuki, Hanatsuki, Yoitsuki, Harutsuki, Natsutsuki*

TYPE AND SIGNIFICANCE: These vessels were among the last fleet destroyers built by the Imperial Japanese Navy.

DATES OF CONSTRUCTION: These units were launched between 1941 and 1944.

HULL DIMENSIONS: 440'3" × 38'1" × 13'7"

DISPLACEMENT: 2,701 tons

ARMOR: None

ARMAMENT: Eight dual-purpose 3.9" guns in dual-gunned mounts that were fully enclosed by gun houses with two each sited in the bow and stern. In addition, four 24" torpedo tubes, four 25mm AA weapons, and 72 depth charges.

MACHINERY: Turbines powered by three oil-fired boilers capable of 52,000 shaft horsepower.

SPEED: 33 knots

COMPLEMENT: 300

SUMMARY: The Japanese specifically designed these vessels to provide AA defense for aircraft carriers. *Akitsuki, Terutsuki, Hatsusuki, Niitsuki, Wakatsuki,* and *Shimotsuki* were destroyed in World War II. *Suzutsuki, Fuyutsuki, Hanatsuki,* and *Natsutsuki* were scrapped in 1948. In 1947, the other two units, *Yoitsuki* and *Harutsuki,* were transferred to China and the Soviet Union, respectively. The Chinese scrapped their vessel in 1963; the Soviets expended their unit as a missile target ship sometime in the late 1960s.

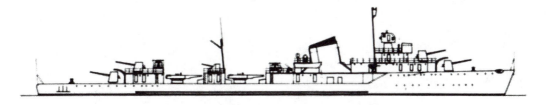

SOVIET UNION: *GNEVNYI* CLASS

Courtesy of Art-Tech/Aerospace/M.A.R.S./TRH/Navy Historical

UNITS: This class comprised 31 units.

TYPE AND SIGNIFICANCE: These Soviet vessels were indicative of Stalin's desire to revive Russia's destroyer program in the years after the 1917 revolution.

DATES OF CONSTRUCTION: All units were launched between 1936 and 1941.

HULL DIMENSIONS: 370'7" × 22'6" × 13'5"

DISPLACEMENT: 1,855 tons

ARMOR: None

ARMAMENT: Four 5.1" guns in single mounts housed in gun shields with two each being located in the bow and stern. In addition, two 3" guns, six 21" torpedo tubes, two 45mm and four .5" guns for AA defense, and 56 mines.

MACHINERY: Turbines powered by oil-fired boilers that generated 48,000 shaft horsepower.

SPEED: 37 knots

COMPLEMENT: 240

SUMMARY: Although being constructed entirely in Russian shipyards, the *Gnevnyi* class relied heavily on Italian naval engineering. All but one unit, *Reshitelnyi* (which ran aground in 1938), served in World War II. Operations in World War II claimed 10 of the vessels. The Soviets removed most of the others from the navy in the 1950s, while four units were transferred to China in 1955. These vessels served the People's Republic of China until the mid-1980s.

SOVIET UNION: *STOROZHEVOI* CLASS
Courtesy of Art-Tech/Aerospace/M.A.R.S./TRH/Navy Historical

UNITS: This class consisted of 19 units.

TYPE AND SIGNIFICANCE: These ships were the first completely Russian designed and built destroyers of the postrevolution era in Russia.

DATES OF CONSTRUCTION: All units were launched between 1938 and 1940.

HULL DIMENSIONS: 370'1" × 33'6" × 13'1"

DISPLACEMENT: 2,192 tons

ARMOR: None

ARMAMENT: Four 5.1" guns in single mounts protected by gun shields. The bow and stern each carried two of these. In addition, two 3" guns, three 37mm AA weapons, four .5" machine guns, six 21" torpedo tubes, and 60 mines.

MACHINERY: Turbines powered by four oil-fired boilers that yielded 54,000 shaft horsepower.

SPEED: 36 knots

COMPLEMENT: 207

SUMMARY: Service in World War II led to the destruction of nine of these vessels. All of the other units, except for *Soobrazitelnyi*, were taken out of service by 1959. In 1966, the one surviving unit became a museum ship.

UNITED STATES: *FARRAGUT* CLASS
Courtesy of Art-Tech/Aerospace/M.A.R.S./TRH/Navy Historical

UNITS: *Hull, Farragut, Aylwin, Dewey, MacDonough, Worden, Dale, Monaghan*

TYPE AND SIGNIFICANCE: These U.S. destroyers were the first in the United States produced to a post–World War I design.

DATES OF CONSTRUCTION: These ships were launched between 1934 and 1935.

HULL DIMENSIONS: 341'3" × 34'3" × 11'7"

DISPLACEMENT: 1,358 tons

ARMOR: None

ARMAMENT: The original armament consisted of five 5" guns in single mounts with the forward two guns being protected by partially enclosed gun houses. In addition, four .5" machine guns and eight 21" torpedo tubes. Owing to the threat of enemy aircraft, during World War II the armament included additional AA weapons at the cost of one aft 5" gun. They also shipped depth charges for ASW operations.

MACHINERY: Turbines powered by two oil-fired boilers that produced 42,800 shaft horsepower.

SPEED: 36.5 knots

COMPLEMENT: 160

SUMMARY: These ships proved to be the template for all U.S. destroyer production before World War II. All units served in World War II. In 1943, *Worden* was sunk; *Hull* and *Monaghan* followed the next year. The other units went to the scrap yard in 1947.

UNITED STATES: *SIMS* CLASS
Courtesy of Art-Tech/Aerospace/M.A.R.S./TRH/Navy Historical

UNITS: *Sims, Hughes, Anderson, Hammann, Mustin, Russell, O'Brien, Walke, Morris, Roe, Wainwright, Buck*

TYPE AND SIGNIFICANCE: This class of U.S. destroyer serves as an example of U.S. destroyer design upon the outbreak of World War II.

DATES OF CONSTRUCTION: All units were constructed between 1938 and 1939.

HULL DIMENSIONS: 348'4" × 36' × 12'10"

DISPLACEMENT: 1,764 tons

ARMOR: None

ARMAMENT: Five 5" guns, four .5" AA weapons, eight 21" torpedo tubes, and 10 depth charges.

MACHINERY: Turbines powered by three oil-fired boilers that produced 50,000 shaft horsepower.

SPEED: 35 knots

COMPLEMENT: 190

SUMMARY: All of the vessels in the class served in World War II. *Sims, Hammann, O'Brien, Walke,* and *Buck* were destroyed in the conflict. By 1948, the others were either scrapped or destroyed as test ships.

UNITED STATES: *BENSON/GLEAVES* CLASS
Courtesy of U.S. Naval Institute

UNITS: This class comprised 95 units.

TYPE AND SIGNIFICANCE: This class was both the last design produced before World War II and the last to adhere to the stipulations of the 1930 London Treaty, despite the fact that the agreement had expired.

DATES OF CONSTRUCTION: The first of these units was launched in 1939 and construction continued on the class through 1943.

HULL DIMENSIONS: 348'4" × 36'1" × 13'2"

DISPLACEMENT: 1,839 tons

ARMOR: None

ARMAMENT: As designed, five 5" guns in single mounts enclosed in gun houses. Two each of these were located in the bow and stern while the fifth was sited aft amidships. In addi-tion, six .5" AA guns, 10 21" torpedo tubes, and depth charge racks. The actual armament following the first 24 units varied, and many were refit-ted with different armaments during World War II.

MACHINERY: Turbines powered by four oil-fired boilers that generated 50,000 shaft horsepower.

SPEED: 35 knots

COMPLEMENT: 208

SUMMARY: These vessels served exten-sively in World War II. Fourteen of the class were sunk in the war. Most of the others operated far past World War II, the last in U.S. service being scrapped in 1972. The United States transferred several units to other powers following the war. Taiwan op-erated one of them until 1976.

UNITED STATES: *FLETCHER* CLASS
Courtesy of Art-Tech/Aerospace/M.A.R.S./TRH/Navy Historical

UNITS: This class comprised 178 ships.

TYPE AND SIGNIFICANCE: This class of destroyer is the largest, in terms of the number of units, ever produced in the world.

DATES OF CONSTRUCTION: Construction of the vessels in this class spanned from 1942 to 1944.

HULL DIMENSIONS: 376'5" × 39'7" × 13'9"

DISPLACEMENT: 2,325 tons

ARMOR: Side armor .75" thick and .5"-thick deck protection protected the machinery spaces and engines.

ARMAMENT: The original armament consisted of five 5" guns in single mounts that were completely enclosed by gun houses. The bow and the stern contained two each of these weapons. The fifth mount was located aft amidships. In addition, four 1.1" weapons and four 20mm guns for AA defense, 10 21" torpedo tubes, and depth charges.

MACHINERY: Turbines fed by four oil-fired boilers that generated 60,000 shaft horsepower.

SPEED: 38 knots

COMPLEMENT: 273

SUMMARY: The *Fletcher* class was an impressive design that incorporated the rare feature (for a destroyer) of armor protection. Most operated in World War II. Fifteen of them were sunk from various causes. Many of them also served in the Korean War for the purpose of gunfire support. In 1975, the U.S. Navy removed the last *Fletcher*-class destroyer from service. Units of this class ended up in

the service of Argentina, Brazil, Chile, Columbia, Greece, Japan, Mexico, Peru, South Korea, Spain, Taiwan, Turkey, and West Germany. None remain in service, but three survive as museums. *Kidd* is part of the Louisiana Veterans Memorial and Museum at Baton Rouge, Louisiana. The *Sullivans* is preserved as part of the Buffalo and Erie County Naval and Military Park in Buffalo, New York. *Cassin Young* was preserved in 1978 as a museum in the Boston Navy Yard.

UNITED STATES: *GEARING* CLASS
Courtesy of Art-Tech/Aerospace/M.A.R.S./TRH/Navy Historical

UNITS: This class comprised 108 units.

TYPE AND SIGNIFICANCE: The *Gearing* class was the last fleet destroyer design of the United States in World War II.

DATES OF CONSTRUCTION: All units were launched between 1944 and 1946.

HULL DIMENSIONS: 390'6" × 40'10" × 14'4"

DISPLACEMENT: 2,616 tons

ARMOR: None

ARMAMENT: The original armament consisted of six 5" guns in dual mounts enclosed by gun houses. Two were sited in the bow while the third was located on the stern. In addition, the vessel carried 12 40mm guns and 11 20mm weapons for AA defense, 10 21" torpedo tubes, and depth charge racks or depth charge throwers. Most of those vessels receiving the FRAM I modernization between 1959 and 1964 had one of the 5" guns and its gun house removed as well as all smaller weaponry. In its place were substituted one ASROC ASW system, six 12.75" homing torpedo tubes, and a DASH ASW system.

MACHINERY: Turbines powered by four oil-fired boilers capable of 60,000 shaft horsepower.

SPEED: 36.8 knots

COMPLEMENT: 336

SUMMARY: These destroyers represented the pinnacle of U.S. destroyer design in World War II and were extremely good craft. None were sunk in World War II, and all served during the Cold War era. Those in U.S. service received FRAM I conversions; others were transferred to Brazil, Ecuador, Egypt, Greece, Iran, Pakistan, South Korea, Spain, Taiwan, and Turkey. In 2004, Taiwan had most of the surviving Gearing-class destroyers, being seven units that received FRAM I conversions. Mexico maintains two vessels in its navy. Other vessels survive as museums. *Orleck* is maintained as a museum by the Southeast Texas War Memorial and Heritage Foundation in Orange, Texas. *Joseph P. Kennedy Jr.* is preserved in Battleship Cove at Fall River, Massachusetts. *Eversole (II)* was transferred to Turkey in 1973 and renamed *Gayret*. It was stricken in 1995 and is now preserved as a museum at Izmit, Turkey.

DESTROYERS AND FRIGATES,

1946–2004

FRANCE: *SUFFREN* CLASS
Courtesy of Art-Tech/Aerospace/M.A.R.S./TRH/Navy Historical

UNITS: *Suffren, Duquesne*

TYPE AND SIGNIFICANCE: These vessels were the first French purpose-built guided missile destroyers.

DATES OF CONSTRUCTION: *Suffren* was laid down in 1962 and completed in 1967; *Duquesne* was laid down in 1964 and completed in 1970.

HULL DIMENSIONS: 517' × 51' × 20'

DISPLACEMENT: 5,335 tons

ARMOR: None

ARMAMENT: The original armament consisted of one Mascura SAM launcher located in the stern, one Malafon ASW launcher sited amidships, two 3.9" guns, two 30mm weapons, and four torpedo tubes that fire ASW homing torpedoes. Currently, the Duquesne retains the Mascura system, the two 3.9" guns, and the four torpedo tubes and carries four Exocet SSM, six 20mm guns, and two 12.7mm weapons.

MACHINERY: Two turbines powered by four oil-fired boilers that produce a maximum power output of 72,500 shaft horsepower.

SPEED: 34 knots

COMPLEMENT: 355

SUMMARY: The *Suffren* class provided the French with a template for future warship design in their navy. *Suffren* was decommissioned in 2001; *Duquesne* is scheduled to follow in 2007.

FRANCE: *TOURVILLE* CLASS
Courtesy of Art-Tech/Aerospace/M.A.R.S./TRH/Navy Historical

UNITS: *Tourville, Duguay-Trouin, De Grasse*

TYPE AND SIGNIFICANCE: These ships were the first destroyers designed to carry the French Exocet SSM.

DATES OF CONSTRUCTION: *Tourville, Duguay-Trouin,* and *De Grasse* were laid down in 1970, 1971, and 1972, respectively. *Tourville* and *Duguay-Trouin* were completed in 1974 and 1975, while the other unit followed in 1977.

HULL DIMENSIONS: 501' × 50' × 19'

DISPLACEMENT: 4,580 tons

ARMOR: None

ARMAMENT: Six Exocet SSM, a Crotale SAM launcher, one Malafon ASW system, two 3.9" guns mounted in single-piece gun houses in the bow, two torpedo tubes that fire ASW homing torpedoes, and two ASW helicopters that operate off a flight deck on the stern. Currently, *Tourville* and *De Grasse* have the same armament with the exception of the Malafon ASW system, which has been removed.

MACHINERY: Two turbines powered by four oil-fired boilers capable of 58,000 shaft horsepower.

SPEED: 31 knots

COMPLEMENT: 303

SUMMARY: *Duguay-Trouin* was removed from service in 1999. The other two units remain in service, but *Tourville* and *De Grasse* are scheduled for deactivation in 2008 and 2009, respectively.

FRANCE: *D'ESTIENNE D'ORVES* CLASS
Courtesy of Art-Tech/Aerospace/M.A.R.S./TRH/Navy Historical

UNITS: This class comprised 17 vessels.

TYPE AND SIGNIFICANCE: These ships are indicative of the reliance of many naval powers, like France, on frigates as they are smaller and cheaper to construct than destroyers.

DATES OF CONSTRUCTION: These units were laid down between 1972 and 1981, with the final unit being ready for service in 1986.

HULL DIMENSIONS: 262' × 34' × 10'

DISPLACEMENT: 950 tons

ARMOR: None

ARMAMENT: Originally, two Exocet SSM, one 3.9" gun in a single-piece gun house mounted forward, one ASW mortar, and four torpedo tubes that fire ASW homing torpedoes. The units that remain in service carry four Exocet SSM, one Matra Simbad SAM system, one 3.9" gun, two 20mm pieces, one ASW mortar, and four torpedo tubes.

MACHINERY: Two diesel engines that generate 12,000 horsepower.

SPEED: 23 knots

COMPLEMENT: 79

SUMMARY: These vessels are designed primarily for coastal defense. The French sold three to Argentina, two being existing units sold in 1978, while the third was a specially built ship additional to the original number. In 2000, the French sold another six vessels to Turkey. Nine units remain in service and are scheduled for decommissioning in 2015.

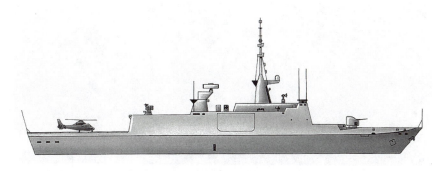

FRANCE: *LAFAYETTE* CLASS

Courtesy of Art-Tech/Aerospace/M.A.R.S./TRH/Navy Historical

UNITS: *Lafayette, Surcouf, Courbet, Aconit, Guépratte*

TYPE AND SIGNIFICANCE: These vessels are among the newest frigates of the French Navy.

DATES OF CONSTRUCTION: These units were laid down between 1990 and 1998 with the last unit, *Guépratte*, being ready for service in 2001.

HULL DIMENSIONS: 407'6" × 50'6" × 15'8"

DISPLACEMENT: 3,600 tons (full load)

ARMOR: Machinery spaces and magazines are protected by steel plate 10mm thick.

ARMAMENT: Eight Exocet SSM, one Crotale SAM launcher, one 3.9" gun located in the bow, two 20mm weapons, two 12.7mm guns, and one helicopter that operates off a flight deck located on the stern.

MACHINERY: Diesel engines capable of 21,107 horsepower.

SPEED: 25 knots

COMPLEMENT: 139

SUMMARY: The design of these frigates was viewed with interest by foreign powers. Saudi Arabia, Taiwan, and Singapore have placed orders for units of this type.

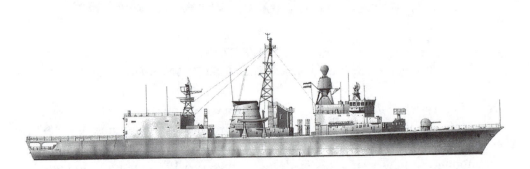

GERMANY: *BREMEN* CLASS
Courtesy of Art-Tech/Aerospace/M.A.R.S./TRH/Navy Historical

UNITS: *Bremen, Nieddersachsen, Reinland-Pfalz, Emden, Koln, Karlsruhe, Augsburg, Lübeck*

TYPE AND SIGNIFICANCE: These German frigates were the first warships produced for West Germany since the 1960s.

DATES OF CONSTRUCTION: The units were laid down between 1979 and 1987 with the last, *Lübeck,* entering service in 1990.

HULL DIMENSIONS: 420' × 47'10" × 19'9"

DISPLACEMENT: 3,700 tons (full load)

ARMOR: None

ARMAMENT: Eight Harpoon SSM, one Sea Sparrow SAM system, one 3" gun located in the bow, four ASW torpedo tubes, and two ASW helicopters contained in a hanger that forms the vessel's aft superstructure.

MACHINERY: Gas turbines and diesel engines that produce 10,400 brake horsepower.

SPEED: 30 knots

COMPLEMENT: 200

SUMMARY: All units are currently in service.

GREAT BRITAIN: *COUNTY* CLASS
Courtesy of Art-Tech/Aerospace/M.A.R.S./TRH/Navy Historical

UNITS: *Devonshire, Hampshire, London, Kent, Fife, Glamorgan, Antrim, Norfolk*

TYPE AND SIGNIFICANCE: These ships were the first purpose-built guided missile destroyers of the British Royal Navy

DATES OF CONSTRUCTION: These units were laid down between 1959 and 1966, with the ships being completed between 1962 and 1970.

HULL DIMENSIONS: 521'6" × 54' × 20'6"

DISPLACEMENT: 6,200 tons

ARMOR: None

ARMAMENT: The original armament consisted of one Seaslug SAM launcher located in the stern, two Seacat SAM launchers, four 4.5" guns mounted in dual-gunned turrets located in the bow, two 20mm weapons, and one ASW helicopter that operated on a flight deck located on the stern. This was later changed to four Exocet SSM, one Seaslug SAM launcher, two Seacat SAM launchers, two 4.5" guns in a single turret in the bow, and one helicopter. The surviving units currently carry four Exocet SSM, two 4.5" guns in the bow turret, and six 324mm torpedo tubes.

MACHINERY: Steam and gas turbines that produced 30,000 shaft horsepower.

SPEED: 30 knots

COMPLEMENT: 440

SUMMARY: *Antrim* and *Glamorgan* operated in the 1982 Falklands War, in which both were damaged by bombs and, in the case of the latter unit, one Exocet SSM as well. None remain in service in the British Royal Navy. As of 2004, Chile operates *Norfolk, Antrim,* and *Fife* as *Capitán Prat, Almirante Cochrane,* and *Almirante Blanco Encalada,* respectively.

GREAT BRITAIN: *LEANDER* CLASS
Courtesy of Art-Tech/Aerospace/M.A.R.S./TRH/Navy Historical

UNITS: *Leander, Ajax, Dido, Penelope, Aurora, Euryalus, Galatea, Arethusa, Naiad, Phoebe, Cleopatra, Minerva, Sirius, Juno, Argonaut, Danae* (broad-beam version: *Andromeda, Jupiter, Charybdis, Hermione, Bacchante, Scylla, Achilles, Diomede, Apollo, Ariadne*)

TYPE AND SIGNIFICANCE: Many naval officials and scholars consider these frigates to be among the best of their type ever built in the missile age.

DATES OF CONSTRUCTION: The original units of this class were completed between 1963 and 1967, with the broad-beam ships following between 1969 and 1973.

HULL DIMENSIONS: 372' × 41' × 18' (broad-beam version: 372' × 43' × 19')

DISPLACEMENT: 2,350 tons (broad-beam version: 2,500 tons)

ARMOR: None

ARMAMENT: The original armament consisted of two 4.5" guns in a dual-piece mount enclosed by a gun house that was located in the bow, two 40mm guns, two 20mm guns, one Limbo system, and one helicopter. During refits, various units received one or a combination of the Exocet SSM, Seacat SAM system, or Sea Wolf SAM system.

MACHINERY: Turbines powered by two boilers that generated 40,000 shaft horsepower.

SPEED: 28.5 knots

COMPLEMENT: 250

SUMMARY: These ships proved to be successful and were frequently rearmed over the course of their careers. None remain in service in the British Royal Navy. Most have been either scrapped outright or sunk as targets, but some were sold to other nations, and some powers contracted for the construction of units. In 2004, of the original group, India, operates the former *Andromeda* as the training vessel *Krishna*. The former *Achilles* is now *Ministro Zenteno* in the service of Chile. The former *Diomede* and former *Apollo* are now the Pakistani warships *Shamsher* and *Zulfiguar*, respectively. In addition to these, on 27 March 2004, one decommissioned British vessel, *Scylla*, was towed into Whitsand Bay off the coast of Cornwall, England, and scuttled for the purpose of creating Britain's first artificial diving reef.

GREAT BRITAIN: *AMAZON* CLASS

Courtesy of Art-Tech/Aerospace/M.A.R.S./TRH/Navy Historical

UNITS: *Amazon, Antelope, Active, Ambuscade, Arrow, Alacrity, Ardent, Avenger*

TYPE AND SIGNIFICANCE: These frigates are indicative of a general-purpose design for escort duty.

DATES OF CONSTRUCTION: All units were laid down between 1969 and 1974, with the last units being completed in 1978.

HULL DIMENSIONS: 384' × 41'9" × 19'

DISPLACEMENT: 3,100 tons

ARMOR: None

ARMAMENT: One 4.5" gun mounted in the bow, four Exocet SSM, one Seacat SAM system, two 20mm guns, six 12.75" ASW torpedo tubes, and one helicopter that operated on a flight deck situated on the stern.

MACHINERY: Gas turbines that produced 56,000 shaft horsepower.

SPEED: 30 knots

COMPLEMENT: 180

SUMMARY: These ships suffered from the fact that their hulls were very lightly built. Two of the units, *Antelope* and *Amazon*, were lost in the 1982 Falklands War. The first ship sank from damage sustained by air-launched rockets, while bomb damage destroyed the other. The British have retired all the units of this class.

GREAT BRITAIN: *SHEFFIELD* CLASS
Courtesy of Art-Tech/Aerospace/M.A.R.S./TRH/Navy Historical

UNITS: *Sheffield, Birmingham, Cardiff, Coventry, Newcastle, Glasgow, Exeter, Southampton, Nottingham, Liverpool*

TYPE AND SIGNIFICANCE: Guided missile destroyers.

DATES OF CONSTRUCTION: *Sheffield* was laid down in 1970 and completed in 1975. The other units were laid down between 1972 and 1978 and completed between 1976 and 1982.

HULL DIMENSIONS: 410 × 46' × 19'

DISPLACEMENT: 3,850 tons

ARMOR: None

ARMAMENT: The original armament consisted of one 4.5" gun in a gun house situated in the bow, one Sea Dart SAM system, two 20mm guns, six 12.75" torpedo tubes, and one helicopter operating on a flight deck situated on the stern. The units that remain in operation carry one Sea Dart SAM system, one 4.5" gun, and four 12.75" torpedo tubes as well as one helicopter.

MACHINERY: Gas turbines that generated 50,000 shaft horsepower.

SPEED: 30 knots

COMPLEMENT: 280

SUMMARY: At the time of their completion, these vessels comprised the largest class of guided missile destroyers launched by Great Britain.

The design was extremely cramped for the crew and did not incorporate sufficient defense systems. As a result, both *Sheffield* and *Coventry* were lost in 1982 in the Falklands War, the former by an Exocet SSM, the latter by bombs. *Cardiff, Newcastle, Glasgow, Exeter, Southampton, Nottingham,* and *Liverpool* remain in service. *Cardiff* and *Newcastle* are slated for removal from service in 2007, while *Glasgow* is due for decommissioning in 2009.

GREAT BRITAIN: *DUKE* CLASS
Courtesy of Art-Tech/Aerospace/M.A.R.S./TRH/Navy Historical

UNITS: *Norfolk, Argyll, Lancaster, Marlborough, Iron Duke, Monmouth, Montrose, Westminster, Northumberland, Richmond, Somerset, Grafton, Sutherland, Kent, Portland, St. Albans*

TYPE AND SIGNIFICANCE: These frigates are the newest ships of their type in the British Royal Navy.

DATES OF CONSTRUCTION: Construction of the first unit, *Norfolk,* began in 1985, with the ship being commissioned in 1990. All other units were ready for service between 1991 and 2002.

HULL DIMENSIONS: 436'2" × 52'9" × 18'

DISPLACEMENT: 3,500 tons

ARMOR: None

ARMAMENT: Eight Harpoon SSM in two quadruple-cell launchers located in the bow, a Sea Wolf SAM system in the bow, one 4.5" gun, two 30mm guns, four torpedo tubes, and one helicopter that operates off a flight deck located on the stern.

MACHINERY: Gas turbines that can produce 31,000 horsepower. Also diesel engines that generate 8,100 horsepower. Finally, the vessel mounts electric motors that can yield 4,000 horsepower.

SPEED: 28 knots. Diesel-electric propulsion generates 15 knots.

COMPLEMENT: 181

SUMMARY: These impressive ships incorporate stealth technology into their design to conceal the vessel from enemy detection systems. All units are currently in service.

ITALY: *ANIMOSO* (DE LA PENNE) CLASS
Courtesy of Art-Tech/Aerospace/M.A.R.S./TRH/Navy Historical

UNITS: *Luigi Durand De La Penne* (former *Animoso*), *Francesco Mimbelli* (former *Ardimentoso*)

TYPE AND SIGNIFICANCE: Currently these ships are the newest guided missile destroyers of the Italian Navy.

DATES OF CONSTRUCTION: *Luigi Durand De La Penne* (former *Animoso*) was laid down in 1988 and commissioned in 1993. *Francesco Mimbelli* (former *Ardimentoso*) was laid down in 1991 and was ready for service in 1993 also.

HULL DIMENSIONS: 487'5" × 52'10" × 28'2"

DISPLACEMENT: 4,330 tons

ARMOR: Kevlar armor over vital areas.

ARMAMENT: One 5" gun mounted in the bow, three 3" guns with one being mounted astern amidships and one each being placed on the sides, eight Ottomat SSM, one Standard SAM system, six 12.6" torpedo tubes, and two helicopters.

MACHINERY: Combined diesel and gas machinery capable of 54,000 horsepower.

SPEED: 31 knots

COMPLEMENT: 377

SUMMARY: These destroyers are in active service and rank as two of the best surface combatants of the Italian Navy.

ITALY: *ARTIGLIERE* CLASS
Courtesy of Art-Tech/Aerospace/M.A.R.S./TRH/Navy Historical

UNITS: *Artigliere, Aviere, Bersagliere, Granatiere*

TYPE AND SIGNIFICANCE: These frigates are the newest vessels of their type in the Italian Navy.

DATES OF CONSTRUCTION: Construction on all four vessels commenced between 1982 and 1984, with the last unit being commissioned for service in 1996.

HULL DIMENSIONS: 371'4" × 37'1" × 12'1"

DISPLACEMENT: 2,208 tons

ARMOR: None

ARMAMENT: One 5" gun mounted in the bow, eight Ottomat SSM, four 40mm guns, and one helicopter that operates on a flight deck situated on the stern.

MACHINERY: Gas turbines and diesel engines that can produce a maximum power output of 50,000 horsepower.

SPEED: 35 knots

COMPLEMENT: 185

SUMMARY: The Italians built these vessels for sale to Iraq but transferred the vessels to its own navy in lieu of international arms embargoes that prohibited the sale. All units are currently in service.

JAPAN: *AMATSUKAZE*

Courtesy of Art-Tech/Aerospace/M.A.R.S./TRH/Navy Historical

TYPE AND SIGNIFICANCE: This vessel was the first guided missile destroyer built in Japan.

DATES OF CONSTRUCTION: *Amatsukaze* was laid down in 1962 and completed in 1965.

HULL DIMENSIONS: 429'9" × 43'11" × 13'9"

DISPLACEMENT: 3,050 tons

ARMOR: None

ARMAMENT: The original armament consisted of four 3" guns, one Terrier SAM system, one ASROC ASW launcher, two Hedgehog devices, and six 12.75" torpedo tubes. In 1978, the Terrier system was offloaded in favor of a Standard SAM system.

MACHINERY: Turbines powered by oil-fired boilers that produced a maximum output of 60,000 shaft horsepower.

SPEED: 33 knots

COMPLEMENT: 290

SUMMARY: This vessel is one of several built by Japan that shows the reliance of the Japanese on U.S. missile technology. *Amatsukaze* was withdrawn from service in 1995.

JAPAN: *HARUNA* CLASS
Courtesy of U.S. Navy

UNITS: *Haruna, Hiei*

TYPE AND SIGNIFICANCE: These ships were the first destroyers in the world to carry three full-sized helicopters for ASW operations.

DATES OF CONSTRUCTION: *Haruna* was laid down in 1970; *Hiei* followed two years later. The former unit was completed in 1973, the latter in 1974.

HULL DIMENSIONS: 501'11" × 57'5" × 16'8"

DISPLACEMENT: 4,950 tons

ARMOR: None

ARMAMENT: The original armament consisted of two 5" guns in two single mounts located in the bow, one ASROC ASW system, six 12.75" torpedo tubes, and three helicopters. These ships now carry one Sea Sparrow SAM system and two 20mm Phalanx cannons.

MACHINERY: Turbines powered by two oil-fired boilers that are capable of 70,000 shaft horsepower.

SPEED: 31 knots

COMPLEMENT: 370

SUMMARY: These ships and an enlarged version of their type are the only destroyers in the world that carry three helicopters. Both units remain in service.

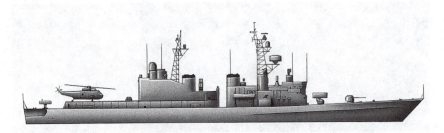

JAPAN: *ASAGIRI* CLASS
Courtesy of Art-Tech/Aerospace/M.A.R.S./TRH/Navy Historical

UNITS: *Asagiri, Yamagiri, Yuugiri, Amagiri, Hamagiri, Setogiri, Sawagiri, Umigiri*

TYPE AND SIGNIFICANCE: These destroyers represent some of Japan's more recent warship construction.

DATES OF CONSTRUCTION: These units were laid down between 1985 and 1988, with the last unit being commissioned in 1991.

HULL DIMENSIONS: 449'5" × 48' × 14'7"

DISPLACEMENT: 3,500 tons

ARMOR: None

ARMAMENT: One 3" gun mounted in the bow, eight Harpoon SSM, one Sea Sparrow SAM system, one ASROC ASW launcher, two 20mm Phalanx cannon, six 12.75" torpedo tubes, and one helicopter operating on a flight deck situated on the stern.

MACHINERY: Gas turbines capable of 53,000 horsepower.

SPEED: 30 knots

COMPLEMENT: 220

SUMMARY: All ships are currently in service.

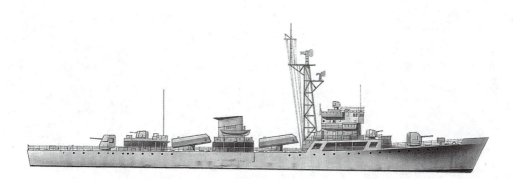

PEOPLE'S REPUBLIC OF CHINA: *JIANGHU I* CLASS
Courtesy of Art-Tech/Aerospace/M.A.R.S./TRH/Navy Historical

UNITS: This class comprised 30 units.

TYPE AND SIGNIFICANCE: These frigates were the first Chinese warships to carry SSMs.

DATES OF CONSTRUCTION: The first of these units was launched in 1975 while the last was completed in 1984.

HULL DIMENSIONS: 337'9" × 39'4" × 13'2"

DISPLACEMENT: 1,800 tons

ARMOR: None

ARMAMENT: The original armament consisted of two 3.9" guns, four SS-N-2 SSM, two RBU-1200 ASW launchers, twelve 37mm guns, and depth charges. In 2004, the surviving units carried two HY-2 SSM launchers amidships, two 3.9" guns, two RBU-1200 ASW launchers, twelve 37mm guns, and depth charges.

MACHINERY: Diesel engines that were capable of 16,000 horsepower.

SPEED: 25 knots

COMPLEMENT: 195

SUMMARY: The design of this vessel attracted foreign interest, and improvements on the design have led to additional, improved batches of the type both in China and through contracts abroad. In 1984, the Chinese transferred two of these units to Egypt, and in 1989 a further unit of the class was procured by Bangladesh. In 2004, the Chinese maintained 27 vessels of the class in service.

SOVIET UNION: *KILDIN* CLASS
Courtesy of Art-Tech/Aerospace/M.A.R.S./TRH/Navy Historical

UNITS: *Neulovimyy, Prozorlivyy, Bedovyy, Neuderzhimmy*

TYPE AND SIGNIFICANCE: These destroyers were the first in the world armed with missiles that had offensive capability against other warships.

DATES OF CONSTRUCTION: All were launched in 1958 and the first unit was completed by 1960.

HULL DIMENSIONS: 415'1" × 42'8" × 15'1"

DISPLACEMENT: 2,850 tons

ARMOR: None

ARMAMENT: One SS-N-1 SSM launcher mounted in the stern, two RBU-2500 ASW launchers, four 3" guns, sixteen 2.2" pieces, and four 21" torpedo tubes.

MACHINERY: Turbines powered by four oil-fired boilers that generated 72,000 shaft horsepower.

SPEED: 38 knots

COMPLEMENT: 285

SUMMARY: These vessels were modified units of another type, the Kotlin class, that were fitted to mount the SSM weaponry. All have been scrapped.

SOVIET UNION: *KRUPNY* CLASS
Courtesy of Art-Tech/Aerospace/M.A.R.S./TRH/Navy Historical

UNITS: *Boiki, Derzkiy, Gnevnyy, Gordyy, Gremyashchiy, Upornyy, Zhguchiy, Zorkiy*

TYPE AND SIGNIFICANCE: These destroyers were the succeeding class to the *Kildin* class and represent the continued Soviet drive for warships equipped with SSM weaponry.

DATES OF CONSTRUCTION: The first of these units was laid down about 1958 and completed by 1961. The other units were constructed during the same period.

HULL DIMENSIONS: 452'2" × 48'11" × 10'6"

DISPLACEMENT: 4,500 tons

ARMOR: None

ARMAMENT: The original armament consisted of two SS-N-1 missile launchers, one each being located fore and aft, two RBU-2500 ASW launchers, sixteen 2.2" guns, and six 21" torpedo tubes. In 1968, a refit commenced that transformed the vessels into ASW craft armed with one SA-N-1 SAM system, three RBU-6000 ASW launchers, 14 2.2" guns, and six 21" torpedo tubes.

MACHINERY: Turbines powered by four oil-fired boilers that were capable of 80,000 shaft horsepower.

SPEED: 36 knots

COMPLEMENT: 350

SUMMARY: In May 1975, *Boiki* and

Zhuguchiy became the first Russian warships to visit a U.S. harbor when they arrived in Boston to celebrate the thirtieth anniversary of the end of World War II. All have been removed from service and scrapped.

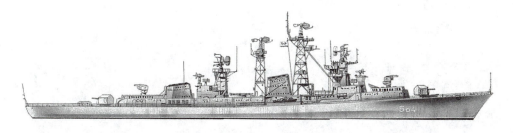

SOVIET UNION: *KASHIN* CLASS

Courtesy of Art-Tech/Aerospace/M.A.R.S./TRH/Navy Historical

UNITS: *Obraztsovyy, Odarennyy, Stereguschchiy, Ognevoy, Provornyy, Komsomolets Ukrainyy, Krasnyy Kavkaz, Krasnyy Krym, Reshitelnyy, Skoriy, Smetlivvyy, Soobrazitelnyy, Sposobnyy, Strogiy, Sderzhannyy, Smelyy, Smyshlennyy, Stroynyy*

TYPE AND SIGNIFICANCE: These were the first AAW destroyers in the Soviet Navy and the first warships of a significant size in the world that used gas-powered turbine engines.

DATES OF CONSTRUCTION: The first unit entered service in 1963, while the last was ready for duty in 1972.

HULL DIMENSIONS: 472'5" × 51'10" × 15'5"

DISPLACEMENT: 3,750 tons

ARMOR: None

ARMAMENT: The original armament comprised two SA-N-1 SAM launchers, two RBU-6000 and two RBU-1000 ASW systems, four 3" guns, and five 21" torpedo tubes.

MACHINERY: Gas turbines capable of 96,000 shaft horsepower.

SPEED: 38 knots

COMPLEMENT: 300

SUMMARY: On 31 August 1974, *Otvazhnyy* was sunk in the Black Sea by a fire that detonated the magazine for the SAM launcher. In 1988, the Soviets transferred *Smelyy* to Poland. Currently, all units but one are retired from service; most have been scrapped. *Smetlivvyy* is the only remaining vessel of the class still in service.

SOVIET UNION: *KRIVAK* CLASS
Courtesy of Art-Tech/Aerospace/M.A.R.S./TRH/Navy Historical

UNITS: This class comprised 42 units.

TYPE AND SIGNIFICANCE: This design was a large frigate that was unusual for the Soviet Union, which constructed mostly small frigates for coastal defense.

DATES OF CONSTRUCTION: All units were laid down and completed between 1970 and 1991.

HULL DIMENSIONS: 405'3" × 46'3" × 15'1"

DISPLACEMENT: 3,300 tons

ARMOR: None

ARMAMENT: One SS-N-14 SAM launcher located on the bow, two SA-N-4 SAM launchers, four 3" guns, two RBU-6000 ASW launchers, eight 21" torpedo tubes, and 20 mines. Some of these ships, known as *Krivak II*, have 4" guns in place of the 3" weapons. In 2004, most of the surviving units carried eight SS-N-25 SSM in two quadruple-cell launchers, two SA-N-4 SAM systems, four 3" guns, eight 21" torpedo tubes, and two RBU-6000 ASW launchers.

MACHINERY: Diesel and gas plant capable of 48,600 shaft horsepower.

SPEED: 32 knots

COMPLEMENT: 200

SUMMARY: On 8 November 1975, a portion of the crew of one of these vessels, *Storozhevoy,* staged a mutiny in an effort to seize the ship and defect from the Soviet Union. Their endeavor ultimately failed. Today, 15 of these units remain in service. Of the others, three were transferred to Ukraine in 1997, and many of the others have been scrapped.

SWEDEN: *HALLAND* CLASS
Courtesy of Sjöhistoriska Museet, Stockholm

UNITS: *Halland, Smaland*

TYPE AND SIGNIFICANCE: These destroyers were the first in the world outside the Soviet Union to carry antiship missiles.

DATES OF CONSTRUCTION: Both units were laid down in 1951, with *Halland* being completed in 1955 and *Smaland* following the next year.

HULL DIMENSIONS: 397'2" × 41'4" × 18'

DISPLACEMENT: 2,630 tons

ARMAMENT: Four 4.7" guns in dual-gunned gun houses with one each being located in the bow and stern, one Saab Rb08A SSM launcher, two 14.6" ASW rocket launchers, two 2.2" guns, six 40mm weapons, eight 21" torpedo tubes, and mines.

MACHINERY: Turbines powered by two oil-fired boilers that produced 58,000 shaft horsepower.

SPEED: 35 knots

COMPLEMENT: 290

SUMMARY: These vessels are prime examples of the fact that technological innovation was present in countries other than the major NATO powers and the Soviet Union. The design proved successful and attracted interest from other nations. The Swedes constructed two more units for Columbia. In 1985, the Swedes removed *Halland* from service. *Smaland* was retired a year earlier but preserved for the nation as a museum ship at Gothenburg, Sweden.

UNITED STATES: *GYATT*

Courtesy of Art-Tech/Aerospace/M.A.R.S./TRH/Navy Historical

TYPE AND SIGNIFICANCE: This World War II–era destroyer was refitted to become the world's first guided missile destroyer.

DATES OF CONSTRUCTION: *Gyatt* was launched in 1945, refitted after World War II, and recommissioned in 1956.

HULL DIMENSIONS: 390'6" × 40'10" × 14'4"

DISPLACEMENT: 2,616 tons

ARMOR: None

ARMAMENT: The original armament consisted of six 5" guns in dual-mount gun houses. Two of these were located in the bow and the last was sited in the stern. The ship also carried 12 40mm guns, 11 20mm weapons, and 10 21" torpedo tubes. The armament after the refit consisted of the four 5" guns mounted in the bow, a portion of the AA weaponry, and one Terrier SAM launcher mounted in the stern in place of the original 5" gun house.

MACHINERY: Turbines powered by four oil-fired boilers that produced a maximum power output of 60,000 shaft horsepower.

SPEED: 36 knots

COMPLEMENT: 336

SUMMARY: This ship was not only the world's first guided missile destroyer, but it was also a prototype for the inclusion of stabilization gear in the U.S. Navy. The ship itself did not prove a great success in the sense that it could not carry the large radar set needed to properly control the Terrier missile. The hull could not support the weight of such equipment without endangering the stability. Nevertheless, *Gyatt* proved the feasibility of mounting missiles on relatively small craft the size of destroyers. Despite its shortcomings, *Gyatt* served in the U.S. Navy and participated in the 1962 blockade of Cuba during the Cuban Missile Crisis. The ship was scrapped in 1969.

UNITED STATES: *COONTZ* CLASS
Courtesy of Art-Tech/Aerospace/M.A.R.S./TRH/Navy Historical

UNITS: *Dewey, Coontz, Preble, Mahan, King, Farragut, Luce, MacDonough, Dahlgren, William V. Pratt*

TYPE AND SIGNIFICANCE: These destroyers, originally designated as frigates, were the world's first purpose-built guided missile destroyers.

DATES OF CONSTRUCTION: All units were laid down in 1957 and 1958 and completed between 1959 and 1961.

HULL DIMENSIONS: 512'6" × 52'4" × 17'9"

DISPLACEMENT: 4,167 tons

ARMOR: None

ARMAMENT: The original armament consisted of one 5" gun mounted forward, one Terrier SAM launcher located in the stern, one ASROC ASW launcher, and six 12.75" ASW torpedo tubes. Following refits, the armament consisted of eight Harpoon SSM, one Standard SAM launcher, one 5" gun, one ASROC launcher, and six 12.75" torpedo tubes.

MACHINERY: Turbines powered by four oil-fired boilers capable of 85,000 shaft horsepower.

SPEED: 32 knots

COMPLEMENT: 360

SUMMARY: All have been removed from service; most have been scrapped.

UNITED STATES: *SPRUANCE* AND *KIDD* CLASSES
Courtesy of Art-Tech/Aerospace/M.A.R.S./TRH/Navy Historical

UNITS: *Spruance, Paul F. Foster, Kinkaid, Hewitt, Elliott, Arthur W. Radford, Peterson, Caron, David R. Ray, Oldendorf, John Young, Comte de Grasse, O'Brien, Merrill, Briscoe, Stump, Conolly, Moosbruger, John Hancock, Nicholson, John Rodgers, Leftwich, Cushing, Harry W. Hill, O'Bannon, Thorn, Deyo, Ingersoll, Fife, Fletcher*

KIDD CLASS: *Kidd, Callaghan, Scott, Chandler, Hayler*

TYPE AND SIGNIFICANCE: These two groups combined constitute one of the two largest post–World War II destroyer groups in the U.S. Navy.

DATES OF CONSTRUCTION: All units were laid down between 1972 and 1980 and completed between 1975 and 1983.

HULL DIMENSIONS: 563'4" × 55' × 20'6"

DISPLACEMENT: 5,826 tons

ARMOR: Kevlar armor added to the Spruance class while the Kidd class were constructed with armor included over vital spaces.

ARMAMENT: The original armament consisted of two 5" guns, one each being located fore and aft, one Sea Sparrow SAM launcher, one ASROC ASW launcher, six 12.75" torpedo tubes, and one helicopter operating on a flight deck sited in the stern. All but seven of the Spruance class were refitted in major overhauls that began in 1986. When they emerged, the ships were armed with one 61-cell VLS launcher in the bow that is capable of Tomahawk missiles and ASROC weapons, eight Harpoon SSM, one Sea Sparrow SAM system, two 5" guns located one each fore and aft, two 20mm Phalanx cannon, six 12.75" torpedo tubes, and one helicopter. The other vessels of the class as well as those of the Kidd class were refitted to include eight Harpoon SSM.

MACHINERY: Gas turbines capable of 80,000 shaft horsepower.

SPEED: 30 knots

COMPLEMENT: 296

SUMMARY: At present, *Spruance, Elliot, O'Brien, Briscoe, Stump, Cushing, O'Bannon, Thorn, Deyo,* and *Fletcher* remain in service. The other vessels, including all those that did not receive the VLS upgrade, are decommissioned. The last warships of the class are scheduled for removal from service by 2007. All of the vessels of the *Kidd* class have been removed from service and will be sold to Taiwan. They will reenter service in the Taiwanese Navy by 2006.

UNITED STATES: *OLIVER HAZARD PERRY* CLASS
Courtesy of Art-Tech/Aerospace/M.A.R.S./TRH/Navy Historical

UNITS: This class comprised 54 units.

TYPE AND SIGNIFICANCE: These frigates constitute both the largest class of this type built by the United States in the post–World War II era and the only class of frigate remaining in the U.S. Navy.

DATES OF CONSTRUCTION: These units were laid down between 1975 and 1987 and completed between 1977 and 1988.

HULL DIMENSIONS: 445' × 45' × 22'; 455' × 45' × 22' (long-hulled version that comprises the majority of the class)

DISPLACEMENT: 2,650 tons (2,750 tons for long-hulled craft)

ARMOR: None

ARMAMENT: The original armament comprised one 3" gun located aft amidships, one Standard SAM system, six 12.75" torpedo tubes, and two helicopters that operate on a flight deck sited on the stern. The SAM launcher is capable of firing both SAM ordnance and the Harpoon SSM. A 20mm Phalanx cannon has been added to the armament. In 2004, those vessels that remain in the U.S. Navy are armed with four Harpoon SSM and Standard SAM missiles that can both be fired from a twin launcher located in the bow, one 3" gun, one 20mm Phalanx cannon, six 12.75" torpedo tubes, and one helicopter.

MACHINERY: Gas turbines capable of 41,000 horsepower.

SPEED: 29 knots

COMPLEMENT: 200

SUMMARY: The design for these vessels called for a cheap, mass-production type of craft. One of the units in this group was *Stark,* which was nearly sunk on 17 May 1987, in the Persian Gulf by two Exocet SSMs fired from an Iranian warplane. Of the original 54 units, the U.S. Navy continued to operate 33 in 2004. Many of the units that have been removed from service have either been transferred or sold to other countries that include Taiwan, Turkey, Egypt, Bahrain, Poland, Australia, and Spain.

UNITED STATES: *ARLEIGH BURKE* CLASS
Courtesy of Art-Tech/Aerospace/M.A.R.S./TRH/Navy Historical

UNITS: In 2004, this class remained under production and currently comprises 38 units.

TYPE AND SIGNIFICANCE: The *Arleigh Burke* class of destroyer is the newest of the type built by the United States and among the most advanced destroyers in the world.

DATES OF CONSTRUCTION: *Arleigh Burke* was laid down in 1988 and commissioned in 1991. All other units have followed since, the most recent being *Mason,* which was laid down in 2000 and launched in 2003.

HULL DIMENSIONS: 504'6" × 66'8" × 32'7"

DISPLACEMENT: 8,315 tons

ARMOR: Kevlar armor covers vital spaces.

ARMAMENT: One 29-cell VLS housed in the bow and a 61-cell VLS positioned aft. The VLS can fire Standard SAM weaponry and Tomahawk cruise missiles. In addition, eight Harpoon SSM, one 5" gun in an automated gun house located in the bow, six 12.75" torpedo tubes, one 20mm Phalanx cannon, and one helicopter that operates off the flight deck sited on the stern.

MACHINERY: Gas turbines that can produce 105,000 horsepower.

SPEED: 32 knots

COMPLEMENT: 346

SUMMARY: In addition to their weaponry, these ships are regarded as very advanced due to the inclusion of the Aegis Combat System. It is designed to control and coordinate the defense of the ship that carries it, as well as to command the defense of entire task forces through the use of its complex computers. The system can track more than 100 targets simultaneously and feed data to the ship's command-and-control center, where a computer evaluates which targets pose the greatest threat to the ship or task force and uses the vessel's weapons accordingly.

Among the units of this class is *Cole,* which was damaged by a terrorist attack on 12 October 2000, in the port of Aden, Yemen. The United States currently plans to construct another 24 of these vessels.

GLOSSARY

AA   antiaircraft

abaft   "farther aft than"; in or toward the stern

ABDA   World War II designation for a force of U.S., British, Dutch, and Australian warships

adrift   a term meaning a vessel is not under control or has come loose from its moorings

aft   near or at the rear portion of a ship's hull

Allies, Allied Powers   Allies being the most commonly used as the collective term for the belligerent states of the United States, Great Britain, France, and Russia in World War II; Allied Powers also used as a collective term for those nations arrayed against the Central Powers in World War I

amidships (midships)   center part of a ship that is located between the bow and stern

antiaircraft battery   all the weapons aboard a vessel that are used to defend it against attacking enemy aircraft

AP   armor-piercing; a type of shell

astern   behind a ship

ASROC   antisubmarine rocket

ASDIC   Allied Submarine Detection Investigation Committee, the body that produced an experimental submarine detection set in 1918; that equipment became known as SONAR

ASW   antisubmarine warfare

Axis Powers   collective term for the belligerent powers of Germany, Italy, and Japan in World War II

ballast   weight additional to the ship itself carried low in a hull to provide greater stability while a ship is at sea

battery   group of guns or missile launchers; also refers collectively to the entire armament of a vessel

beach   as verb, means to run a ship onto a shore, sometimes a deliberate act by a captain to prevent a ship from sinking when flooding

beam   width of the hull of a ship measured at the widest point

bilges   lowest interior portion of a vessel's hull

bow   forward end of a vessel

bridge   main center of control for a vessel

broadside   generally, refers to the sides of a vessel that are above the water; it is also used to define a tactic where all of a warship's guns on one side are fired simultaneously

bulkhead   vertical partition that separates one compartment from another in the hull of a vessel

bulwark   side of a ship that rises above the upper deck

buoyancy   ship's capacity to remain afloat

CA   cruiser (oftentimes used to denote a heavy cruiser)

CAG   original term for a guided missile cruiser

caliber   internal diameter of a gun; also used to refer to the diameter of shells and bullets

capital ship   a warship of the largest or most powerful type

Central Powers   the belligerent nations of Germany, Austria-Hungary, and the Ottoman Empire in World War I

CGN   nuclear-powered guided missile cruiser

cockpit   compartment within ships of the Age of Fighting Sail where surgeons treated sailors wounded in battle

commissioning   the official act through which a warship is made an active unit of a nation's navy

conning tower   battle station for commanding officers of a battleship, battle cruiser, or cruiser when in action; normally located forward of the bridge.

COSAG   designation for combined steam and gas propulsion

course   direction in which a vessel is steaming or sailing; dependent on the manner of instrument used in the determination, as the course can refer to a magnetic, compass, or gyro course

DC   depth charge

DCT   depth charge thrower

DD   designation for a destroyer

DDR   designation for a destroyer radar picket

displacement   weight of water in tons that is displaced by a ship's hull

DL   designation for a destroyer leader

DLG   designation for a guided missile destroyer

draft   depth of water at which a vessel floats

DSMAC   digital scene matching area correlation; a targeting system used in cruise missiles

executive officer   second in command of a vessel or squadron

flagship   the ship carrying the overall commander of a fleet or squadron

fore   toward or near the bow

full displacement   displacement of a ship when fully equipped and fueled

galley   kitchen of a ship

general quarters   an order, i.e., to battle stations on a vessel in preparation for combat

GPS   global positioning system

guerre de course   French, "commerce warfare" (or "war on commerce")

gun deck   in the Age of Fighting Sail, the main deck of a frigate that houses the battery of the vessel

HE   high-explosive; a type of shell

head   ship's toilet

heading   direction in which a ship's bow is pointing

horsepower (hp)   measurement of power that is equal to about 750 watts

hull   the body of a vessel that includes the keel, frames, bulkheads, side plate or planking, and deck

international waters   areas of the world's oceans that fall outside the waters within the territorial boundaries of nations

keel   wooden or steel plate that runs down the centerline of a hull at the lowest point of the structure

knot   unit of speed at sea that is equal to one nautical mile per hour

laid down   the beginning of construction on a ship

list   as verb, means the act of a vessel leaning over to one side as a result of flooding or a shifting of cargo within the hull

Mach   the ratio of the speed of an object to the speed of sound; the actual number value varies based on the temperature of the air through which the sound passes; for purposes of reference, Mach 1 in an environment of 75 degrees Fahrenheit is 769.5 miles per hour

magazine   compartment in a warship that stores projectiles and propellant for use in its guns

main battery   group of the biggest guns aboard a warship

mess deck   deck on a vessel that houses the tables and chairs for eating and congregating

moor   as verb, means the act of fixing a ship to a stationary object by means of a cable to a dock or an anchor to the bottom of a shallow body of water

nautical mile   unit of measurement at sea that is equal to 6,076 feet

overhaul   an extended procedure whereby a warship is taken into a dockyard and its machinery, weapons, and equipment are examined and repaired if necessary; technological improvements are oftentimes added during this process; also: the act of one ship overtaking another at sea

portside (port)   left-hand side of a ship when one faces toward the bow

pp   abbreviation for the length of a ship from the perpendicular bulkhead in the bow to that of the stern; beyond these bulkheads are the prow and stern tip, respectively

QF   quick-firing; a type of naval gun

retrofit   in warships, the process of adding new technology that did not exist or was not included at the time of initial construction

rigging   originally referred collectively to all the masts, spars, and sailing accoutrements of a vessel, in latter ages, signal lines and radio wires

round shot   ball of iron used as a projectile in the Age of Fighting Sail; its size was dependent on that of the weapon that fired it; also known as solid shot

rudder   device for steering a vessel that is normally situated in the stern

salvo   the firing of several guns at once

SAM   surface-to-air missile

scrapping   the process of dismantling a ship

scuttling   purposely flooding a vessel to sink it

shaft horsepower (shp)   the net power available at the propeller shaft after losing some power to friction generated by the machinery that transfers the power of the engine to the shaft that turns the propeller of a ship

ship-of-the-line (line-of-battle ship)   in the Age of Fighting Sail, term referred to the most powerful vessels of a battle fleet that formed up in a line against an opposing like formation of enemy vessels

SLBM   submarine-launched ballistic missile

spar   in the Age of Fighting Sail a pole comprised of wood that was used for masts and yards

SSM   surface-to-surface missile

standard displacement   displacement of a ship when fully equipped but without fuel

STAAG   stabilized tachymetric anti-aircraft gun

starboard   right-hand side of a vessel when one faces toward the bow

stern   aft end of a ship

superstructure   structure that is built on top of the main deck of a ship; in a warship, this area includes the command and control facilities

TERCOM   terrain contour matching; a targeting system used in cruise missiles

TBD   designation for torpedo boat destroyer; this was eventually shortened to the modern term "destroyer"

TGB   British designation of the nineteenth century that stood for a torpedo gunboat

Triple Entente   belligerent powers of Great Britain, France, and Russia in World War I

USSR   Union of Soviet Socialist Republics

VLS   vertical launch system

V/STOL   vertical/short takeoff and landing

yard   unit of measurement equal to 3 feet; in nautical terms, refers to a spar attached lengthways across a mast from which a sail is hung

SELECTED BIBLIOGRAPHY

Baer, George W. *One Hundred Years of Sea Power: The U.S. Navy, 1890–1990*. Stanford, CA: Stanford University Press, 1994.

Baker, A. D. *The Naval Institute Guide to Combat Fleets of the World 1995: Their Ships, Aircraft, and Armament*. Annapolis, MD: Naval Institute Press, 1995.

Birkler, J. L. *The Royal Navy's New-Generation Type 45 Destroyer: Acquisition Options and Implications*. Santa Monica, CA: RAND Europe, 2002.

Brown, David K. *Before the Ironclad: Development of Ship Design, Propulsion, and Armament in the Royal Navy, 1815–1860*. London: Conway Maritime Press, 1990.

Brown, David K. *Warrior to Dreadnought: Warship Development, 1860–1905*. London: Chatham Publishing, 1997.

———. *Warship Losses of World War II*. London: Arms and Armour Press, 1990.

Brown, William David Seton. *Propelling Machinery of a Torpedo-Boat Destroyer*. London: Institute of Civil Engineering, 1900.

Bruce, Anthony and William Cogar. *An Encyclopedia of Naval History*. New York: Facts on File, 1998.

Burt, R. A. *British Destroyers in World War One*. Warships Illustrated, No. 7. London: Arms and Armour Press, 1986.

Busquets, Camil. *Destroyers, Frigates, and Corvettes: The Encyclopedia of Armament and Technology*. Barcelona, Spain: Lema, Poole, Chris Lloyd, 1999.

Buxton, Ian. *Metal Industries: Shipbreaking at Rosyth and Charlestown*. Kendal, UK: World Ship Society, 1992.

Chant, Christopher. *Destroyers and Frigates*. London: Brassey's, 1994.

———. *The History of the World's Warships*. Edison, NJ: Chartwell Books, 2000.

Chesneau, Roger, ed. *Conway's All the World's Fighting Ships, 1922–1946*. London: Conway Maritime Press, 1980.

Cocker, Maurice. *Destroyers of the Royal Navy, 1893–1981*. London: Ian Allan, 1981.

Coe, James B. *Projected Manpower Requirements of the Next Generation U.S. Navy Destroyer.* Monterey, CA: Naval Postgraduate School, 1995.

Colledge, J. J. *Ships of the Royal Navy: The Complete Record of All Fighting Ships of the Royal Navy from the Fifteenth Century to the Present.* Annapolis, MD: Naval Institute Press, 1987.

Cosentino, Michele and Ruggero Stanglini. *The Italian Navy.* Italy: Edizioni Aeronautiche Italiane, 1994.

Couhat, Jean Labayle. *Combat Fleets of the World 1986/1987: Their Ships, Aircraft, and Armament.* Translated by A. D. Baker III. Annapolis, MD: Naval Institute Press, 1986.

Fabb, John, and A. P. McGowan. *Victorian and Edwardian Navy from Old Photographs.* London: B. T. Batsford, 1976.

Friedman, Norman. *U.S. Destroyers: An Illustrated Design History.* Annapolis, MD: Naval Institute Press, 1982.

———. *U.S. Naval Weapons: Every Gun, Missile, Mine, and Torpedo Used by the U.S. Navy from 1883 to the Present Day.* Annapolis, MD: Naval Institute Press, 1982.

———. *World Naval Weapons Systems.* Annapolis, MD: Naval Institute Press, 1989.

———. *Seapower and Space: From the Dawn of the Missile Age to Net-Centric Warfare.* Annapolis, MD: Naval Institute Press, 2000.

Gardiner, Robert, ed. *Conway's All the World's Fighting Ships, 1860–1905.* London: Conway Maritime Press, 1979.

———. *Conway's All the World's Fighting Ships, 1947–1982, Part 1: The Western Powers.* London: Conway Maritime Press, 1983.

Gates, P. J. *Surface Warships: An Introduction to Design Principles.* London: Brassey's Defense Publishers, 1987.

George, James L. *The History of Warships: From Ancient Times to the Twenty-First Century.* Annapolis, MD: Naval Institute Press, 1998.

Gray, Randal, ed. *Conway's All the World's Fighting Ships, 1906–1921.* London: Conway Maritime Press, 1985.

———. *Conway's All the World's Fighting Ships, 1947–1982, Part 2: The Warsaw Pact and Non-Aligned Nations.* London: Conway Maritime Press, 1983.

Green, Michael. *Destroyers.* Mankato, MN: Capstone High/Low Books, 1999.

Gröener, Erich. *German Warships, 1815–1945.* Annapolis, MD: Naval Institute Press, 1990.

Hague, Arnold. *The Allied Convoy System, 1939–1945: Its Organization, Defense, and Operation.* Annapolis, MD: Naval Institute Press, 2000.

Halpern, Paul. *A Naval History of World War I.* Annapolis, MD: Naval Institute Press, 1994.

Harding, Richard. *Seapower and Naval Warfare, 1650–1830.* Annapolis, MD: Naval Institute Press, 1999.

Hastings, Max, and Simon Jenkins. *The Battle for the Falklands.* New York: W. W. Norton, 1983.

Hawkins, Ian, ed. *Destroyer: An Anthology of First-Hand Accounts of the War at Sea, 1939–1945*. London: Conway Maritime Press, 2003.

Herne, Jeffrey J. *Fletcher, Gearing, and Sumner Class Destroyers in World War II*. New York: W. R. Press, 1998.

Hodges, Peter, and Norman Friedman. *Destroyer Weapons of World War II*. Annapolis, MD: Naval Institute Press, 1979.

Hogg, Ian, and John Batchelor. *Naval Gun*. Poole, Dorset, UK: Blandford Press, 1978.

Hooter, E. R. *Destroyers, Frigates, and Corvettes: The World Market*. Coulsdon, Surrey, UK: Jane's Information Group, 1995.

Hovgaard, W. *Modern History of Warships*. New York: Spon and Chamberlain, 1920.

Howarth, Stephen. *The Fighting Ships of the Rising Sun: The Drama of the Imperial Japanese Navy, 1895–1945*. New York: Atheneum, 1983.

Hoyt, Edwin Palmer. *Destroyers: Foxes of the Sea*. Boston: Little, Brown, 1969.

Humble, Richard. *United States Fleet Carriers of World War II "in Action."* New York: Blandford Press, 1984.

Jackson, Robert. *Destroyers, Frigates, and Corvettes*. Alcobendas, Madrid, Spain: Editorial Libsa, 2002.

Jane's Fighting Ships of World War II. New York: Crescent Books, 1992.

Japanese Aircraft Carriers and Destroyers. London: MacDonald, 1964.

Jenkins, E. H. *A History of the French Navy: From Its Beginnings to the Present Day*. Annapolis, MD: Naval Institute Press, 1973.

Jentchura, Hansgeorg, Dieter Jung, and Peter Mickel. *Warships of the Imperial Japanese Navy, 1869–1945*. Translated by Anthony Preston and J.D. Brown. Annapolis, MD: Naval Institute Press, 1977.

Keegan, John. *The Price of Admiralty: The Evolution of Naval Warfare*. New York: Viking, 1989.

Kemp, Peter. *The British Sailor: A Social History of the Lower Deck*. London: Aldine Press, 1970.

King, Dean, and John Hattendorf, eds. *Every Man Will Do His Duty: An Anthology of Firsthand Accounts from the Age of Nelson, 1792–1815*. New York: Henry Holt, 1997.

Lambert, Andrew D. *Steam, Steel, and Shellfire: The Steam Warship, 1815–1905*. London: Conway Maritime Press, 1992.

Langtree, Christopher. *The Kelly's: British J, K, and N Class Destroyers of World War II*. Annapolis, MD: Naval Institute Press, 2002.

Lavery, Brian. *Nelson's Navy: The Ships, Men, and Organisation, 1793–1815*. London: Conway Maritime Press, 1989.

Leith, Craig. *Two Honourable Years*. Waterlooville, UK: C. Leith, 1993.

Lenton, H. T. *British and Empire Warships of the Second World War*. Annapolis, MD: Naval Institute Press, 1998.

Lenton H. T., and J. J. Colledge. *Warships of World War II, Part II: Destroyers and Submarines*. London: Ian Allan, 1962.

Lewin, Ronald. *Ultra Goes to War*. London: Random House, 1978.

Lyon, David. *The First Destroyers*. London: Chatham Publishing, 1996.

Manning, T. D. *The British Destroyer*. London: Godfrey Cave Associates, 1961.

March, Edgar. *British Destroyers: A History of Development, 1892–1953*. London: Seeley Service, 1966.

Marder, Arthur. *The Anatomy of British Sea Power: A History of British Naval Policy in the Pre-Dreadnought Era, 1880–1905*. Hamden, CT: Archon Books, 1964.

Marriott, Leo. *Royal Navy Destroyers Since 1945*. London: Ian Allan, 1989.

Millet, Allen, and Peter Maslowski. *For the Common Defense: A Military History of the United States of America*. New York: Free Press, 1994.

Moore, John, ed. *Jane's Fighting Ships, 1986–1987*. London: Jane's Publications, 1986.

———. *Jane's Fighting Ships of World War I*. New York: Military Press, 1990.

Newcomb, Dick. *U.S. Destroyers of the World Wars: History of the "Tin Cans."* Paducah, Kentucky: Turner Publishing, 1994.

Paine, Lincoln P. *Warships of the World to 1900*. Boston: Houghton Mifflin, 2000.

Parker, Robert S. *Blood on the Sea: American Destroyers Lost in World War II*. Cambridge, MA : DaCapo, 2001.

Polmar, Norman. *Guide to the Soviet Navy*. Annapolis, MD: Naval Institute Press, 1986.

———. *The Naval Institute Guide to the Ships and Aircraft of the U.S. Fleet*. 16th ed. Annapolis, MD: Naval Institute Press, 1997.

Pope, Dudley. *Life in Nelson's Navy*. Annapolis, MD: Naval Institute Press, 1981.

Preston, Anthony. *Destroyers*. Englewood Cliffs, NJ: Prentice-Hall, 1977.

———. *Super-Destroyers: The Big Destroyers Built in the 1930s for Britain, France, Germany, Italy, Japan, and the United States*. London: Conway Maritime Press, 1978.

Pretty, R. T. and D. H. R. Archer. *Jane's Weapons Systems, 1972–1973*. New York: McGraw-Hill, 1973.

Prézelin, Bernard, ed. *The Naval Institute Guide to Combat Fleets of the World 1993: Their Ships, Aircraft, and Armament*. Translated by A. D. Baker III. Annapolis, MD: Naval Institute Press, 1993.

Rohwer, Jurgen. *Stalin's Ocean-Going Fleet: Soviet Naval Strategy and Shipbuilding Programs, 1922–1953*. London: Frank Cass, 2001.

Ropp, Theodore. *The Development of a Modern Navy: French Naval Policy, 1871–1904*. Annapolis, MD: Naval Institute Press, 1987.

Ross, Al. *The Destroyer, the Sullivans*. London: Conway Maritime Press, 1988.

Sanders, Michael S. *The Yard: Building a Destroyer at the Bath Iron Works*. New York: Perennial, 2001.

Saunders, Stephen, ed. *Jane's Fighting Ships, 2001–2002*. Alexandria, VA: Jane's Information Group, 2001.

———. *Jane's Fighting Ships, 2002–2003.* Alexandria, VA: Jane's Information Group, 2002.

———. *Jane's Fighting Ships, 2003–2004.* Alexandria, VA: Jane's Information Group, 2003.

Schofield, William G. *Destroyers, 60 Years.* New York: Rand McNally, 1962.

Scutts, Jerry. *Fletcher DDs in Action.* Carollton, TX: Squadron/Signal Publications, 1995.

Sharpe, Richard. *Jane's Fighting Ships, 1987–1988.* London: Jane's Publications, 1987.

———. *Jane's Fighting Ships, 1989–1990.* London: Jane's Publications, 1989.

———. *Jane's Fighting Ships, 1990–1991.* London: Jane's Publications, 1990.

———. *Jane's Fighting Ships, 1991–1992.* London: Jane's Publications, 1991.

———. *Jane's Fighting Ships, 1992–1993.* Alexandria, VA: Jane's Information Group, 1992.

———. *Jane's Fighting Ships, 1993–1994.* Alexandria, VA: Jane's Information Group, 1993.

———. *Jane's Fighting Ships, 1994–1995.* Alexandria, VA: Jane's Information Group, 1994.

———. *Jane's Fighting Ships, 1995–1996.* Alexandria, VA: Jane's Information Group, 1995.

———. *Jane's Fighting Ships, 1996–1997.* Alexandria, VA: Jane's Information Group, 1996.

———. *Jane's Fighting Ships, 1997–1998.* Alexandria, VA: Jane's Information Group, 1997.

———. *Jane's Fighting Ships, 1998–1999.* Alexandria, VA: Jane's Information Group, 1998.

———. *Jane's Fighting Ships, 1999–2000.* Alexandria, VA: Jane's Information Group, 1999.

———. *Jane's Fighting Ships, 2000–2001.* Alexandria, VA: Jane's Information Group, 2000.

Smith, Peter Charles. *Hard Lying: The Birth of the Destroyer, 1893–1913.* Annapolis, MD: Naval Institute Press, 1971.

Spector, Ronald H. *At War at Sea: Sailors and Naval Combat in the Twentieth Century.* New York: Viking, 2001.

Sumida, Jon Tetsuro. *In Defense of Naval Supremacy: Finance, Technology, and British Naval Policy, 1889–1914.* Boston: Unwin, Hyman, 1989.

Sumrall, Robert F. *Sumner-Gearing-Class Destroyers: Their Design, Weapons, and Equipment.* Annapolis, MD: Naval Institute Press, 1995.

Thrower, W. R. *Life at Sea in the Age of Sail.* London: Phillimore, 1972.

Tomajczyk, Stephen F. *Modern U.S. Navy Destroyers.* Osceola, WI: MBI Publishing, 2001.

Tucker, Spencer C. *A Handbook of 19th Century Naval Warfare.* Thrupp, Stroud, Gloucestershire, UK: Sutton, 2000.

———. *A Short History of the Civil War at Sea.* Wilmington, DE: Scholarly Resources, 2002.

———. *The Great War, 1914–1918.* Bloomington: Indiana University Press, 1998.

United States Department of the Navy. *Main Propulsion Plant DD45 and 692 Classes and Converted Types.* Washington, DC: U.S. Navy Bureau of Ships, 1946.

United States Department of the Navy. *"The Oldest and the Best" Decommissioning: United States Ship Prairie, March 26, 1993, Long Beach, California.* Washington, DC: Department of the Navy, 1993.

Van der Vat, Dan. *The Atlantic Campaign: World War II's Great Struggle at Sea.* New York: Harper and Row, 1988.

Vego, Milan. *The Soviet Navy Today.* London: Arms and Armour Press, 1986.

Walmer, Max. *Destroyers.* Vero Beach, FL: Rourke, 1989.

Wells, John. *The Royal Navy: An Illustrated Social History.* Gloucestershire, UK: Alan Sutton, 1994.

Whitley, Michael J. *Destroyer! German Destroyers in World War II.* Annapolis, MD: Naval Institute Press, 1983.

———. *Destroyers of World War II: An International Encyclopedia.* London: Cassell Military, 2002.

Wiper, Steve. *Benson-Gleaves Class Destroyers.* Tucson, AZ: Classic Warships Publications, 2001.

INDEX

ABOUT THE AUTHOR

ERIC W. OSBORNE, Ph.D., is adjunct professor in history at the Virginia Military Institute, Lexington, Virginia. His published works include *Britain's Economic Blockade of Germany, 1914–1919* (2004) and *Cruisers and Battle Cruisers* (ABC-CLIO, 2004).